UNDERSTANDING SHARIA PROCESSES

Sharia family law processes have attracted increasing debate and controversy in the United Kingdom, Canada and Australia in recent years. While the reasons for opposition to sharia processes are complex, they often feature the concern that sharia processes disadvantage Muslim women. However, to date there has been inadequate attention to the experiences of participants in sharia processes. This book studies women's experiences with these processes in Australia, with attention to the question of how religious communities and liberal legal systems can best respond to the needs of Muslim women who use these processes. In doing so, this book offers unique evidence to inform future policy developments in Australia that will also have implications for other liberal jurisdictions. In this way, this book makes a significant contribution to the international discussion and response to sharia processes.

Understanding Sharia Processes

Women's Experiences of Family Disputes

Farrah Ahmed
and
Ghena Krayem

•HART•
OXFORD • LONDON • NEW YORK • NEW DELHI • SYDNEY

HART PUBLISHING
Bloomsbury Publishing Plc
Kemp House, Chawley Park, Cumnor Hill, Oxford, OX2 9PH, UK
1385 Broadway, New York, NY 10018, USA
29 Earlsfort Terrace, Dublin 2, Ireland

HART PUBLISHING, the Hart/Stag logo, BLOOMSBURY and the Diana logo are trademarks of Bloomsbury Publishing Plc

First published in Great Britain 2021

A catalogue record for this book is available from the British Library.

Library of Congress Cataloging-in-Publication data

Names: Ahmed, Farrah, author. | Krayem, Ghena, author.

Title: Understanding sharia processes : women's experiences of family disputes / Farrah Ahmed, Ghena Krayem.

Description: Gordonsville : Hart Publishing, an imprint of Bloomsbury Publishing, 2021. | Includes bibliographical references and index.

Identifiers: LCCN 2021004212 (print) | LCCN 2021004213 (ebook) | ISBN 9781509920730 (hardback) | ISBN 9781509949489 (paperback) | ISBN 9781509920754 (pdf) | ISBN 9781509920747 (Epub)

Subjects: LCSH: Islamic law—Non-Islamic countries. | Domestic relations (Islamic law)—Non-Islamic countries. | Women (Islamic law)—Non-Islamic countries. | Islamic law—Reception—Non-Islamic countries. | Domestic relations (Islamic law)—Australia. | Women (Islamic law)—Australia.

Classification: LCC KBP69.5 .A36 2021 (print) | LCC KBP69.5 (ebook) | DDC 346.01/5—dc23

LC record available at https://lccn.loc.gov/2021004212

LC ebook record available at https://lccn.loc.gov/2021004213

ISBN: HB: 978-1-50992-073-0
ePDF: 978-1-50992-075-4
ePub: 978-1-50992-074-7

Typeset by Compuscript Ltd, Shannon

FOREWORD

Krayem and Ahmed's comprehensive and compelling analysis of the practice and use of Islamic family processes is important and timely for several reasons.

First, this project adds significantly to our understanding of the use of Islamic family processes inside Muslim communities, and their meaning for Australian Muslims. Krayem and Ahmed squarely confront the four major concerns often raised in majority non-Muslim countries like Australia about the use of these informal, non-legal processes. Islamic marriage and divorce traditions, and family and community management of marital disputes, are practices that that place outside the courts and they constitute an informal dispute resolution culture that is usually 'under the radar'.

Bringing these processes into the light of day means asking some tough questions about them. Are these processes fair to women? Do they respond adequately (not that the legal system necessarily does) to domestic violence? Do they conflict with or undermine domestic law, and persuade women to accept less than may be due to them in the event of divorce? Finally, can procedures that have historically privileged male decision-makers recognise gender equality rather than imposing conservative ideas of women's roles?

Ahmed and Krayem have conducted in-depth interviews with participants in Islamic family processes as well as with imams, who play a special role for Australian Muslims seeking an authority figure. Their findings illustrate the range of experiences of the women who use such processes, as well as their multiple and deeply embedded motivations. Contemporary media often suggests a simplistic and inadequate understanding of Islamic religious and cultural traditions. In this 'sound bite' assessment, Islam universally oppresses women who are wholly unable to stand up for themselves and what they want. If you are interested in getting beyond this 'sound bite', the real story, of course, is much more complicated.

As Ahmed and Krayem show, Islamic family processes do sometimes rely on gender stereotypes and exhibit a lack of appreciation for women's lived experiences, especially in domestic violence situations, in the processes they studied. A lack of women in positions of authority around marital conflict is a further problem. These issues are certainly a part of the story they tell. But – and this is where this gets really interesting – this is nowhere approaching the whole story of shari'a processes.

Many women, including those without strong religious practices themselves, describe positive experiences that are meaningful to them. Obtaining an Islamic divorce from an authoritative figure (usually their imam) is extremely important to their sense of closure and a new beginning when they end their marriage. It is often critical to their family relationships and to achieving their goal (divorce/separation) without creating a larger family schism. Contrary to the depiction of shari'a in the media, Ahmed and Krayem show that there are a wide range of practices, rather than a single immutable 'shari'a law'. Instead, they point to changes and modifications that aim to adapt shari'a to the modern context of women in Australia. For example, some women describe the traditional assumption that only their husband can grant them a divorce – known as *talaq* – being used as a means of controlling and exploiting them emotionally. Yet some imams – and a growing number of modern Islamic legal systems – reject the triple, unilateral *talaq*. Some imams are more responsive to domestic violence, and other types of abusive behaviours inside marriage, than others. It is of course critical that women facing violence and abuse have a safe place to go to, and it essential to involve women as responders and decision-makers (this reflects the same struggle we see in non-Muslim communities and cultures to properly confront sexual violence). The evolution of the practice of family shari'a in twenty-first century Australia is inevitable, and it is critical for Australian Muslim communities. To maintain their own distinctive identity(ies) within a non-Muslim secular society, Australian Muslims need to reach for greater clarity about what is important to them and what needs to change.

Ahmed and Krayem meticulously document the range of shari'a practices inside Australian Muslim communities, and show how some approaches come out far better than others when evaluated against criteria of fairness, appropriateness of response and outcomes. They have carefully and without judgment interrogated the experience of Muslim family processes and then evaluated them according to principles of equality and fairness, especially as this affects women participants. Ahmed and Krayem also identify and challenge patriarchy within the Muslim culture. They find many things that could be done better, and they say so. But their account maintains a crucial commitment to understanding this cultural and religious phenomenon as important and meaningful to many.

Beyond evaluating the current practices, Ahmed and Krayem give voice to the women who use them. In doing so, they demonstrate the importance of understanding before judging. Behind each individual who turns to an Islamic family process there is a history, a personality, an experience of marriage, a relationship with faith, and usually an extended family to manage. Feminists as well as conservatives need to recognise that these experiences are important and valid, even where they confound our expectations. The stories about the ending of a marriage described in this book reflect both the sameness and the differences in our human experiences.

This is the second way in which this book is important. The events of this year, 2020 – among many, the re-emergence of the Black Lives Matter movement, and the COVID-19 pandemic and its unequal impact on different communities – have highlighted the importance of our collective commitment to understanding and respecting our differences. Differences mean that we all have learning to do about others. Differences often mean inequality and unfair treatment. Why are Australian Muslim family processes sometimes singled out as 'scary' and 'threatening' when similar processes exist in many other religious and cultural groups? As Krayem and Ahmed show, there is little if any interest among Australian Muslims in substituting Islamic processes for those of the state; they are simply using a parallel process that aligns with their religious and cultural values and has important meaning for them. Rather than fearing or stigmatising these differences, our goal should be to better understand and then – ideally collaboratively – evaluate them.

Ahmed and Krayem's methodology offers a model for how we should learn about and seek to understand other groups who are demonised in the media, and who experience unfairness and discrimination. Instead of 'othering', our goal should be understanding and responding. Only then can we answer some of the plethora of questions crowding in on us this year. Why are Black and South Asian communities experiencing a higher incidence of COVID and death than white communities? Why do Black children grow up being given 'The Talk' about dealing with police, when this is an unknown issue for other children with different coloured skin? Why does fatal violence disproportionately affect transgendered people?

2020 is making us increasingly aware of the need to replace a narrative which relates and compares everyone's experience – in countries like Australia, Canada, the UK and the US and beyond – to the experience of white people, and especially white men. An alternative narrative both respects, and aims to better understand, other life experiences, beliefs and values. Ahmed and Krayem's work challenges the expectation that everyone will think and behave like the dominant white community. Yet at the same time, it reminds us of our many similarities when it comes to choosing a life partner and our despair when our choice turns out to be the wrong one. Many of the descriptions of marital strife in this book will resonate with anyone who has ever been in a long-term relationship, Muslim or non-Muslim. Domestic violence is endemic, and no community is untouched by this. Many of the problems the authors identify in Islamic family processes – assumptions about a women's role in the family, patriarchal norms, and a preponderance of male decision-makers – will be all too familiar to those who have used other religious or cultural processes, or even the courts.

At a time of confusion, strife and often hastily formed judgements, Ahmed and Krayem's book is a light that shines brightly reminding us of how much better we can do.

Julie Macfarlane
Professor of Law and Distinguished University Professor,
University of Windsor
October 2020

ACKNOWLEDGEMENTS

This book was made possible by a generous Australian Research Council Discovery grant. It could not have been completed without the constant help, guidance and support of our co-investigators on that grant, Carolyn Evans and Helen Rhoades. Carolyn and Helen guided and encouraged our earliest articulations of the idea for this project with wisdom, kindness and generosity. We remain deeply grateful to them.

We have been fortunate to work on this project with dedicated, knowledgeable, collegial and brilliant research fellows who oversaw the complicated logistics of fieldwork over two cities and significant time period, assisted with conducting and coding interviews, undertook research on specialist topics, edited the manuscript and served as sounding boards for our ideas about the project. Amira Aftab, Anisa Buckley, Tamana Daqiq, Mehal Krayem, Balawyn Jones, Mohamed Hamed and Helen McCue have made vital and valuable contributions to the project. We also benefitted from excellent assistance from Ken Kiat of the Academic Research Service at Melbourne Law School and Samantha Hinderling in preparing this manuscript.

We benefitted greatly from feedback from a range of scholars. Carolyn Evans helped us shape the initial contours of the plan for this book. Helen Rhoades provided foundational guidance on the methodology. An entire draft book manuscript was generously reviewed by Adam Possamai, Julie Macfarlane, Jeff Redding, Helen Rhoades and Ihsan Yilmaz. We are particularly grateful for Julie's continued support for the project over many years.

The research for this book is based on fieldwork in Sydney and Melbourne which would not have been possible without the assistance of community organisations such as the Board of Imams Victoria, the Australian National Imams Council, the Muslim Women's Association, the Australian Muslim Women's Centre for Human Rights, the Lebanese Muslim Association and the Islamic Council of Victoria. In giving us their time and support, these organisations demonstrated their commitment to research and learning. We offer them our sincere thanks.

Most of all, we owe thanks to the women with direct experience of engaging with sharia processes who agreed to be interviewed by us. Their experiences form the very heart of this book and we hope that we have done justice to the experiences they shared with us.

We would like to thank our families and friends, whose patience and support have made this book possible.

CONTENTS

Foreword ... *v*
Acknowledgements ... *ix*
Glossary: Arabic and Islamic Terms ... *xv*

1. Introduction ... **1**
I. Concerns about Sharia Processes ... 2
II. Why Sharia Processes Exist ... 4
III. The Importance of Women's Experiences ... 7
IV. Methodology ... 8
V. Significance and Outline ... 12

2. People, Procedures and Practices ... **15**
I. Introduction ... 15
II. British Institutions and Processes ... 15
A. Key Organisations, Procedures and Practices ... 16
III. Canadian Institutions and Processes ... 19
A. Key Organisations ... 20
B. Procedures and Practices ... 21
IV. Australian Institutions and Processes ... 23
A. Key Organisations, Procedures and Practices ... 24
V. Conclusion ... 33

3. Women's Perspectives and Experiences ... **34**
I. Introduction ... 34
II. Before Sharia Processes ... 34
A. Family ... 34
B. Professionals and Community Workers ... 36
III. Reasons for Seeking a Religious Divorce ... 37
A. Spiritual Motivations ... 37
B. Ending Emotional Exploitation ... 39
C. Closure and 'Moving On' ... 40
D. Avoiding Stigma ... 41
IV. Women's Experiences of Sharia Processes ... 42
A. Emphasis on Reconciliation ... 42
B. A Lack of Skills and Training ... 44
C. A Lack of Transparency ... 45
D. Responding to Domestic Violence ... 46

E. Acknowledgement of Injustice 49
F. Gender Imbalance on Panels 50
G. Re-traumatisation, Privacy and Forum-shopping 51
H. Impact on Faith 53
V. Conclusion 53

4. Imams' Roles and Perspectives 55
I. Introduction 55
II. Imams' Understanding of their Role in Reconciliation 55
III. Imams' Understanding of their Role in Divorce 59
A. Role as Service-Providers and Advocates for Women 59
B. Backlash for Carrying Out Roles in Divorce Proceedings 60
IV. Responding to the Concerns of Women and Professionals 62
A. The Need for Training and Resources 62
B. Responding to Domestic Violence 63
C. Gender Imbalance in Sharia Processes 67
V. Conclusion 68

5. Outcomes of Sharia Processes 70
I. Introduction 70
II. Divorce Outcomes 70
A. Summary of the Types of Islamic Divorce 71
B. Divorce Outcomes from Sharia Processes 73
III. Financial Outcomes 78
A. Imams' Limited Advisory Role in Financial Matters 79
IV. Child Custody 90
V. Conclusion 94

6. Evolution and Change 96
I. Improving Sharia Processes 96
A. Pre-marriage Briefing and Counselling 97
B. Rethinking Marriage Contracts and Delegated Divorce Rights – *Talaq Tafweedh* 97
C. Financial Agreements 98
D. The Initial Stages of Sharia Processes 99
E. Women on Panels 101
F. Professionals on Panels 104
G. Education and Transparency about Divorce Options and Financial Entitlements 105
H. Clearer Processes and Procedures 106
I. Acknowledgement and Response to Injustice, Abuse and Harm 107
J. Domestic Violence 108

K. Referral and Integration of Support Services 111
L. Sensitivity to Cultural and Linguistic Diversity 114
M. Support and Resources for Religious Divorce 116
N. Enhanced Role for Muslim Women's Organisations 117
O. Tracking the Australian Legal System....119
II. Improving the Family Law System 120
A. Better Enforcement of Orders against Former Partners 120
B. Better Tailored Legal Aid....120
C. Enhancing the Cultural Sensitivity of Mainstream Services 121
D. Legal Recognition of the *Mahr* 121
E. A Muslim Family Relationship Centre/Service: A One Stop Shop for Muslim Families 122
III. Conclusion....124

7. Conclusion **125**

Appendix A: Methodology and Project Phases.... **130**
Appendix B: Board of Imams Victoria Marriage Contract.... **137**
Appendix C: Board of Imams Victoria Islamic Mediation/ Reconciliation Application.... **139**
Appendix D: Board of Imams Islamic Divorce Application **145**
Appendix E: Lebanese Muslim Association Application **151**
Appendix F: Summary of Key *Sunni* Positions on Islamic Divorce.... **153**
Appendix G: Qatari Family Law Code.... **161**

Bibliography....*172*
Index *179*

GLOSSARY: ARABIC AND ISLAMIC TERMS

***faskh* (or *tafriq*)** – a type of Islamic divorce. *Faskh* is granted by a religious 'court' and is a type of divorce used when the husband is seen to be at fault, for example, due to mistreatment of his wife. See Appendix F for details.

fatwa – a formal ruling or interpretation on a point of Islamic law given by a qualified legal scholar (known as a mufti).

iddah – maintenance owed by the husband to the wife during the period of separation.

khulah – a woman's right to release herself from marriage. In contrast to *talaq*, some scholars believe that this type of divorce does not require the husband's consent (though there are scholars who believe the husband's consent is still required). See Appendix F for details.

mahr – marriage-gift received by the wife. See chapter five for details.

mutah (in the context of divorce) – a post-divorce financial settlement made by the husband to the wife, seen as a 'gift of consolation paid to divorced women'.

***tafriq* (or *faskh*)** – a type of Islamic divorce. *Tafriq* is granted by a religious 'court' and is a type of divorce used when the husband is seen to be at fault, for example, due to mistreatment of his wife. See Appendix F for details.

talaq – the right held by a husband to issue a unilateral divorce to their wife. See chapter five and Appendix F.

talaq tafweedh – (delegated divorce) a woman's right to effect a *talaq* divorce if her husband has delegated his power of *talaq*. See chapter five and Appendix F.

1

Introduction

Religion plays a role in regulating family life in many societies. One-third of the world's population live under personal law systems which govern family life and are informed by religious norms.[1] Even in states without personal laws, ecclesiastical courts, rabbinical tribunals, sharia councils, groupings of priests or elders may informally regulate the family life of religious communities.[2] In recent decades, institutions and processes associated with Muslim communities across Western liberal states have come under particular scrutiny.

Sharia processes – Muslim community processes, informed by Islamic norms, which informally regulate family life – have created controversies in Canada, the United Kingdom and Australia, among other states. For example, in 2003, in Ontario, an organisation called the Islamic Institute of Civil Justice announced that it would conduct arbitrations – enforceable by Ontario courts – according to principles of Islamic family law, for Muslims who approach it. Amidst the resulting media storm and public opposition to the idea of religious arbitration of family disputes, Ontario decided, in 2005, that it would no longer enforce such arbitrations.[3] A few years later, in February 2008, Rowan Williams, the Archbishop of Canterbury, explored the possibility of greater recognition of sharia in English law in a lecture,[4] which also saw a strong and largely hostile media reaction. In Australia, Pauline Hanson's One Nation Political Party, and politicians like Cory Bernardi and Jacqui Lambie, have expressed concern about, and opposition to, sharia.[5] In 2011, the Australian Attorney-General, Robert McClelland, said '[t]here is no place for sharia law in Australian society and the Government strongly rejects any proposal for its introduction'.[6] In 2012, former High Court Judge,

[1] Y Sezgin, *Human Rights under State-Enforced Religious Family Laws in Israel, Egypt, and India* (Cambridge, Cambridge University Press, 2013); F Ahmed, *Religious Freedom under Personal Law System* (Oxford, Oxford University Press, 2016).

[2] R Sandberg et al, 'Britain's Religious Tribunals: "Joint Governance" in Practice' (2013) 33 *Oxford Journal of Legal Studies* 263.

[3] AC Korteweg, 'The Sharia Debate in Ontario: Gender, Islam, and Representations of Muslim Women's Agency' (2006) 18 *ISIM Review* 50; see M Boyd, 'Dispute Resolution in Family Law: Protecting Choice, Promoting Inclusion' (Ministry of the Attorney General 2004) <www.attorneygeneral.jus.gov.on.ca/english/about/pubs/boyd> accessed 26 October 2020.

[4] R Williams, 'Civil and Religious Law in England: A Religious Perspective' (2008) 10 *Ecclesiastical Law Journal* 262.

[5] G Krayem and F Ahmed, 'Islamic Community Processes in Australia: An Introduction' in S Bano (ed), *Gender and Justice in Family Law Disputes: Women, Mediation, and Religious Arbitration* (Waltham MA, Brandeis University Press, 2017).

[6] J Hole, 'Muslim Group Wants Sharia Law in Australia', *ABC News*, May 17, 2011.

Gerard Brennan argued against the suggestion that there was room for the operation of sharia within Australian law because it inevitably reflected 'different fundamental standards'.[7] News reports have been critical of Australian sharia processes relating to religious divorce.[8]

This book enriches our understanding of sharia processes through an empirical study focused on women's experiences with these processes. The book goes beyond standard criticisms of sharia processes to reveal the subtleties and nuances of women's experiences. The book also challenges important preconceptions about sharia processes and about how Muslim communities understand the relationship between these processes and the state. Significantly, the book offers concrete suggestions for how sharia processes and state family law systems should change to improve women's experiences, drawing comparative insights from studies of sharia processes across Australia, the United Kingdom and Canada.

Sharia processes are described in different ways in different jurisdictions: sharia councils, religious tribunals, Islamic arbitration, Islamic divorce panels, and so on. The sharia processes that we studied primarily involved imams dealing with Muslims facing marital difficulties; the processes often included attempts to reconcile the parties and mediate conflicts, but the raison d'être of most sharia processes is the facilitation or grant of religious divorce for Muslim women. This study of sharia processes included only Muslim community processes that deal with family matters. In what follows, we explain why sharia processes are controversial, why they exist, the need to understand them better, and how this book hopes to contribute to our understanding of these processes.

I. Concerns about Sharia Processes

There are complex reasons for opposition to sharia processes. While some opposition to sharia processes comes from parties with a clearly Islamophobic agenda (Pauline Hanson being an example), this is not the whole story. One set of concerns relates to whether women *freely* choose to engage with sharia processes. For instance, during the Ontario religious arbitration controversy, a Canadian women's organisation – Women's Legal Education and Action Fund ('LEAF') – raised concerns that women may face strong cultural or religious pressures to use religious arbitration. LEAF raised concerns that religious or cultural communities might exclude, shun or condemn women who do not engage in religious arbitration, which in turn might compound their alienation after a family break-up and

[7] G Brennan, 'Lessons from a Life in the Law', Hal Wootten Lecture (UNSW 23 August 2012) <www.law.unsw.edu.au/sites/default/files/imce/files/wootten/hal_wootten_lecture_-_sir_gerard_brennan_0.pdf> accessed 5 November 2020.

[8] H Gleeson, J Baird and S Malik, '"I'm Not His Property": Abused Muslim Women Denied Right to Divorce', *ABC News*, April 18 2018; H Gleeson and J Baird, '"Now Is the Time for Change": Politicians and Advocates Call for an Urgent Review of the Islamic Divorce Process', *ABC News*, April 19 2018.

have adverse impacts on their social, financial and immigration interests.[9] LEAF argued that these concerns were particularly strong in cases where women might lack resources or information about their options, concluding that '[w]hen these conditions are present it is not accurate or reasonable to suggest that arbitration is being chosen freely'.[10] Similar concerns have been raised in the United Kingdom where commentators have suggested that some women were coaxed into participating in reconciliation sessions with their husbands, even when they had existing injunctions issued against their husbands on the grounds of violence.[11]

A second set of concerns relates to how sharia processes respond to situations of family violence. In Australia, a series of in-depth articles from ABC News reported that although imams involved in sharia processes claim that women who provide proof of domestic violence through intervention orders or photographs of injuries are entitled to an immediate Islamic divorce, many survivors of violence and their advocates say that imams deny them the right to divorce.[12] One woman quoted in the article claimed that imams dismissed evidence presented to them, such as an audio recording of the husband's violent outburst, and told her to give the marriage another chance.[13] Some imams reportedly did not recognise emotional, psychological and financial abuse as valid grounds for a divorce, or equivalent to physical domestic abuse, as they reportedly claimed, 'he doesn't hit you'.[14] Many imams reportedly failed to refer women in family violence situations to support services or police.[15] Imams reportedly requested husbands and wives be present in the same room, including in a case of alleged violence where an intervention order was in place.[16] Commentators have expressed similar concerns that mediation in UK sharia councils is conducted in accordance with religious principles that prioritise keeping a marriage together even where there are allegations of spousal abuse.[17] They raise concerns that mediation by sharia councils in England 'can render some women vulnerable to physical and emotional abuse'.[18]

[9] Statement of the Women's Legal Education and Action Fund ('LEAF') in Boyd (n 3) 50–51.

[10] ibid. See also N Bakht, 'Family Arbitration Using Sharia Law: Examining Ontario's Arbitration Act and its Impact on Women' (2004) 1 *Muslim World Journal of Human Rights* 1; A Shachar, 'Privatizing Diversity: A Cautionary Tale From Religious Arbitration in Family Law' (2008) 9 *Theoretical Inquiries in Law* 573, 588–90.

[11] See F Ahmed and JC Norton, 'Religious Tribunals, Religious Freedom, and Concern for Vulnerable Women' (2012) 24 *Child and Family Law Quarterly* 383.

[12] Gleeson, Baird and Malik (n 8).

[13] ibid.

[14] ibid.

[15] ibid.

[16] ibid.

[17] ibid; SN Shah-Kazemi, *Untying the Knot: Muslim Women, Divorce, and the Shariah* (Signal Press, 2001), <www.nuffieldfoundation.org/project/untying-the-knot-muslim-women-divorce-and-the-shariah> accessed 1 November 2020; JR Bowen, 'Private Arrangements: "Recognizing Sharia" in England', *Boston Review*, 1 March 2009, <www.bostonreview.net/john-bowen-private-arrangements-sharia-England> accessed 1 November 2020.

[18] S Bano, 'In Pursuit of Religious and Legal Diversity: A Response to the Archbishop of Canterbury and the "Sharia Debate" in Britain' (2008) 10 *Ecclesiastical Law Journal* 283, 300.

A third set of concerns relates to the outcomes of sharia processes. In the UK, decisions of sharia councils are said to harm, discriminate against and disadvantage women.[19] Commentators have expressed the concern that women may not be aware of their entitlements under civil family law and thus accept decisions or recommendations from sharia councils that are inconsistent with these entitlements. There are reports of husbands using sharia councils in order to negotiate for increased access to children even in cases where injunctions have been issued by civil law mechanisms to prohibit access.[20] While sharia processes often exist primarily to facilitate or grant religious divorces to Muslim women, some women are reportedly never granted a divorce or are not granted a divorce for a long period of time, due to the imam failing to track the husband down to gain his approval.[21]

A fourth set of concerns relates to the fairness of sharia processes. There are complaints that these processes lack procedural fairness and have no oversight or accountability.[22] There are also concerns that 'participation takes place in a space that is … male dominated and is often imbued with conservative interpretations regarding the position of women in Islam (as mothers, wives and daughters)'.[23]

Finally, implicit in some criticism of sharia processes is a concern that these processes compete with, challenge and may supplant the state.[24] This concern often stems from views about the desirability of state courts maintaining exclusive authority to adjudicate disputes,[25] views that sit uneasily with the recent push towards alternative dispute resolution across many jurisdictions.

II. Why Sharia Processes Exist

Given these concerns, it would be natural to ask why so many people, particularly women, engage with sharia processes. Many (but not all) Muslim women seeking a religious divorce turn to sharia processes to effectuate or facilitate a religious divorce. To appreciate why they do so, and why sharia processes are significant to some women, it is important to understand the different types of religious divorce in Islamic religious traditions. Appendix F offers a detailed account of types of

[19] F Ahmed and JC Norton, 'Religious Tribunals, Religious Freedom, and Concern for Vulnerable Women' (2012) 24 *Child and Family Law Quarterly* 363.

[20] Bano (n 18) 301.

[21] Gleeson, Baird and Malik (n 8).

[22] ibid.

[23] Bano (n 18) 302.

[24] See K Mendecka, 'Sharia Councils in Western Society: Compromise or Surrender (With Particular Reference to the United Kingdom)' (4th International Conference – Interdisciplinary Approach to Law in Modern Social Context, 21–22 April 2016) <www.tf.vu.lt/wp-content/uploads/2016/04/Interdisciplinary-Approach-to-Law-in-Modern-Social-Context_Pranešimų-rinkinys.pdf> accessed 1 November 2020, for some of the tropes about sharia processes vis-à-vis the state legal system.

[25] J Redding, *A Secular Need: Islamic Law and State Governance in Contemporary India* (University of Washington Press 2020) 57, 59, 63–64.

Islamic divorce and their different implications, but at this point it is important to understand the difference between four major types of divorce:

Talaq – This type of divorce spans a broad range of arrangements; however, this type of divorce is pronounced by the husband and requires his consent.

Talaq tafweedh – Islamic marriage contracts may contain a clause that gives the woman the right to effectuate a type of *talaq* divorce known as *talaq tafweedh*. The potential for greater use of this under-used clause is discussed further in chapter six. Appendix B contains an example of a *talaq tafweedh* in a marriage contract offered by the Board of Imams Victoria.

Khulah – This is the woman's right to release herself from the marriage. In contrast to *talaq*, some scholars believe that this type of divorce does not require the husband's consent (though there are scholars who believe the husband's consent is required).

Tafriq or Faskh – In this type of divorce, the marriage is dissolved by a religious court, usually because the husband has committed a wrong, including mistreatment of the wife.

The different types of divorce have different implications, for instance, for the *mahr* or the marriage-gift received by the wife, which will be explored later in this book. But to understand why women turn to sharia processes, it is important to appreciate that when the wife seeks a *tafriq or faskh* religious divorce due to abuse (which was the case for many of the women we interviewed), this requires a decision from a religious 'court'. Sharia processes sometimes serve the functions of such a religious court (though as we will see in chapter five, some imams are uncomfortable characterising sharia processes in this way). Even where a woman seeks a *khulah* divorce, which may not strictly *require* the involvement of a religious court, the divorce is generally facilitated through sharia processes. This is seen in the UK, Australia and Canada.

It is important to note, however, that sharia processes are not always regarded as essential for women to effectuate a religious divorce, and not all Muslim women view a religious divorce facilitated through a sharia process as essential. A *talaq* divorce may not require any kind of sharia process. Further, Anisa Buckley's work has highlighted ways in which Muslim women have gained religious divorces without sharia processes of the kind studied in this book, even in cases where their husband would not consent to a divorce or agree to initiate a *talaq* divorce. Some scholars have expressed the view that a civil divorce also serves as a religious divorce;[26] based on this ruling, some women have been able to fast-track their

[26] A Buckley, *Not 'Completely' Divorced: Muslim Women in Australia Navigating Muslim Family Laws* (Melbourne, Melbourne University Publishing, 2019) 159–61; M Jaraba, 'The Practice of Khulʿ in Germany: Pragmatism versus Conservatism' (2019) 26 *Islamic Law and Society* 83, 87. Unfortunately, the full text of the European Council for Fatwa and Research fatwa is no longer available online. However, relevant sections are available in V Sisler, 'European Courts' Authority Contested? The Case of Marriage

religious divorce through sharia processes[27] or circumvent the processes entirely.[28] However, this view – that a civil divorce is equivalent to a religious divorce – is heavily contested.[29] So many women may still prefer to approach sharia processes for a religious divorce.

The chapters that follow will discuss in more detail why women seek a religious divorce, even where they can gain a civil divorce. In short:

a. religious divorce is important to women who seek to fulfil their religious obligations or to 'do the right thing' from a religious perspective. Research shows that even women who do not identify as deeply religious seek out religious divorces for this reason;[30]
b. some women sought a religious divorce for closure, a definitive end to the relationship and to solidify 'boundaries' between them and their former spouses;
c. in some cases, the validation provided by a panel of imams helps to ease guilt that women might feel about ending the marriage;
d. a sense of closure and the definitive ending of the marriage by a religious authority is sometimes identified as important before women can pursue new relationships;
e. it has been argued that Muslim women seek out religious processes because they find civil court systems intimidating and foreign, and religious options more familiar and comfortable;[31] and
f. some of these reasons why women seek an Islamic divorce are particularly salient for women who are not in civil marriages; a religious divorce may be the only way to symbolically mark the end of a significant relationship.

and Divorce Fatwas On-Line' (2009) 3 *Masaryk U. J.L. & Tech.* 51 and J Macfarlane, *Islamic Divorce in North America: A Shari'a Path in a Secular Society* (Oxford, Oxford University Press, 2012). This fatwa is also discussed in L Larsen, *How Muftis Think: Islamic Legal Thought and Muslim Women in Western Europe* (Leiden, Brill, 2018) 92.

[27] John Bowen's research noted that the Islamic Sharia Council has continued to take this approach to fast-track women's religious divorce applications, as well as the Sharia Council of Birmingham, as long as the husband did not contest the civil divorce. JR Bowen, *On British Islam: Religion, Law, and Everyday Practice in Shari'a Councils* (Princeton NJ, Princeton University Press, 2016) 217.

[28] Buckley (n 26) 222. Our interviews also include cases where women took it upon themselves to determine they were divorced, eg, Interview 45.

[29] SH Al-Haddad, 'Fatwa: A Civil Divorce Is Not a Valid Islamic Divorce' (2010) Islam21c: <www.islam21c.com/fataawa/912-fatwa-a-civil-divorce-is-not-a-valid-islamic-divorce/> accessed 1 November 2020.

[30] J Macfarlane, 'Understanding Trends in American Muslim Divorce and Marriage: A Discussion Guide for Families and communities' (2012) *Institute for Social Policy and Understanding* 33: '[f]or others, their connection to Islam as a matter of personal identity is more significant than their formal obeisance to God. These individuals may lead a relatively secular lifestyle yet continue to embrace some critical rituals, usually associated with times of crisis and personal transition'. There are similar findings in the UK: R Parveen 'Do Sharia Councils Meet the Needs of Muslim Women?' in Bano (n 5) 147; T Walker, *Shari'a Councils and Muslim Women in Britain: Rethinking the Role of Power and Authority* (Leiden, Brill, 2017) 22.

[31] R Griffith-Jones, *Islam and English Law: Rights, Responsibilities and the Place of Shari'a* (Cambridge, Cambridge University Press, 2013) 395; Walker (n 30) 81.

Thus, while sharia processes have attracted widespread public criticism, they are also regarded by many women who use them as serving important purposes.

III. The Importance of Women's Experiences

Given the concerns and controversies that have surrounded sharia processes, it is unsurprising that they have received much recent scholarly attention in contemporary Western societies. Sharia processes in some states, including the UK and Canada, have been the subject of substantial and rigorous scholarly studies, which can inform public discourse. This is not true of sharia processes in Australia. There is little scholarly empirical evidence with which to assess claims made in the media about contemporary Australian sharia processes.[32] As a literature review report conducted for the Australian Human Rights Commission found: 'the research required to identify and analyze the patterns and dynamics of alternative dispute resolution related to family law matters in Islamic communities in Australia does not yet exist'.[33] This report also found:

> [w]hat is notably absent … is published empirical research … that demonstrates: how and why current family law and mediation provisions are failing Australian Islamic communities; the extent to which members of Australian Islamic communities engage in and support alternative dispute resolution processes related to divorce and family matters; the extent to which members of Australian Islamic communities eschew and reject alternative dispute resolution processes related to divorce and family matters; and how and why the existing operation of alternative dispute resolution processes related to divorce and family matters in Islamic communities do or do not serve their rights and interests.[34]

The need for such research is pressing. In particular, given that the main criticisms of sharia processes relate to their impacts on the women who engage with them, there is a particularly urgent need for scholarly attention to the *experiences* of women in sharia processes in Australia. This book will provide a much-needed, empirically informed account of how sharia processes are experienced by women.

[32] G Krayem, *Islamic Family Law in Australia: To Recognise or Not to Recognise* (Melbourne, Melbourne University Publishing, 2014) was the first empirical study of sharia processes in the Australian context, offering valuable insights into the workings of these processes. Krayem's research, based on interviews with 65 participants, focused on the Muslim community in New South Wales. This book builds upon Krayem's work by addressing the gender concerns which make these processes controversial, and by expanding the scope of the interviews, the sample of communities accessed, numbers of interviewees, and geographical locations within Australia, as well as the breadth of family law issues studied.

[33] Schofield King Lawyers, 'Intersections between the Law, Religion and Human Rights Project' (January 2011) <www.humanrights.gov.au/our-work/intersections-between-law-religion-and-human-rights-project-literature-review-prepared> accessed 1 November 2020.

[34] ibid 4.

Debates, controversies and tropes about sharia processes are truly transnational. Public, scholarly and media discussions about these processes in one Western liberal jurisdiction are explicitly and implicitly influenced by discussions in others.[35] An account of Australian sharia processes is therefore necessary for a more informed public and political discourse about sharia processes, and Islam, not just in Australia, but across Western liberal states.

IV. Methodology

The account of sharia processes in this book is also significant for its methods. It is based on insider and outsider research,[36] produced through in-depth interviews and analysed through constructivist grounded theory methods[37] of analysis. These methods made it possible for us to reveal the experiences of Muslim women as

[35] For example, A Buckley, 'What Are Muslim Women's Options in Religious Divorce?', *ABC Religion & Ethics*, 6 March 2020 discusses the Islamic status of Muslim civil divorce in Australia based on a 2002 ruling by the European Council for Fatwa and Research, 'The European Council for Fatwa and Research: Renewed Leadership, Renewed Hopes' <www.e-cfr.org/blog/2018/12/16/european-council-fatwa-research/> accessed 1 November 2020, as well as on divorces through the Fiqh Council of Birmingham, <www.fiqhcouncilbirmingham.com> accessed 27 October 2020. M Bhatti, 'What Is Islamic Dispute Resolution and Why Is It Controversial in Australia?' (*The Conversation*, 7 February 2019) <www.theconversation.com/what-is-islamic-dispute-resolution-and-why-is-it-controversial-in-australia-110497> accessed 27 October 2020, discusses women's concerns about patriarchal interpretations of Islamic divorce rules in Australia against similar reports in the UK. Scholarly work like A Aftab, 'Religious Accommodation in the Secular State: The Sharia Debates in Australia, Canada, and the United Kingdom' (2019) 79 *Studies in Law, Politics, and Society* 85 discusses sharia law in relation to multiculturalism and religious freedom in the jurisdictions of Australia, UK and Canada; I Uddin, 'Islamic Family Law: Imams, Mosques, and Sharīʿa Councils in the UK (2020) 8 *Electronic Journal of Islamic and Middle Eastern Law* 25 draws on an empirical study on marriage and divorce in the UK and Australia; I Uddin, 'Nikah-only Marriages: Causes, Motivations, and Their Impact on Dispute Resolution and Islamic Divorce Proceedings in England and Wales' (2018) 7 *Oxford Journal of Law and Religion* 401 discusses empirical studies in Canada and Australia compared to the UK; S Farrar and G Krayem, *Accommodating Muslims under Common Law: A Comparative Analysis* (Abingdon, Routledge, 2017) 206, studies the relationship between Muslims and the common law jurisdictions of Australia, Canada, England and Wales, and the USA; Bano (n 5) describes sharia processes in a number of jurisdictions including in Australia, Canada and the UK; N Aroney and R Ahdar, 'The Accommodation of the Shari'a within Western Legal Systems' (2012) 13 *Rutgers Journal of Law and Religion* 387 discusses the accommodation of sharia in Western jurisdictions including Australia.

[36] T Brannick and D Coghlan, 'In Defense of Being "Native": The Case for Insider Academic Research' (2007) 10 *Organizational Research Methods* 59.

[37] Grounded theory can be thought of as the systematic gathering and analysis of data which stresses the formation of theory informed by conceptual analysis, making it more than a description of the data gathered. It is suitable for 'studying individual processes, interpersonal relations and the reciprocal effects between individuals and larger social processes': Anselm Strauss and Juliet Corbin, 'Grounded Theory Methodology: An Overview' in NK Denzin and YS Lincoln (eds), *The SAGE Handbook of Qualitative Research* (London, Sage Publications, 2011) 273–85. Grounded theory emerged from the 1967 work of social scientists Barney Glaser and Anselm Strauss: BG Glaser and AL Strauss, *The Discovery of Grounded Theory* 7th edn (Piscataway NJ, Aldine Transaction, 2012). In their seminal work *The Discovery of Grounded Theory: Strategies for Qualitative Research*, Glaser and Strauss advocate for the generation of theory through the systematic interpretation of empirical data. Grounded theory as a methodology has been widely utilised in feminist scholarship, critical race scholarship, journalism, nursing, education and psychology (VB Martin et al, 'What Is Grounded Theory Good For?' (2018) 95

they engage with sharia processes in ways that would not have otherwise been possible.

Using grounded theory methods, this project took an inductive approach to understanding women's experiences of sharia processes at particular points of time. Rather than testing a specific hypothesis or answering a specific set of queries, it pieced together a picture of sharia processes through ongoing analysis of interviews.[38] Taking a constructivist approach, this project acknowledges that data analysis is located in a specific time, place, culture and context, 'but also reflect[s] our social, epistemological and research locations. Thus, our standpoints, starting points, and end points influence our data analyses'.[39] Our conscious and reflective approach to our identities influenced – and, we argue, benefitted – the generation and interpretation of data throughout the course of this project.

The research team associated with the project was diverse in terms of age, ethnicity and religious identity, but all researchers identified as women. This research was conducted against a background where Islamophobia is prevalent and normalised,[40] where Australian Muslims suffer from discrimination and are heavily 'over-researched'.[41] This has created a climate in which many potential research participants may be mistrustful of 'outsider' media organisations, government departments, universities and academics. The 'research fatigue'[42] that goes along with over-research means that potential participants are excessively exposed to participation in research projects and may have a sense of the:

> redundancy of research presence, as well as the sense that research fails to bring any tangible or substantive change or benefit … In some cases, research may be seen as constituting part of a system of surveillance and control that leads directly to the disadvantage and disempowerment of … community members … In other cases, research may be seen as benefiting the lives and careers of researchers but leaving the lives of those being researched unimproved in any significant way, regardless of the time, energy and resources they have contributed to the research effort.[43]

Journalism and Mass Communication Quarterly 11). While its application in legal theory appears quite limited, the multi-disciplinary nature of our research lends itself to an application of grounded theory. This approach benefits the research greatly due to its emphasis on fluidity and ongoing comparison between data, throughout the data collection phase.

[38] K Charmaz and L Belgrave, 'Qualitative Interviewing and Grounded Theory Analysis' in JF Gubrium et al (eds), *The Sage Handbook of Interview Research: The Complexity of the Craft* 2nd edn (London, Sage Publications, 2012) 347–66.

[39] ibid 349.

[40] S Poynting and L Briskman, 'Islamophobia in Australia: From Far-Right Deplorables to Respectable Liberals' (2018) 7 *Social Sciences* 213.

[41] J Koen, D Wassenaar and N Mamotte, 'The "Over-Researched Community": An Ethics Analysis of Stakeholders Views at Two South African HIV Prevention Research Sites' (2017) 194 *Social Science and Medicine* 1. Minority communities, along with Indigenous, low-income, post-crisis (war or genocide, for example) communities and those living in poverty, are among the most prevalent research participants the world over (M Sukarieh and S Tannock, 'On the Problem of Over-Researched Communities: The Case of the Shatila Palestinian Refugee Camp in Lebanon' (2012) 47 *Sociology* 494. For Muslims living in the West, the increased political and media interest in Islam has added a layer of keen academic interest.

[42] Koen, Wassenaar and Mamotte (n 41).

[43] Sukarieh and Tannock (n 41) 497.

These factors mean that there was a high risk that potential research participants would be disinclined to participate in research on topics like sharia processes.

Researching Muslim communities in this climate required community members to overcome this mistrust to participate in the research project. The project members who identified as Muslim women played a key role in overcoming this mistrust. These insider researchers[44] had a level of understanding and familiarity with research participants and lived experience of Islamophobia, leading to increased credibility, rapport and trust.[45] As such, they were able to access communities in ways an outsider would not have been able to, yielding richer data. Their knowledge and understanding also allowed them to provide a deeper, more nuanced analysis of the interview data.

From a constructivist perspective, our findings were shaped by the position of the researchers vis-à-vis the individuals and communities whose practices were being studied. We gained knowledge through interactions between participants and researchers, who related to participants – and Muslim communities – in many ways. The fact that all interviewers were women, and some researchers were Muslim and identifiable through the wearing of the *hijab*, facilitated rapport with women who had struggled through their divorce experiences. Further, some of the research team involved in the project were already widely connected and respected across the Muslim communities in New South Wales and Victoria through their active roles in community organisations. Women who had experienced sharia processes may have been more comfortable discussing specific cultural and religious perspectives with our interview team, given that it included people who are embedded and known within Muslim communities. The position of some of the research team within Muslim communities also allowed us trusted access to community organisations, imams and community leaders.

While the religious identity of the Muslim researchers played a vital role in accessing individuals, groups and institutions with experience of sharia processes, we remained alert and sensitive to the challenges and potential problems with insider research. First the Muslim researchers were aware that they occupied what Brannick and Coghlan call 'role duality' in that they are both insiders and outsiders at once, intertwining the narrative of the researched and the researcher.[46] As researchers and interviewers, they emphasised to participants their 'outsider' role as researchers associated with multiple public universities. They repeatedly underscored the implications of this 'outsider' role: that they were researchers, not community workers; that they were obliged to report their findings impartially; and that information collected in these interviews would be made available to the

[44] A Griffith, 'Insider/Outsider: Epistemological Privilege and Mothering Work' (1998) 21 *Human Studies* 361.

[45] S Unluer, 'Being an Insider Researcher While Conducting Case Study Research' (2012) 17 *Qualitative Report* 1, 5.

[46] T Brannick and D Coghlan, 'In Defense of Being "Native": The Case for Insider Academic Research' (2007) 10 *Organizational Research Methods* 59.

public through presentations in academic forums, a community report and in the publication of a book and journal articles.

Second, it is sometimes feared that insiders may lack objectivity, miss nuances, take things for granted, avoid sensitive issues or leave their assumptions unchallenged.[47] Three researchers – including two senior academics – who do not identify or present as Muslim played key roles in the project. Further, one researcher with expertise on comparable sharia processes in other jurisdictions was unfamiliar with the Australian Muslim communities at the centre of this research. These relative outsiders were variously involved in the project planning from the very earliest stage, and advised the team on methodology, conducted interviews, and analysed data. Their involvement acted to check concerns – for example around taking facts for granted or objectivity – relating to insider research.

Whilst Appendix A explains in greater detail the different stages of the empirical research undertaken for this book, it is important to outline some key aspects of the way in which we conducted the interviews. We interviewed across three different groups of participants:

- women who have engaged with sharia processes due to marital breakdown;
- imams and community leaders who have experience and knowledge of these processes; and
- professionals, including lawyers, mediators, psychologists and social workers, who have worked with clients who have experienced these processes.

It was an important part of our methodology to understand sharia processes from multiple perspectives, giving us as researchers a 'bird's eye' view of the way in which the processes operated, and in particular the experiences of those who use them. Our findings throughout the book are informed by all these perspectives. The interviews gave us a unique understanding of how sharia processes were operating in Sydney and Melbourne, being the cities with the largest Muslim communities in Australia. The 2016 Australian Census recorded 2.6 per cent of the population as Muslim.[48] The biggest concentration of Muslim communities is in New South Wales (44 per cent of Muslims in Australia, around 268,000 people live there) and Victoria (33 per cent of Muslims in Australia, around 197,000 people live there), specifically in the Greater Sydney and Greater Melbourne areas.[49]

[47] Unluer (n 45) 6.

[48] Australian Bureau of Statistics, Religion in Australia: 2016 Census Data Summary (28 June 2017) <www.abs.gov.au/ausstats/abs@.nsf/Lookup/by%20Subject/2071.0~2016~Main%20Features~Religion%20Data%20Summary~70> accessed 1 November 2020.

[49] K Dekker, W Brouwer and V Colic-Peisker, *Suburbs with a Higher Concentration of Muslim Residents in Sydney and Melbourne: Spatial concentration, community, liveability and satisfaction* (RMIT, Social and Global Studies Centre, 2019) 11–12; see also J Forrest, 'Suburbs "swamped" by Asians and Muslims? The data show a different story' (*The Conversation*, 5 July 2017) <https://theconversation.com/suburbs-swamped-by-asians-and-muslims-the-data-show-a-different-story-79250> accessed 1 November 2020.

Finally, our study used comparative methods as a tool for understanding sharia processes. As already mentioned, the project findings contribute to transnational discussions about sharia processes. Equally, the literature on these processes in the UK and Canada helped shape our earliest inquiries – including interviews – as well as our proposals for change. Studies of sharia councils and Islamic divorce in the UK and Canada shaped our inquiry by highlighting likely points of interest and concern in Australian sharia processes.

The comparative method allows us to paint a nuanced picture of sharia processes through comparative description of these processes across three states which share common law legal systems, established multicultural populations and histories of controversy around sharia processes. Reflecting on shared and distinctive features of sharia processes across these similar jurisdictions deepens our understanding of the processes in each of these jurisdictions and of sharia processes in the West, more generally. The significance of our findings from our fieldwork in Australia is made clearer by setting it against what we know about sharia processes across these broadly similar jurisdictions. The broadly similar legal[50] and social contexts also facilitate comparative reflection with the aim of making recommendations for change.

V. Significance and Outline

The next chapter provides an outline of the key groups, institutions and individuals – imams and groupings of imams – who offer sharia processes, as well as an outline of the stages and steps in the processes themselves. We set our new findings about the people, procedures and practices associated with sharia processes against existing research on these processes in the UK and Canada.

Chapter three offers an account of women's experiences of sharia processes based on extensive interviews with women who used these processes in Australia, and the professionals who supported them, contextualised against empirical research from the UK and Canada. The chapter explores why women sought a religious, as well as a civil, divorce. It traces their experiences attempting to resolve marital difficulties through mediation with community leaders, professionals and families, right up to their experience with sharia processes, typically in order to secure a religious divorce. The chapter highlights the challenges that women faced, including the lack of gender representation on the divorce panels, imams' responses to domestic violence and the lack of transparency in the divorce process.

In chapter four, based on in-depth interviews with imams, we explore their roles and perspectives in sharia processes. The chapter focuses on the issues faced by imams in what they see as their key roles of facilitating reconciliation

[50] The similarity of legal systems is salient as sharia processes arguably operate in the shadow of the law: see RH Mnookin and L Kornhauser, 'Bargaining in the Shadow of the Law: The Case of Divorce' (1979) 88 *Yale Law Journal* 950.

and (failing that) facilitating divorce. The chapter explores imams' responses to the experiences of women, and the professionals who support them which were detailed in chapter three. We also identify the many challenges faced by imams in the administration of sharia processes.

Chapter five offers an account of the outcomes – in a broad sense – of sharia processes, including outcomes relating to divorce, financial settlements and arrangements for children. We explore how different divorce outcomes – different types of Islamic divorce – have repercussions for women's financial entitlements. We offer an account of the advice that imams give regarding women's potential financial entitlements in Islamic jurisprudence. We find that imams are reluctant to offer advice on child custody[51] and financial issues (apart from the *mahr* – the marriage gift from the husband to the wife), so we offer an account of how women who use sharia processes seek outcomes on these issues from mediation or state processes.

Chapter six details the changes that have taken place in Australian sharia processes over the five years of our study. The improvements in the sharia processes of important bodies such as the Centre for Arbitration and the Resolution Disputes (CARD) and the Board of Imams in Victoria (BOIV) are significant. This chapter documents those changes, and we offer suggestions for improvements, particularly relating to women's experiences, that are relevant for the providers of sharia processes. We also recommend broader changes directed to Muslim community organisations and the Australian legal system. The comparative experiences of sharia processes in the UK and Canada inform our suggestions, and some of our suggestions may be relevant to the providers of sharia processes in those countries.

Overall, this book offers three main sets of insights about sharia processes. While scholarly research and media investigations have found instances of women being dismissed, discriminated against and harmed by sharia processes, this book adds depth and nuance to our understanding through its multi-perspective focus on women's experiences. Common criticisms of sharia processes centre on perceived problems with the norms they adopt, for example religious rules on property or custody, or their outcomes, for example failure or delay in receiving a divorce. Our study reveals subtler aspects of women's experiences with these processes. Some of the women we interviewed described how their experience affected their ability to practice and stay connected with their faith. Others expressed anguish and profound disappointment that imams did not – even informally – acknowledge the injustice done to them or rebuke or chastise their husbands. Others, still, were disconcerted by different languages spoken in the course of some sharia processes. Significantly, some women had positive experiences of sharia processes, describing imams as their advocates and as playing a familial supportive role. Thus, the book enriches our understanding of sharia processes by revealing a fuller and

[51] While we use the term child custody because that is widely recognised as a descriptor of the disputes about parenting that arise upon separation, we acknowledge that the *Family Law Act (1975)* (Cth) uses the terms parenting orders and time spent with the child.

more nuanced range of women's experiences, which are not reducible to the standard criticisms levelled at these processes.

Secondly, this book challenges some important preconceptions about sharia processes. A widespread implicit assumption is that sharia processes – based on religious law – are immutable and unchanging.[52] This book overturns that assumption. Through staggered interviews, we capture how the processes have changed and evolved over time. The book shows sharia processes to have more capacity for evolution, even dynamism, than previously understood.

Thirdly, the book challenges preconceptions about attitudes within the Muslim community about the relationship between sharia processes and the state. It is sometimes reported that the Muslim community favours the legal recognition of decisions and settlements reached in community forums.[53] However, our interviews with community leaders, imams, Muslim lawyers, psychologists, social workers and the women who engaged with sharia processes revealed very little appetite – indeed very little interest – in state recognition for sharia processes. Contrary to public discourse, which characterises sharia processes as being in tension or competition with the Australian legal system, we found that imams and other community actors explicitly and implicitly deferred to the Australian legal system and accepted its authority.

Finally, our interviews elicited suggestions for how sharia processes and the Australian family law system should be changed in order to improve women's experiences. These suggestions came from imams; from women with first-hand experience of the processes; and from legal, mental health and social work professionals, who together provide multi-perspectival views on best practices. The book draws on these views, as well as studies of different practices in sharia processes in the UK and Canada, to offer recommendations on how sharia processes and the state family law system should change.

[52] See A Emon, 'Islamic Law and the Canadian Mosaic: Politics, Jurisprudence, and Multicultural Accommodation' (2009) 37 *Canadian Bar Review* 391, 395; A El Shamsy and NJ Coulson, 'Sharīʿah', *Encyclopædia Britannica*, 25 August 2020 <www.britannica.com/topic/Shariah> accessed 27 October 2020; A A Engineer, 'Is Sharia immutable?', *Dawn*, 1 February 2003 <www.dawn.com/news/782766/is-sharia-immutable> accessed 27 October 2020.

[53] Hole (n 6); N Berkovic, 'Hyder Gulam Calls for Australia to Embrace Legal Pluralism', *The Australian*, 28 September 2012; P Hanson, The senate first speech. Commonwealth of Australia Senate, 14 September 2016. For instance, the submission by the Australian Federation of Islamic Councils (AFIC) to the Parliamentary Joint Standing Committee on Migration asks for 'legal pluralism', possibly suggesting greater recognition of Islamic decision-makers (Australian Federation of Islamic Councils, 2011); A Black, 'Legal Recognition of Sharia Law: Is This the Right Direction for Family Law Matters?' (2010) 84 *Family Matters* 65: 'Among Australian Muslims, there exists a strong preference to have legal questions answered and disputes settled by person with Islamic credentials'; M Ozalp, 'Do Australian Muslims want Shari'ah Law in Australia?' (2012) 221(3) *St Mark's Review* 66, 67.

2

People, Procedures and Practices

I. Introduction

This chapter provides an introductory overview of Muslim community organisations, groups and individuals who offer sharia processes, as well as the procedures and practices they adopt, in the UK, Canada and Australia. The discussion of Australian processes is informed by fieldwork conducted in Muslim communities in Sydney and Melbourne. Surveying different sharia processes across these jurisdictions enriches our understanding of these processes by revealing their diversity as well as points of convergence. This chapter offers an overview of some of the main institutions and groups and their procedures and practices, acknowledging that comprehensive coverage of all sharia processes would be impossible. It also discusses how sharia processes interact with the state family law system, particularly civil divorce. In later chapters, the different procedures and practices across these jurisdictions will be used to recommend changes to sharia processes in Australia.

II. British Institutions and Processes

In the UK, institutions or groupings that deal with Islamic divorce and ancillary matters are usually called 'sharia councils'.[1] While some councils are quite informal, others like the Sharia Council of the Birmingham Central Mosque, the

[1] There is no definitive information on the number of sharia councils that operate in the UK. A report published by thinktank Civitas in 2009 claimed that at least 85 sharia councils were in operation: D MacEoin and DG Green, *Sharia Law or 'One Law for All'?* (CIVITAS: Institute for the Study of Civil Society, 2009) 69. Another independent review into sharia law in England and Wales in 2018 noted that research and anecdotal estimates vary between 30 sharia councils currently in existence to the 85 councils noted in the Civitas report: M Siddiqui, A-M Hutchinson, S Momtaz and Sir M Hedley, 'The Independent Review into the Application of Sharia Law in England and Wales' (Presented to Parliament by the Secretary of State for the Home Department by Command of Her Majesty, February 2018). Meanwhile, in an interview conducted by John Bowen, it was claimed that there are 'probably about a dozen' across the country: JR Bowen, *On British Islam: Religion, Law, and Everyday Practice in Shari'a Councils* (Princeton NJ, Princeton University Press, 2016) 61.

Islamic Sharia Council (ISC) and the Muslim Law Sharia Council (MLSC) are more formal with written procedural rules, websites, regular meetings and fees for service.[2] The councils all have a shared purpose and offer similar services, namely, religious guidance on a range of issues, mediation and counselling services for marital disputes, and facilitation of religious divorce.[3] There is an enormous diversity amongst the councils not only in terms of the number of religious scholars offering advice but also in terms of the theological orientations of the scholars within these councils (based on their formal training in Islamic jurisprudence).[4]

Sharia councils are often closely associated with local mosques, which are spread out geographically across the UK. The councils therefore tend to be shaped by the localised (ethnic) cultures of the mosque communities, in addition to the diverse Islamic schools of thought.[5] Despite the differences in their theological orientations, scholars work together to reach consensus through discussions and debate.[6] Further, even councils with different theological orientations, like ISC and MLSC, have 'friendly relations' and recognise each other's procedures.[7]

A. Key Organisations, Procedures and Practices

Sharia processes vary between the councils described above, though bodies like the ISC and MLSC implement formal procedures that must be followed before a determination can be made about a divorce application, and any divorce certificates issued.[8] These administrative procedures are much the same across the more formally structured sharia councils. The general steps in UK sharia processes are outlined in Figure 1.

i. Islamic Sharia Council

In line with the process outlined in Figure 1, ISC follows a defined procedure, open to some variation, and records the procedure and documentation in a file.[9] When the wife submits a form to ISC requesting a divorce, the ISC sends out letters to the husband up to three times before the divorce process begins.[10]

[2] R Dalph Grillo, *Muslim Families, Politics and the Law: A Legal Industry in Multicultural Britain* (Farnham, Ashgate, 2015) 19; T Walker, Shari'a Councils and Muslim Women in Britain: Rethinking the Role of Power and Authority (Leiden, Brill, 2017) 45.

[3] Walker (n 2) 45.

[4] S Bano, *Muslim Women and Shari'ah Councils: Transcending the Boundaries of Community and Laws* (Basingstoke, Palgrave Macmillan, 2012) 85–86.

[5] ibid 87.

[6] Bowen (n 1) 61.

[7] ibid.

[8] Bano (n 4) 108.

[9] Bowen (n 1) at 67.

[10] ibid 71.

Interviews with both spouses then take place, but more often than not the parties are interviewed separately.[11] However, even before the proceedings begin, the ISC requires a civil divorce proceeding to be initiated if the marriage was registered in the UK or conducted overseas. Additionally, it requires proof that couples have been separated (that is, have not had sex) for one year through a document signed by two witnesses[12] – a lower requirement than the civil divorce requirement of two- and five-year separation periods depending on whether the divorce is contested.[13]

Figure 1 Overview of UK Sharia Processes[14]

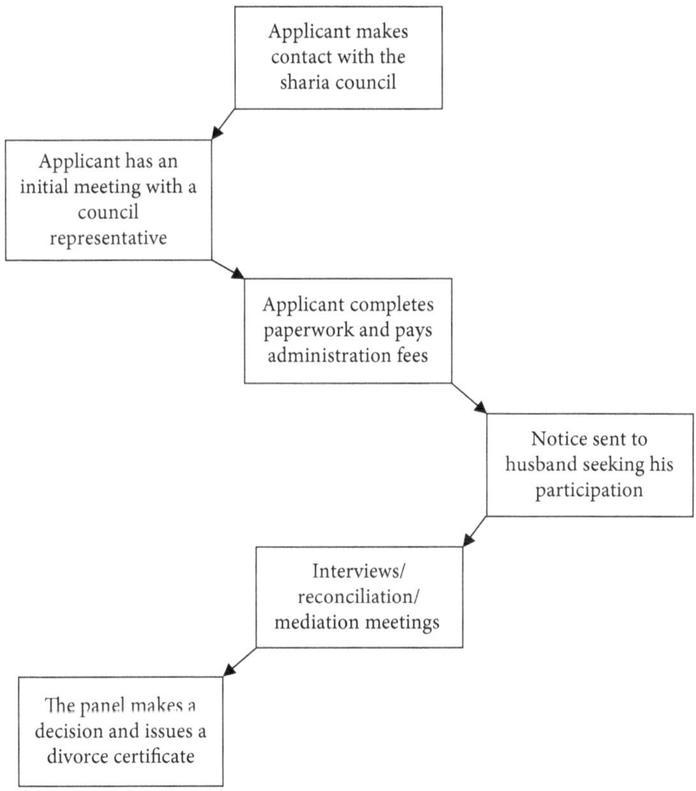

[11] ibid.
[12] ibid 72.
[13] ibid 73.
[14] ibid 109; S Bano, 'An Exploratory Study of Shariah Councils in England With Respect to Family Law' (Centre for Islamic and Middle Eastern Law, University of Reading 2012) 20.

ii. Sharia Council of the Birmingham Central Mosque

In contrast to ISC, the Sharia Council of the Birmingham Central Mosque only hears cases from women seeking an Islamic divorce if the civil divorce has been completed. In this sharia council, female staff engage in most of the discussions with clients, with applicants attending three counselling sessions with a female counsellor before their application can proceed.[15] The parties must attend reconciliation meetings, and only once it is established that reconciliation is unlikely to occur does the file proceed to the council panel to determine whether a divorce certificate should be issued.[16] It is only when all the facts have been ascertained and dossiers prepared that the panel of scholars become involved in order to make a decision.[17] In 2013, the council decided that where a civil divorce was awarded and the husband did not contest the Islamic divorce, the scholars did not need to consider the case, and other staff at the council could confirm the Islamic divorce.[18]

iii. Muslim Law Sharia Council

At MLSC, potential applicants are not required to go through reconciliation processes like those carried out at the ISC and Sharia Council of the Birmingham Central Mosque. It is only if applicants wish to attempt reconciliation that the MLSC will offer counselling with a qualified Muslim counsellor.[19]

iv. The Muslim Arbitration Tribunal

The Muslim Arbitration Tribunal (MAT) at Hijaz offers the possibility of resolving commercial and other kinds of disputes through binding arbitration under the terms of the *Arbitration Act 1996* (UK). Since 2012, even financial and property disputes arising from a divorce may be resolved by arbitration.[20] This is perhaps the most formal process compared to the other councils.[21] Otherwise, it largely follows similar processes to the other sharia councils.[22]

The cost of obtaining a religious divorce in the UK varies amongst the councils. For instance, the ISC charges £400 for a *khulah* or *talaq* with additional costs for other services;[23] while the Sharia Council of the Birmingham Central Mosque charges a

[15] Bano (n 4) 123.
[16] ibid 127.
[17] Bowen (n 1) 61.
[18] ibid.
[19] Bano (n 4)130.
[20] Bowen (n 1) 155. See also MAT website, which outlines the services offered <www.matribunal.com/services.php> accessed 1 November 2020.
[21] Walker (n 2) 45.
[22] ibid 53.
[23] The Islamic Shari'a Council, 'Prices' <www.islamic-sharia.org/services/prices/> accessed 1 November 2020.

fee of £300 for the whole proceeding and divorce certificate (£200 if a civil divorce has already been obtained).[24] Similarly, the MLSC has an all-inclusive fee of £325 for a *khulah* divorce.[25] Some Muslim women and men have been critical of these charges.[26] The outcomes of sharia processes in the UK, including with respect to divorce, custody and property and financial settlements, are discussed in chapter six.

III. Canadian Institutions and Processes

In 2003, an Islamic arbitration tribunal was established by the Canadian Society of Muslims (CSM), an Islamic group headed by Syed Mumtaz Ali, through the Institute of Islamic Civil Justice (IICJ).[27] Following the establishment of the IICJ, Ali announced that the IICJ would arbitrate family disputes and inheritance matters in line with sharia, and that the decisions would be enforceable under the *Ontario Arbitration Act 1991*.[28] This set off a heated debate about the nature of sharia-based arbitration and eventually led to the law being amended so that religious arbitrations were not recognised in 2006.[29]

The media coverage which followed created the (incorrect) impression that the amendment to the *Arbitration Act* also banned 'sharia law' implying that any Muslim who sought Islamic divorce through private processes was committing an illegal act.[30] Existing private processes for religious divorce taking place with imams and self-described 'arbitrators' were inaccurately described as 'arbitration tribunals'. In reality, these did not fulfil the prerequisites to be legally recognised as arbitration processes.[31] Despite popular perception, the 2006 policy change had little or no impact upon the most pressing issue for Muslim women – religious divorce.[32]

[24] Birmingham Central Mosque, 'Birmingham Sharia Council' <https://centralmosque.org.uk/wp-content/uploads/2019/03/Birmingham-Shariah-Council-Prospectus-March-2019.pdf> accessed 1 November 2020.

[25] The Muslim Law Sharia Council UK, 'Khula (Divorce)' <www.shariahcouncil.org/khula-divorce/> accessed 1 November 2020.

[26] Secretary of State for the Home Department, *The Independent Review into the Application of Sharia Law in England and Wales* (February 2018) 14.

[27] SM Ali, 'Why Was the Institute Formed?' <www.muslimcanada.org/sufi/mumtaz.htm?> accessed 1 November 2020.

[28] A Macklin, 'Multiculturalism Meets Privatization: The Case of Faith-Based Arbitration' (2013) 9 *International Journal of Law in Context* 343, 345–46; S Razack, 'The Sharia Law Debate in Ontario: The Modernity/Premodernity Distinction in Legal Efforts to Protect Women from Culture' (2007) 15 *Feminist Legal Studies* 3.

[29] AC Korteweg, 'The Sharia Debate in Ontario: Gender, Islam, and Representations of Muslim Women's Agency' (2006) 18 *ISIM Review* 50; C Cutting, 'Sharia and Constraint: Practices, Policies, and Responses to Faith-Based Arbitration in Ontario' (UWSpace 2013) 189.

[30] J Macfarlane, *Islamic Divorce in North America: A Shari'a Path in a Secular Society* (Oxford, Oxford University Press, 2012) 16.

[31] ibid 15.

[32] C Cutting, 'Faith-Based Arbitration or Religious Divorce: What Was the Issue?' in AC Korteweg and JA Selby, *Debating Sharia: Islam, Gender Politics, and Family Law Arbitration* (Toronto, University of Toronto Press, 2012) 66; Cutting (n 29) 189.

The continued presence of Muslim organisations and individuals offering dispute resolution to Muslims in Ontario has recently been highlighted in a study by Cutting.[33] Religious leaders now act more as religious counsellors rather than as adjudicators, imparting their knowledge of religious norms to help mediate disputes between spouses.[34]

A. Key Organisations

Sharia processes in Canada are generally relatively informal in nature, lacking a centralised system and sets of standards, and formal recordkeeping, which means that there are local variations in the practices of imams adjudicating religious divorces.[35] As in the UK, Canadian Muslim community groups present a number of options for women seeking religious divorce or dispute resolution, some of which we discuss below. In addition to the groups discussed below, women seeking divorce may also receive support and advice from the Canadian Council of Muslim Women (CCMW), which is explicitly opposed to faith-based arbitration.[36] The CCMW works to empower and support Muslim women by offering information, tools and resources, including contacts for legal services.[37]

i. Darul Iftaa

Although several organisations and individual imams grant religious divorces in Canada, Darul Iftaa handles the greatest number of divorces.[38] Darul Iftaa was established in 2007 and functions under the umbrella of the Canadian Council of Muslim Theologians (CCMT). Despite being the most preferred organisation for divorce services, the Darul Iftaa muftis state that they do not deal with any monetary issues regarding division of property or financial support.[39] In terms of its theological leanings, Darul Iftaa claims to adhere to an orthodox interpretation of the Hanafi school and caters mostly to those from South Asian backgrounds. However, in matters of 'limping marriages' (where women have a civil divorce but the husband refuses to grant them a religious divorce) the imams have borrowed heavily from the Maliki school to provide women with greater leeway in grounds for *faskh*.[40]

[33] Cutting (n 32) 67.
[34] A Saris, 'Challenging Stereotypes: Gender-Sensitive Imams and the Resolution of Family Disputes Law in Canada Montreal' in F Banda and LF Joffe (eds), *Women's Rights and Religious Law* (Abingdon, Routledge, 2016) 257.
[35] Macfarlane (n 30) 145.
[36] Cutting (n 29) 235; Razack (n 28) 9–10.
[37] See Canadian Council of Muslim Women (CCMW), <www.ccmw.com/resources> accessed 27 October 2020.
[38] Cutting (n 29) 207.
[39] Cutting (n 29) 210; Cutting (n 32) 71.
[40] Cutting (n 29) 205; Cutting (n 32) 72.

Similar to the UK sharia councils, where it was estimated approximately 90 per cent of cases are brought by women seeking religious divorce, all cases brought to Darul Iftaa are by women seeking annulments of their religious marriage.[41]

ii. Islamic Social Services and Resources Association

Unlike Darul Iftaa, the Islamic Social Services and Resources Association (ISSRA) caters to Muslims from diverse ethnic backgrounds and applies the school of Islamic law requested by the client. ISSRA was established in 1990 and provides various services and social programs. The imams do not provide formal arbitration for civil disputes, although they provide mediation services between family members (which are impacted by how families settle divorces in the civil courts regarding financial matters and custody).[42] Couples have to complete the process of civil divorce first if they want to use the services of ISSRA.

iii. Institute of Islamic Civil Justice

The IICJ may have been at the centre of the sharia controversy in the early 2000s that led to legislative changes to the arbitration laws, but many of the mediators and arbitrators associated with the IICJ now work with the Muslim Mediation Services (MMS), which is the only Islamic organisation in Ontario that carries out arbitrations that adhere to the new arbitration provisions, and thus are court enforceable.[43] To comply with the regulations, the MMS has a formal procedure that ensures documentation is kept, that independent legal advice is provided to parties, and that they operate within the limits of the civil family law framework.[44]

B. Procedures and Practices

The procedures and practices used by different imams, whether acting independently or in association with the organisations mentioned above, vary widely. While some imams encourage both parties to engage a family lawyer to finalise the civil process, others work with parties to reconcile or reach a divorce decision.[45] This was seen in cases from Quebec where the role of imams (as religious counsellors) was to enable couples to reconcile and save their marriage if possible. Where attempts to reconcile fail, imams generally advise the spouses to seek a

[41] Cutting (n 32) 72.
[42] ibid 74; Cutting (n 29) 211.
[43] Cutting (n 32) 68.
[44] ibid 69.
[45] J Macfarlane, 'Practising an "Islamic Imagination": Islamic Divorce in North America' in AC Korteweg and JA Selby, *Debating Sharia: Islam, Gender Politics, and Family Law Arbitration* (Toronto, University of Toronto Press, 2012) 56.

civil divorce in court.[46] ISSRA imams require a civil divorce to be secured before an Islamic divorce is granted, although it recommends mediating financial issues before going to court to avoid financial and emotional costs.[47]

Typically, imams approached by women seeking to initiate a religious divorce attempt to contact the husband three times, over a period from six months to a year, before they are comfortable proceeding with the divorce.[48] In most cases, the process followed does not resemble a formal arbitration, rather it is 'a highly informal and idiosyncratic process' marked by the absence of formal processes.[49] Strikingly, not all imams keep records of divorces or provide any written confirmation of divorce, unless the parties request certificates of divorce either for family or for legal purposes, such as for returning to their Muslim countries of origin (for example, Iran).[50] Although individual imams generally handle requests for divorce, of late, panels of imams have also been established. Where panels of imams have emerged within community organisations, they determine whether to approve a divorce by resorting to a paper review process rather than an oral hearing.[51]

To take one instance of practice, couples approaching the imam of the Islamic Centre of Quebec in Montreal[52] are advised to first apply for a civil divorce, as he does not have the legal authorisation to grant a divorce. In cases where the couple has obtained a civil divorce, the imam asks the husband to pronounce three consecutive divorce declarations over three months to make it final. If the couple has not yet obtained a civil divorce, the imam offers to reconcile the parties and if this is rejected (or fails), advises the husband to pronounce *talaq* once a month over three months to finalise the divorce.

The nature of proceedings also varies depending on who initiates the divorce. If the husband initiates the divorce, there is no need for witnesses, and the wife must be informed of the divorce either verbally or in writing. If the wife is not present or not informed, the proceedings become void. On the other hand, the wife can initiate divorce only if civil procedures have already commenced. Generally, she must return her *mahr* and explain her reasons for divorce to the imam. If the reasons are acceptable to the imam, he will then ask the husband to pronounce *talaq*. If the husband refuses, the wife can give her reasons for divorce in the presence of two male or one male and two female witnesses, and the imam would thereafter declare that the Islamic divorce has taken place (either *khulah*, *faskh* or *tafriq*).

[46] Saris, 'Challenging Stereotypes' (n 34) 260.
[47] Cutting (n 32) 75.
[48] Macfarlane (n 45) 59.
[49] Macfarlane (n 30) 155.
[50] ibid 158.
[51] ibid 155.
[52] Immigration and Refugee Board of Canada, *Canada: Information on the Procedures for Securing a Divorce in Islam in Canada, on Whether These Procedures Are Uniform throughout Canada, and on Whether a Record of the Divorce Would Be Kept at a Mosque if the Divorce Took Place in Canada* (1 May 1997) <www.refworld.org/docid/3ae6acf360.html> accessed 27 October 2020.

Even after the completion of proceedings, the imam does not sign a certificate of divorce as only civil authorities can do so. This has led to records of Islamic divorces in Canada being almost non-existent. Nevertheless, if requested by the parties, he will write a letter attesting that the Islamic divorce took place once the civil divorce is awarded and will keep a copy for his records.

While there is a European Council for Fatwa and Research (ECFR) *fatwa* proclaiming civil divorce as an 'equivalent' to Islamic divorce, this has not been completely accepted by the relevant communities. In her study, Macfarlane found that a number of respondents did not accept the *fatwa* completely, as they felt they needed closure by way of a religious divorce and their families and communities would not accept a civil divorce as equivalent to religious divorce.[53] Even the imams who recognised the *fatwa* nonetheless felt that couples needed to consult them to come to an agreement on consent orders and to gain closure, as well as to secure documentation of an Islamic divorce.[54] Moreover, once an Islamic divorce is obtained, the parties can apply for an uncontested civil divorce which does not require lawyers. Thus, an Islamic divorce enables parties to 'reduce the costs of hiring separate lawyers and fighting a protracted legal battle'.[55]

Lastly, obtaining a religious divorce from imams in Canada appears to be virtually cost-free,[56] unlike in Britain. The outcomes of Canadian sharia processes will be discussed further in chapter six.

IV. Australian Institutions and Processes

Sharia processes in Australia are, in comparison with British sharia councils, less formal and more loosely organised. However, over the course of our research, the groups of imams dealing with these issues in Australia became increasingly formalised and institutionalised. Nevertheless, the more informal and ad hoc arrangements still remain, and individual imams continue to deal with issues around marital disputes and breakdown.

Australian sharia processes are also diverse in terms of the theological orientation of those who offer them. Imams often consider all the different schools of thought when making a determination as to what is in the best interests of the couple in dispute.[57] The Board of Imams Victoria rely closely on the Qatari Code of Family Law, extracts from which are reproduced in Appendix G.

The Australian National Islamic Council (ANIC) is the only central Islamic organisation of imams and Islamic scholars with broad representation across Australia. One of its key responsibilities is to elect the Grand Mufti of Australia;

[53] Macfarlane (n 30) 237.
[54] ibid.
[55] Macfarlane (n 45) 55.
[56] Macfarlane (n 30) 154.
[57] Interview 14 (Melbourne, April 2016).

the current Grand Mufti is Dr Ibrahim Abu Mohamed. ANIC has developed the Centre for Arbitration and the Resolution Disputes Ltd (CARD) whose key function is to facilitate the resolution of marital disputes. Each state in Australia has either a Board or Council that meets the needs of the Muslims in that state, except for Tasmania which is directly served by ANIC.[58] The most established groupings of imams working on sharia processes are found in Sydney at ANIC and the Board of Imams Victoria (BOIV) in Melbourne.[59] There are also other 'groupings' of imams who facilitate sharia processes, for example, the imams affiliated with the Lebanese Muslim Association (LMA) in Sydney.

Cultural context plays an important role in understanding how Australian Muslims resolve their family disputes. Across Australia, there is a wide diversity of Muslim communities representing some 62 different ethnicities. These include Aboriginal and non-Aboriginal Australian-born Muslims, established communities of Turkish, Kurdish, Lebanese, Egyptian, Bosnian and Indonesian Muslims and recently arrived communities from Iraq, Somalia, Afghanistan, Pakistan, Bangladesh and India. In some cases, the cultural context of the country of origin influences how couples proceed with disputes that arise in Australia, particularly in newly emerging and migrant communities. The availability of imams from these communities also influences the way in which a divorce is sought as some communities will prefer to approach imams from their cultural group, but not all communities will have an imam from their cultural group. Arabic-speaking communities, such as the Lebanese, Egyptian and more recently Iraqi, will generally use the established imam groupings such as the ANIC, BOIV or LMA. These communities have been in Australia for some time and have well-established family and community networks as well as imams from their cultural background.

A. Key Organisations, Procedures and Practices

i. *Board of Imams Victoria (BOIV)*

The Board of Imams Victoria (BOIV) has established what they call the 'Council of Islamic Family Arbitration and Mediation'. This is a service offered to 'facilitate Islamic divorce for Muslim women',[60] as well as mediation and counselling services. While not all Muslims will approach institutions like BOIV, our research suggests BOIV serves a range of cultural communities. For example, one interviewee explains how a divorce in the Indonesian community is generally sought:

> [I]f they decide to have a divorce, for example, it depends on where they got married. So if they got married in Indonesia, sometimes they just get the divorce, *talaq*, and

[58] See Australian National Imams Council (ANIC) <www.anic.org.au> accessed 27 October 2020.
[59] See Board of Imams Victoria <www.boiv.org.au> accessed 27 October 2020.
[60] Interview 14 (Melbourne, April 2016).

> then … they don't go to the Board of Imams, even though I refer them to them. So in most cases, that's fine. And then everybody knows that, *Okay, that couple is actually divorced*. That's it. But if they were married here … Sometimes they will go to the Board of Imams after I refer them, or they go to the court. But mostly they prefer to go to the court.[61]

The following case of a mixed marriage from that community also illustrates cross-cultural referral to BOIV:

> The woman is Indonesian and the husband is Iraqi or something like that. Along the way, the wife didn't know that the husband is cheating and then there was kind of neglection … and then the wife asked for a divorce but the husband didn't want to. And I referred them to the Board of Imams. I knew that the sheikh [imam or religious scholar] that I referred to tried to call the husband and there was no response, there was no update, there was no follow up. And then, okay, the wife is giving up and then she just, *Okay then, I'll go to the court instead*.[62]

The Board consists of five imams, who are also members of BOIV and meet once a week as a panel. As of 2019, this panel includes a female scholar.[63] In interviews, imams stated that in about half of all cases heard by the Board, a civil divorce has already been finalised.[64] In the remaining cases, a civil divorce has been sought but is still pending, and the applicant wishes to finalise the religious element of the divorce.[65]

BOIV's first form of engagement with couples centres on an attempt to reconcile them. We have access to two application forms provided by BOIV. The form reproduced in Appendix C is an application for 'Mediation/Reconciliation – Family Counselling'. The form reproduced in Appendix D is an application for 'Application for Mediation/Reconciliation, Arbitration or Islamic Divorce'. If the couple agree to reconciliation the imams will suggest counselling if the couple is able to afford it and are willing to attend.

As outlined in Figure 2, to begin the process a spouse must download an application form online or pick up a copy from the head office. The form contains several basic questions, and the spouse is required to submit proof of marriage, preferably a marriage certificate. This might be difficult for couples married overseas or couples who are refugees or asylum-seekers. In such cases, the Board requires a birth certificate of a child (if one exists) or any other document that might offer proof of marriage, including photographs of a wedding or testaments from attendees at the wedding. The form (Appendix D) asks for details of the couples' separation, whether an intervention order exists between the couple and if they have engaged in any previous mediation or counselling.

[61] Interview 56 (Melbourne, January 2020).
[62] Interview 56 (Melbourne, January 2020).
[63] Interview 40 (Melbourne, September 2016).
[64] Interview 14 (Melbourne, April 2016).
[65] ibid.

Figure 2 Overview of BOIV's Sharia Processes

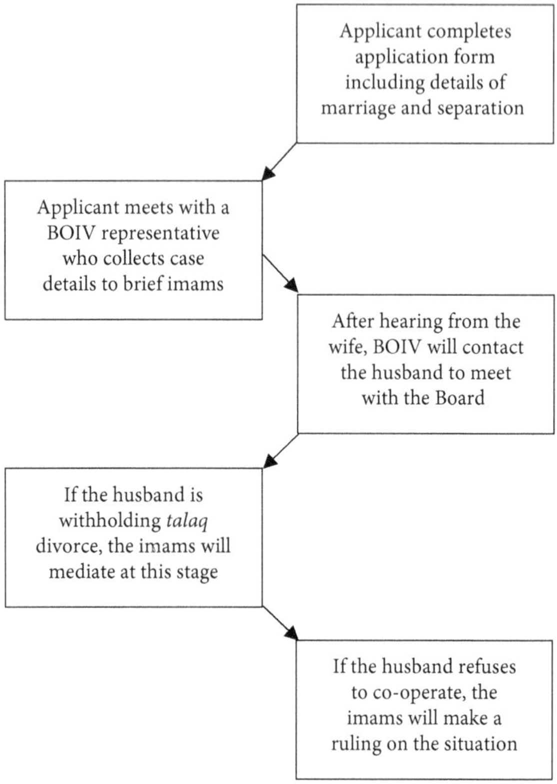

The Board will ask for any claims of fault on behalf of either party to be verified. For example, claims of cheating, gambling or addiction. If claims of domestic violence are being presented, the Board will ask for an affidavit, apprehended violence order, or intervention order as proof. Where no such proof exists, they will see whether the matter has gone to court and what the findings of the court have been. If the wife explains that she did not report the violence, for example, for fear that the husband may be arrested, the imams will encourage the woman to report it.[66] Additionally, the Board will consider how long the couple has been separated and the reasons why, until this point, the divorce has not been finalised.

The wife is usually the one who contacts the Board, and a representative from BOIV will meet with her first to discuss her case. The point of contact is a female staff member, who has been working with BOIV for several years and is considered a respected community figure. She liaises with the women on behalf of the

[66] Interview 16 (Melbourne, May 2016).

Board. The purpose of this initial session is to ensure that the woman is comfortable telling her story and that the staff member has the details needed to brief the imams. It is also an opportunity to refer the woman to any support services, if required.

After this stage of the process, the woman meets with the panel, including a staff member employed by the Board who assists the wife to convey the specifics of her marital problems to the panel. After hearing from the wife, the imams will then contact the husband. The husband will meet with the Board at this stage and tell his side of the story. For men who are withholding *talaq* divorce, this is where the imams 'mediate'.

Imams will attempt to contact the husband three times. The first instance is via SMS. If this fails, they then send a letter through registered mail, and finally they will call him.[67] If at this stage the husband refuses to co-operate, and the marriage has broken down, the imams will make a ruling on the situation. In many cases imams will issue a *tafweedh* divorce (based on the woman's delegated right to divorce, specified in the contract – see Appendix B) or *tafriq* divorce without any further attempts at reconciliation. This is not done lightly. The imams reported that for the immediate issuing of a *tafweedh or tafriq* divorce the husband would need to have been absent for a long period of time, such as being in jail, or there must have been some 'dispute among them [husband and wife] and they can't reconcile [which is] causing harm to the woman'.[68]

Imams may also order a *khulah* divorce in a situation where they feel the husband has not done anything wrong; in such a case, if there is any outstanding *mahr*, the woman will not receive it and any maintenance from the husband will cease. Further if the husband and wife state that the divorce is being withheld or delayed because of issues to do with custody or property, the imams will refer the couple to a family relationship centre where they will recommend mediation, and the couple will continue to work through their issues. Should the couple return to the imams having been unable to resolve their issues, the process will resume, and the divorce will be fast tracked because the process has already been started. The third meeting then brings the husband and wife together (if no intervention order exists), again with the female staff member and the panel of imams, to make a final decision on the religious divorce.[69]

The Board of Imams charges AUD $500 per application for issuing a *tafweedh* or *tafriq* divorce and between AUD $200–$250 for *talaq* and *khulah* divorce applications. They view this as a donation to cover their expenses. For those who cannot afford to pay the set price, a lower price is negotiated, they are put on a payment plan, or the fee is forfeited altogether.[70]

[67] Interview 40 (Melbourne, September 2016).
[68] Interview 14 (Melbourne, April 2016).
[69] Interview 16 (Melbourne, May 2016).
[70] Interview 40 (Melbourne, September 2016).

ii. Australian National Islamic Council (ANIC)

In 2016, ANIC sought to standardise sharia processes for divorce and other Islamic community processes by creating an umbrella service, the Centre for Arbitration and Resolution of Disputes (CARD). CARD aims to streamline divorce proceedings and assist Muslim women and men to either reconcile or dissolve their marriages. This service is made up of both English-speaking and Arabic-speaking imams who focus specifically on family disputes, although they cover other disputes as well. As a service operating across states, CARD imams deal with interstate cases via Skype and phone. In line with this streamlined approach, all other imams are encouraged to refer family disputes to CARD. Although, as will be discussed below, many individual imams continue to resolve family law matters, including conducting divorces. However, for more complex cases, individual imams tend to refer couples either to BOIV, LMA or, more recently, CARD for reconciliation or divorce.

First, as with the BOIV imams discussed above, when a spouse approaches ANIC-CARD for a divorce, the imams believe it is their responsibility to attempt to reconcile the two parties. If it is possible to reconcile the disputing couple, the imams will do so. The imams do not meet with the couple immediately but give them 'at least two or three weeks' to cool off. This forms part of their strategy to encourage reconciliation, believing that if they give the couple space, they may reconsider their want of a divorce. In practice, this is a wait of two or three weeks between the divorce application being submitted and the first meeting being scheduled.

Next, as outlined in Figure 3, the applicant will meet with an imam and a female support worker to explain her current situation. The imams stress that in this session she does not need to answer any questions that she feels uncomfortable answering.[71] She may be alone or with her husband at this session. In practice, the overwhelming majority of couples meet with the imams separately, unless the couple is in agreement on all the issues and are coming to the imams only to formalise the divorce. In particular, if there is an intervention order in place, then the couple cannot be in the same room and the imams will hear from the couple separately.

Finally, the imams come to a decision about the couple's divorce and in doing so stress that this is 'only religious advice, nothing legally binding'.[72] An imam, at this stage, may also refer the couple to other counselling services including qualified psychologists.[73] Additionally, they will encourage the woman to report violence to the police.

[71] Interview 27 (Sydney, September 2016).
[72] Interview 24 (Sydney, May 2016).
[73] Interview 50 (Sydney, October 2016).

Figure 3 Overview of ANIC-CARD's Sharia Processes

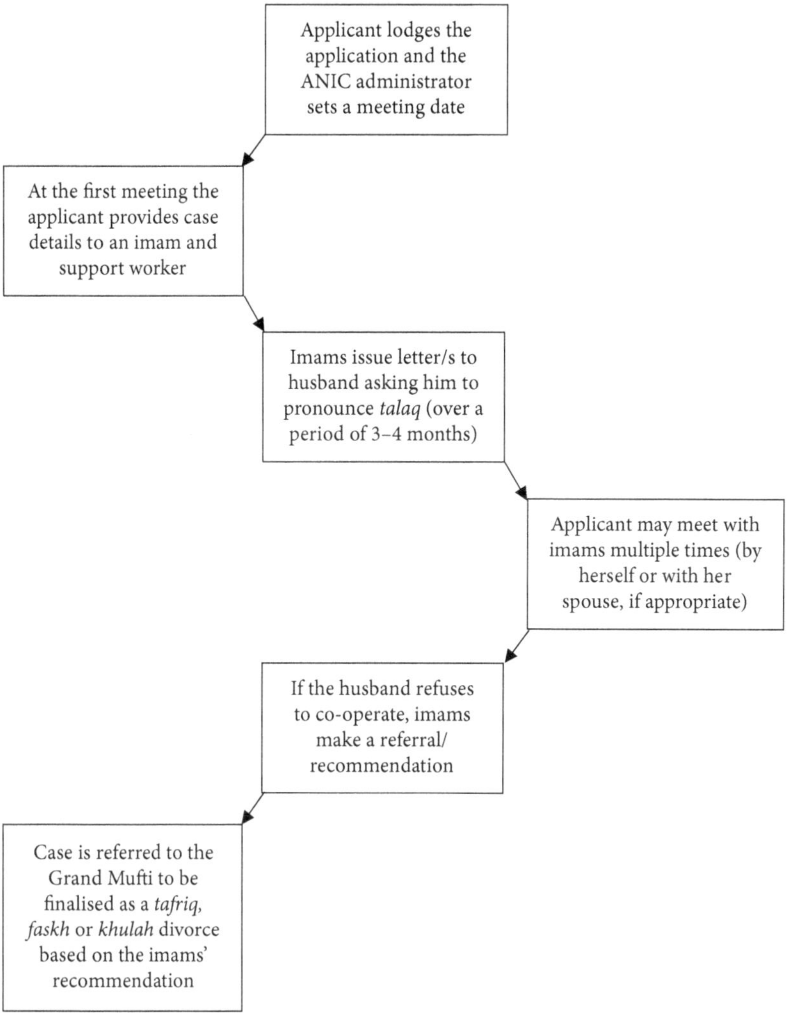

At this stage, the imams may recommend a *talaq*, *khulah*, *tafriq* or *faskh* divorce. The general process is that the imams issue a letter to the husband, asking him to pronounce *talaq*. They send a letter to the husband once a month for three to four months. It is only after four months, if the husband has not responded, that the imams will issue a *tafriq*, *faskh* or *khulah* divorce and release the woman from the marriage.[74] Initially this process took up to six months, but interviews in the later part of our research indicate this time period has been reduced; the maximum period for a divorce to be completed is now four months under the streamlined divorce process. If the husband has not cooperated within these four months, the divorce will be referred to the Grand Mufti for a final divorce determination.

The final stage of ANIC-CARD sharia divorce determinations, for all types of contested divorce applications, is for the application to be forwarded to the Grand Mufti within the four-month timeframe, to be finalised. Imams insist on couples finalising their civil divorce before or alongside sharia processes to ensure that individuals have clarity as to whether they are married or divorced. Therefore, imams generally do not issue a religious divorce certificate without the civil divorce also having been finalised.

ANIC-CARD charges a AUD $150 application fee, and a fee of AUD $350 to be paid upon completion of the process.

iii. Lebanese Muslim Association (LMA)

As noted above, there are a number of different groupings of imams that operate in New South Wales and Victoria outside of the scope of ANIC-CARD and BOIV. One such example is the Lebanese Muslim Associated (LMA) in Sydney. The LMA has been in operation since 1962 and was established by the Lebanese community to provide social, religious, educational and recreational services for New South Wales' Muslim community. The organisation now supports a number of communities and networks across New South Wales. It manages three mosques and is the caretaker of Lakemba Mosque, one of the largest mosques in Australia which attracts a large number of regular worshippers.

As outlined in Figure 4, to seek a divorce through the imams affiliated with LMA, a spouse will make an appointment with the imam's secretary. Sometimes, if the divorce is straightforward, an individual imam will oversee it. If, however, it is more complex, he will sit with a panel of five imams to come to a decision.[75]

When the applicant comes in, they will fill out an application form (Appendix E), detailing the status of their marriage and whether it is registered in Australia or overseas. They will be asked about their residential status, the *mahr*, the number of times they have previously been married, whether there are children from this or previous marriages, if they are separated and (if so) for how long, whether their divorce has been finalised in the civil court, whether they have sought counselling

[74] ibid.
[75] Interview 34 (Sydney, August 2016).

and whether there are any child custody arrangements in place. The applicant(s) will also indicate whether they are interested in reconciliation.

Figure 4 Overview of LMA's Sharia Processes

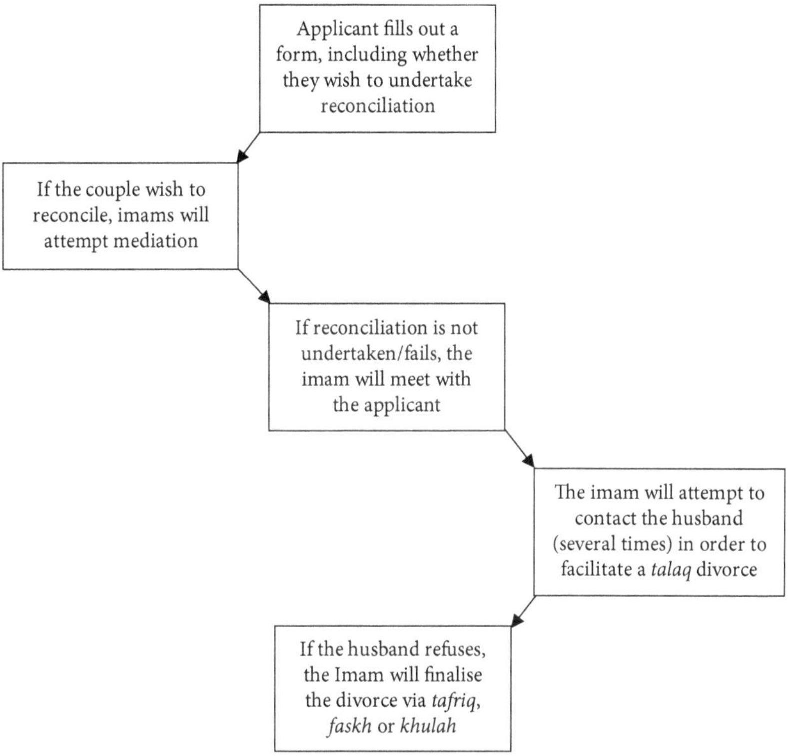

If couples indicate that they wish to reconcile, imams will proceed down this path. They will first attempt to understand whether there are psychological or medical issues, such as addiction. If any of these factors are present, the couple will be referred to professional services. If these are absent, the couple will begin mediation. Imams will also attempt to ascertain whether domestic violence is present in the relationship. If domestic violence is present, the spouse will be referred to counselling and encouraged to report to police.[76]

Imams note that it is mostly women who contact them first. Most women who approach LMA do so because their husband has refused to divorce them (*talaq*). At this point, they hear the woman's side of the story and make attempts to contact the

[76] Interview 29 (Sydney, August 2016).

husband. At times, once the husband has been contacted, he will issue the *talaq* divorce. If this is the case, the imams will make him sign a form and have witnesses sign that they have seen him utter the divorce and the divorce will be finalised.[77]

If the husband refuses to issue a *talaq*, the imams will give him several chances to issue the divorce, and if there is no 'logical'[78] reason that he will not issue the divorce, then they will finalise the divorce via *tafriq*, *faskh* or *khulah*. Like other bodies, if a civil divorce has already been confirmed and the husband has filed the civil divorce application, they will also accept this as a *talaq* divorce.[79] On the other hand, if a civil law divorce has not yet been finalised, couples typically do not receive the official, signed form for their religious divorce until their civil law divorce has been finalised. If for some reason their marriage is not registered under civil law, they will only receive the religious divorce certificate. Recent interviews with imams associated with LMA have indicated that like the other panels they are currently working on various policies to enhance their process, which will be discussed in chapter six.

iv. Individual Imams

While, in recent times, couples with a family conflict or who wish to seek divorce typically use the services of one of the established imam groupings in Victoria or New South Wales, some couples still approach local individual imams known to them. Some women, frustrated with the perceived slow and complicated process of seeking divorce through the established Boards or Councils, will go to individual imams. Typically, the party who approaches the imam with the request for assistance is asked to provide the specifics of their situation. The imam will then approach the second party and seek further details and clarification from them. If the situation is complicated, the imam will refer the case to ANIC-CARD or BOIV. If the couple wishes to reconcile the imam will proceed.

If the matter is 'simple', then the individual imam will ask if the couple would like to involve any other community elders in the reconciliation process.[80] If so, the imam will contact the relevant parties, and the elders and families will sit down to discuss the issue. Some families, understandably, prefer to keep the matter private. One imam noted that due to the standing of that family in the community, they may not want others in the community to know about their dispute.[81]

Some imams, whose focus is on reconciliation, will tell a woman that they only offer services in relation to marriage, but not divorce.[82] Others will tell the woman to be patient with their husbands and to wait.[83] Facing such challenges, some

[77] ibid.
[78] Interview 34 (Sydney, August 2016).
[79] ibid.
[80] Interview 8 (Melbourne, April 2016).
[81] Interview 47 (Melbourne, October 2016).
[82] Interview 12 (Melbourne, April 2016).
[83] ibid.

women will then 'just go overseas, just go to Canada, bypass Australia completely, go online, find an imam that has openly said *I will divorce you, come to me and I will divorce you and I'll give it to you*'.[84]

In instances where the woman has decided to pursue a divorce and the husband will not grant her *talaq*, thus pushing her to request *khulah*, the individual imams will refer the woman to BOIV or ANIC-CARD. This is because most individual imams do not believe that they have the authority to grant a woman *khulah*, *faskh* or *tafriq* and that these types of divorce require a 'court' or the consensus of multiple imams.

V. Conclusion

This chapter has provided an overview of sharia processes – and the people, procedures and practices associated with them – across three jurisdictions. As outlined in this chapter, a considerable amount of research into sharia processes in the UK and Canada already exists. The Australian landscape of sharia processes, set out in this chapter, supplements this literature. Thinking about the features of different sharia processes relative to each other sharpens our understanding of these processes, by identifying both diversity as well as similar or sympathetic features. Thinking about sharia processes comparatively, as we will see in later chapters, also helps us identify practices and procedures which improve women's experiences. We use this comparative insight to offer recommendations for changes to sharia processes.

[84] ibid.

3

Women's Perspectives and Experiences

I. Introduction

This chapter seeks to highlight the experiences and perspectives of women as they navigate sharia processes, usually in order to seek an Islamic divorce. We begin by outlining the experiences of women facing marital difficulties before they engage with sharia processes. Typically, the women we interviewed sought the assistance of their families, approached professionals or participated in informal mediation within their communities. If none of these steps addressed their marital issues, they typically went on to seek a religious divorce from sharia processes. Next, we explore the reasons *why* Muslim women seek religious divorce, either on its own or in addition to civil divorce. Finally, we elaborate on the experiences of women participating in sharia processes. These experiences, drawn from interviews with the women themselves as well as the professionals who support them, also form the basis for our recommendations for changes to sharia processes discussed later in this book, in chapter six.

II. Before Sharia Processes

Before engaging with sharia processes, couples often head down other avenues for assistance, such as asking families or elders in the community to mediate, seeking the support of friends or utilising other professionals (for example, community workers, counsellors and psychologists).

A. Family

Women are often reluctant to involve their families early on in relationship conflicts and hope to resolve their issues themselves. For example, in cases of domestic violence, women explained that they only reached out to their families once the abuse had escalated to an intolerable level.[1] Families are the most common port of call before seeking the advice of an imam or going through sharia processes.

[1] Interview 2 (Sydney, April 2016).

Some women also described family intervention by the husband's family, where his parents or siblings attempt to convince the wife to return to the relationship.[2] Other women sought advice from their own family but did not reveal the full extent of their marital problems until they had consciously decided to leave the relationship. One woman, who was married to her spouse for five years, stated: 'a lot of my family didn't know the extent of the abuse up until the night where I actually booted him out for being physically violent'.[3] This same woman eventually participated in an informal mediation involving community leaders but emphasised that the behaviour of her husband did not change despite community leaders 'siding' with her. She said: 'You know we got back together and the same thing happened, then the same thing happened again'.[4]

Another woman described how her husband made little effort to hide his infidelities. Once she revealed the extent of his behaviour to his family, they were ashamed on his behalf and attempted to forge a path for reconciliation. However, her husband expressed no remorse or desire to reconcile:

> So after that I got my divorce and then the imams sent an email to my husband with divorce papers and the reasoning and they said, *You've got two weeks to reply*, he never replied. And that was the end of my marriage.[5]

While in some cases women reach out to their family or community leaders, in other cases a woman might call on a single relative (often a brother or mother) to support her and assist her to negotiate the divorce proceedings.[6]

The role of family may be particularly important if a woman has come to Australia on a spousal visa (having been married in a foreign country); these women are often in a precarious situation if the husband wants to separate and send them back to their home country. In the case of one Pakistani woman who arrived in Australia on a spousal visa, the involvement of her family was crucial. This woman wanted to remain in Australia to raise her two young daughters. Meanwhile her husband, preferring not to take on the financial burden of a family, wanted to send her back to Pakistan where his family would take financial responsibility for his wife and two daughters.

> He tried his best and he brought his parents into this matter and he started putting pressure on me and my family saying that it was best that we separate but stay married. But my family found that absolutely outrageous and they didn't entertain the proposal.[7]

[2] Interview 66 (Sydney, February 2016).
[3] Interview 18 (Melbourne, April 2016).
[4] Interview 18 (Melbourne, April 2016).
[5] Interview 3 (Sydney, April 2016).
[6] Interview 9 (Melbourne, April 2016); Interview 28 (Sydney, August 2016).
[7] Interview 52 (Sydney, November 2019).

B. Professionals and Community Workers

Many of the women who we interviewed accessed mainstream services, which included mainstream family dispute resolution processes (such as Family Dispute Resolution Practitioners, Family Relationship Centers (FRCs) and marriage counselling) and mediation processes offered by psychologists and community organisations. Our research indicates that women use these services, but often their husbands are reluctant to attend.[8]

Several women stated that prior to seeking a divorce, they asked their husbands to attend counselling. One woman explained that there was prolonged conflict and verbal abuse in the marriage, as well as ongoing infidelity by the husband, and the woman was encouraged to attend a couples counselling session with Relationships Australia.

> [T]hat's when we went to the relationship counselling, to Relationships Australia, and started counselling. And he [the counsellor] ended up splitting us up. He was like, *I can't have you in the same room together*, and I was like, *Why? What's wrong?* And he was like, *We can't condone this type of talking*, and I didn't get it, but [my husband] was just yelling at me and just abusing me and I'd become so numb to it.[9]

As several psychologists in our sample reported, couples will often only see a psychologist when their relationship has deteriorated to the point where the woman is determined to leave the relationship and threatens to do so unless the husband agrees to counselling:

> [U]nfortunately, it's at the point of: *You either come to counselling or it's over*. And most men actually ignore that anyway because they think the women are bluffing, but women have actually [by] then thought about divorce for about three years on average before they divorce anyway. And so by the time that they come, women are basically, like they're basically on the brink anyway.[10]

Social workers and psychologists also play an important role in supporting women and educating them on their options. The complexity of providing support to women from different cultures was explained by one social worker who advises women of their rights under Islamic law:

> Yeah, yeah, because don't forget, we come here saying that *we're all Muslim* but we're still holding onto our [culture] *I am Indonesian*, for example. *I am South African. I am Indian*. So all these will come as part and parcel of the religion … it's embedded within their culture. So the culture and the religion, it's very, very mixed so you need to let her understand what does Islam say at this point, why you don't have to keep nodding your head at every single word he said because this is your right. You've got choices.[11]

[8] Interview 12 (Melbourne, April 2016).
[9] Interview 52 (Sydney, November 2019).
[10] Interview 12 (Melbourne, April 2016).
[11] Interview 20 (Sydney, May 2016).

In addition to professional counsellors, lawyers are used in the divorce process in relation to seeking a civil divorce.

Some imams will refer women to lawyers to help sort out their dispute, especially if they feel that the husband is being unjust or if they have mediated a settlement between the couple that needs to be legally enforceable. Participants have suggested that it would be helpful to women if such lawyers had both cultural and religious understanding.[12] By this, interviewees did not necessarily mean a high level of religious knowledge but rather enough to understand the context of the women's experiences. As one participant noted:

> for me, my legal representative was also a Muslim woman, so she knew how to relate to me and basically how to connect the dots. So I was very fortunate in that matter as I didn't have any concerns trying to make someone understand how things work in my culture, so I was very lucky that way.[13]

Another participant expressed the limitations of cultural understanding within mainstream legal services. Before settling on a solicitor who shared her religious background, this participant attempted to use a solicitor who wasn't Muslim: 'They don't understand … you know with the Islamic contract … that's not acknowledged, that's not even looked at. So [she] couldn't really understand what I was talking about'.[14]

III. Reasons for Seeking a Religious Divorce

When attempts at addressing problems with the marriage failed, there were diverse and complex reasons why women chose to pursue an Islamic divorce. But broadly, there were four interconnected factors why the women in our study decided to engage with sharia processes to seek a religious divorce: religious and spiritual reasons; the need to end emotional manipulation; the need for closure; and a desire to avoid stigma within their community.

A. Spiritual Motivations

Spiritual reasons outlined by women for seeking a religious divorce included the realisation that their spouse was compromising their spiritual connection with God. In some instances, the woman was being asked by her spouse, family, or community to accept, forgive, downplay or turn a blind eye to behaviour that she

[12] Interview 52 (Sydney, November 2019).
[13] ibid.
[14] Interview 18 (Melbourne, April 2016).

considered to be against her beliefs. This included cheating, lying, violence, theft, drug use or alcohol consumption. One woman explained:

> It wasn't until my Iman [faith] was on the line that I thought, I'm going to lose my religion by staying with him and the tensions that the kids might be experiencing, it was better for them to have two households where they could be happy than living in tension.[15]

Another woman discovered that her physically abusive husband was having an affair with another woman and using '*qiyam al layl*' (nightly prayers performed at a mosque or prayer facility) as a cover up for his escapades. She said:

> I hold on to my Islam because I had learnt about it and it was mine and I had taken it for myself and I did not need anyone to diminish it. And now [he] used Islam to hide what he was doing and he was saying that he was going to do *qiyam al layl*, but he was with this other person and that really infuriated me. How dare you use Islam as a cover up?[16]

In that case, the woman felt that her husband was asking her to downplay the severity of his actions with the excuse that she 'wasn't giving him what he wanted at the time … sexually'. In her session with the imams, the woman explained the situation in full:

> So, if I came to touch him, he will say that my hand is too hot. If I call him, he says no you are tired just go to sleep. And he was complaining that I [was] never near him during Ramadan and during that time in the daytime we are fasting [and sexual contact would break the fast] … At the end I am really sorry for this as when he wants something that's *haram* [forbidden] it's not going to happen for him.[17]

As the violence toward her escalated and the cheating continued, the woman sought more guidance from imams. She was assured by the imams that she had every right to leave the marriage. This guidance 'gave [her] the affirmation that [she] was doing the right thing and … was not going against Islam'.[18] She continued, 'it was important to me because I am a revert [a convert to Islam] and at the time I wanted to make sure I was doing the right thing'.[19] In this way, the desire to symbolise their adherence to religious tenets is a motivating reason for some women to turn to religious bodies and processes (as opposed to a desire to save their marriages or reconcile).[20]

[15] Interview 45 (Melbourne, September 2016).
[16] Interview 53 (Sydney, November 2019).
[17] ibid.
[18] ibid.
[19] Interview 53 (Sydney, November 2019).
[20] S Bano, *Muslim Women and Shari'ah Councils* (Basingstoke, Palgrave Macmillan, 2012) 186. See also SN Shah-Kazemi, *Untying the Knot: Muslim Women, Divorce, and the Shariah* (Signal Press 2001) <www.nuffieldfoundation.org/project/untying-the-knot-muslim-women-divorce-and-the-shariah> accessed 1 November 2020.

Further, some Muslim women sought a religious divorce so that the divorce was 'Islamically valid'. A belief in Islam and God was the driving force behind the pursuit of an Islamically valid divorce. One woman indicated:

> [I]t was very important to me. It doesn't feel like the divorce is complete without the Islamic divorce … I just felt that [if I was] still married in the eyes of God [then] a legal divorce is not enough. Just like I needed an Islamic marriage now I need the Islamic divorce.[21]

This was true irrespective of a woman's level of religiosity, in that even women who did not necessarily view themselves as practising other aspects of Islam valued the right to, and process of, obtaining a religious divorce. Many Muslim women, not just in Australia, but also in Canada and the UK, seem to share this desire to comply with religious obligations by obtaining an Islamic divorce.[22]

B. Ending Emotional Exploitation

Women also sought religious divorce in a bid to end emotional manipulation, exploitation and abuse. Emotional exploitation and manipulation were common at the stage where women had been separated from their husbands or had sought outside help or intervention. Emotional exploitation also related to women finding themselves in 'limping marriages' – cases where even though a civil divorce had been granted, the husband refused to grant a religious divorce. Such situations tie the woman to the marriage and leave her in a precarious and vulnerable position,[23] open to the types of manipulation described below.

Several interviewees described instances where they felt emotionally manipulated by their husbands, who sometimes attempted to maintain control over them by refusing to religiously divorce them (*talaq*). Some manipulation related to physical and sexual intimacy. Men often used the fact that they were not yet religiously divorced to try to initiate sexual relations, often accompanied by claims of having changed or wanting to reconcile. These behaviours allowed the manipulation, and in some cases abuse, of the wife to continue. Women therefore felt that having

[21] Interview 51 (Sydney, October 2019).

[22] Shah-Kazemi (n 20) 50–51; J Macfarlane, 'Understanding Trends in American Muslim Divorce and Marriage: A Discussion Guide for Families and Communities' (Institute for Social Policy and Understanding, 2012) 33: '[f]or others, their connection to Islam as a matter of personal identity is more significant than their formal obeisance to God. These individuals may lead a relatively secular lifestyle yet continue to embrace some critical rituals, usually associated with times of crisis and personal transition'. There are similar findings in the UK: R Parveen, 'Do Sharia Councils Meet the Needs of Muslim Women?' in S Bano (ed), *Gender and Justice in Family Law Disputes: Women, Mediation, and Religious Arbitration* (Waltham MA, Brandeis University Press, 2017) 147; T Walker, *Shari'a Councils and Muslim Women in Britain: Rethinking the Role of Power and Authority* (Leiden, Brill, 2017) 22.

[23] Bano (n 20) 187. See also Parveen (n 22) 148, 163; D Pearl and W Menski, *Muslim Family Law* 3rd edn (London, Sweet & Maxwell, 1998); A Buckley, *Not "Completely" Divorced: Muslim Women in Australia Navigating Muslim Family Laws* (Melbourne, Melbourne University Press, 2019).

an Islamic divorce prevented them from being 'used'. One woman explained her experience:

> [I was] uncertain, yeah, because I was – I got sick and tired of like the emotional abuse where he'd come and, you know, be intimate with me and give me hope and then just leave again and not hear from him for another two or three weeks. So it was just like he'd use [me] – and then I'd feel like crap and then I'd try to build myself. It was devastating … it was trauma. Yeah, it was very, very difficult to deal with every single time. It was the same thing and I kind of, like not that I blame myself, but I hated myself for [it] – I just felt cheap. Like, but then I thought well Islamically he's my husband so maybe he might turn and feel what I feel and think, *Okay, this is my wife, and these are my kids …* but it never happened.[24]

The granting of a religious divorce helped this woman to cut ties with her former husband and to expend her energy on finding ways to move forward instead of repeating this cycle of emotional manipulation.

C. Closure and 'Moving On'

An Islamic divorce can mark the end of a significant relationship which may not constitute a civil marriage. For example, those who are in a polygamous relationship, although not common, may be unable to register their marriage under civil law if the husband already has a marriage registered. Others may simply feel that there is no reason to register the marriage because a legal acknowledgement is not important if their marriage is religiously valid. This is a common occurrence in several jurisdictions.[25] For those Muslims who choose not to enter civil marriages, or otherwise do not register their marriage with the state, sharia processes offer a route to dissolving the religious marriage.[26]

The exact numbers of unregistered marriages are difficult to ascertain because there are no official records. However, several community workers reported seeing this issue more regularly, with one stating that 'more and more people are becoming aware that they don't have to register their marriage … it's looked as more burden, more paperwork and just extra money, extra headaches'.[27] This phenomenon has led to greater uncertainty for many women who are unsure about the status of their marriage (ie, whether it is recognised by state law or not).[28]

[24] Interview 4 (Sydney, April 2016).

[25] Bano (n 20) 160–61; G Krayem, *Islamic Family Law in Australia: To Recognise or Not to Recognise* (Melbourne, Melbourne University Press, 2014) 137.

[26] Parveen (n 22) 160–61.

[27] RC Akhtar, 'Non-legally Binding Muslim Marriages in England and Qatar: Circumventing the State' (2020) 8(1) *Electronic Journal of Islamic and Middle Eastern Law* 20; Interview 35 (Sydney, August 2016).

[28] Walker (n 22) 134 (discussing UK law, but applicable issue across the board).

In instances where marriages are not recognised in civil law, some women reported that the Islamic divorce provides them finality and closure. It allows an official board or body to note that this chapter of their lives has drawn to a close. This means that the experience of divorce is not minimised religiously, socially and culturally, even if legally it is not acknowledged.

In reflecting on the process, one interviewee in an unregistered marriage explained that in retrospect, she would have liked to have had both a legal and Islamic divorce: 'I think I'd want to have both'. She stated that 'because being married has ramifications, like for all my super[-annuation] and stuff like that was tied in with him, and I did that all, I changed that all'.[29] This is an important acknowledgement of how, despite not seeking a legal divorce, this woman was able to gain some closure through receiving her Islamic divorce.[30]

The finality and closure of a religious divorce is also important for some because it gives them the freedom to pursue a new relationship. For many Muslim women still tied up in divorce negotiations with a former husband, pursuing a new relationship can be fraught with obstacles. Finalising their divorce Islamically means that, should they wish, they are free to pursue a new relationship, knowing that a religious marriage with a new partner is possible. For many practising Muslim women, this is important because of a belief in the sanctity of marriage and religious restrictions around sexual intimacy outside of marriage. Therefore, being able to religiously marry another partner allows Muslim women to ensure they are abiding by the values that are important to them.

One woman explained how her husband's refusal to divorce her by *talaq*, and her refusal to accept *khulah* as an avenue for securing a divorce, impacted on her ability to move on: 'I want to resolve it [the divorce]. I would like to be able to move on with my life'. When asked 'And is that something that's holding you back?', she replied:

> 'Yeah, I can't. I can't, I haven't … Religiously – I don't care about the legal system. I want to be able – if I get involved in a relationship, I want to know that I'm not doing anything wrong in the eyes of God.[31]

D. Avoiding Stigma

Another reason women in our study sought religious divorce was as a form of protection from community gossip or stigma. Utilising religious processes and obtaining a religious divorce was thought to diminish the stigma of being labelled a 'divorcee' within their families and communities, as they have gone through the 'proper' religious channels to get a divorce.[32]

[29] Interview 13 (Melbourne, April 2016).
[30] ibid.
[31] Interview 6 (Sydney, April 2016).
[32] Bano (n 20) 200–01.

For example, one interviewee described why an Islamic divorce was important for her after her husband was unfaithful:

> It would have given me anxiety to still be married to him … I guess then I knew he wasn't in my life. So, we, because the Arab community talks a lot, so they'd be like *she didn't do this, she didn't do that, she didn't do this* … If we didn't get, I guess, Australian divorced until a year later, I would have gone through hell for another year until that point when it was officially over … because it's just, I guess as sad as it is, it's the community atmosphere that we have.[33]

IV. Women's Experiences of Sharia Processes

We now turn to the issues that arose for women who accessed sharia processes. This section draws on interviews with women who experienced these divorce processes, as well as with lawyers, counsellors, social workers, psychologists, community workers and community leaders who supported these women. The observations from these professionals confirm the data that we obtained from the interviews conducted with women. Together these data provide a holistic picture of women's experiences with these processes.

While existing research has established the pivotal role that imams play in granting Muslim women divorce, as well as their role in addressing family disputes more broadly,[34] interviewees raised several concerns about how sharia processes are conducted in practice. Such concerns included: the emphasis on reconciliation; imams' lack of skills and training; a lack of transparency in decision-making; a failure to respond adequately to domestic violence (as well as a failure to acknowledge and respond to injustice more broadly); gender imbalance on divorce panels; issues relating to privacy and re-traumatisation; and how experiences with sharia processes impacted women's faith and religious practice. The experiences of women, as well as other professionals involved in sharia processes, provide insight into how sharia processes might be improved, which is explored in detail in chapter six.

A. Emphasis on Reconciliation

As mentioned in chapter two, imams generally prioritise reconciliation between the couple before proceeding with divorce processes, unless there is an Apprehended Violence Order (AVO) in place.[35] In their interviews for this study, both imams and professionals who work with women highlighted that reconciliation is always the initial goal. This is reflective of the broader focus on reconciliation within Islam, where Muslims are encouraged to 'seek conciliatory redress in the form of

[33] Interview 68, Sydney, February 2016.
[34] See Krayem (n 25); Bano (n 20); Walker (n 22).
[35] Interview 16 (Melbourne, May 2016).

mediation and arbitration'.[36] It is worth noting that the Australian legal system also places an emphasis on reconciliation, reflected in provisions of the Family Law Act 1975 (Cth). For example, the principles to be applied by the courts note that the Family Court shall have regard for 'the means available for assisting parties to a marriage to consider reconciliation or the improvement of their relationship with each other and to their children'.[37] This is further reflected in the rules around applying for a divorce; where parties have been married for less than two years, they must show that they have considered reconciliation with the assistance of a professional.[38]

Women who initiate contact with imams might express openness to reconciliation. One interviewee reported that she said to the imams: 'I don't want to get divorced. If you can find a solution for me, I'll go back and stay married'.[39] However, for some women, imams' attempts at reconciliation made them feel that they were not being heard or that they were being pressured to reconcile. The focus on reconciliation resulted in a lack of guidance and support for women on other issues, such as domestic violence (which is discussed below).[40]

Some scholars have argued that the language used within reconciliation efforts by imams can exacerbate problematic dynamics of power, emphasising the idea that a woman's role is to maintain familial relations and keep the marriage stable.[41] This distraction from the true causes of conflict means that the root causes are never addressed. For example, if:

> the couple have a situation and they want to seek a divorce, or they want to seek counselling, and the sheikh [imam or religious scholar] pretty much reads out her rights and roles and responsibilities … that she should maintain obedience or all that. And basically, the underlying issues are not addressed, or overlooked based on that overpowering statement.[42]

One young woman, recalling her experience seeking mediation in the first few months after her wedding, said that she made an appointment with an imam of her fiancé's choosing with the initial intention of 'working things out'. However, she felt the imam was not able to address the core problems:

> He [the imam] was saying *there's worse people out there and I think you guys need to work on each other* … it didn't feel like the problem was solved. If anything, I felt like I walked out wanting to leave him but – and then I was scared to leave him so that night … [I sent him a message asking for forgiveness and saying] I forgive you … and he ignored

[36] S Gohir and N Akhtar-Sheikh, 'British Muslim Women and Barriers to Obtaining a Religious Divorce' in S Bano (ed), *Gender and Justice in Family Law Disputes: Women, Mediation, and Religious Arbitration* (Waltham MA, Brandeis University Press, 2017) 171. This principle around reconciliation is found explicitly in the Quran 4:35 as well as discussed in Hadith.
[37] Family Law Act 1975 (Cth), s 43.
[38] Family Law Act 1975 (Cth), s 44(1B).
[39] Interview 13 (Melbourne, April 2016).
[40] Walker (n 22) 168.
[41] Bano (n 20) 211.
[42] Interview 35 (Sydney, August 2016).

> me for four days … I felt he wasn't humbled by it [the visit to the imam] at all. If anything, he became more arrogant and our problems got worse after that because he felt like, *You should be thankful you've got me. Who would want you?* That's the sort of conversations we were having after: *Why would anyone want you?* And it was very demeaning, and it took me a long time … to build myself up.[43]

While imams are often seen as crucial to the negotiation process as parties helping to navigate a religious divorce, many women have expressed concerns about the pressure that was placed upon them to reconcile and accept terms that had been negotiated for them by the imams, without actually giving them a voice or hearing their views.[44]

B. A Lack of Skills and Training

Imams are often expected to provide support services that they are not adequately trained to offer, for instance, serving as marital counsellors or addressing domestic violence. As reported by professionals, this leads to the emergence of a divide between the expectations of those seeking out the services of imams and the outcomes.[45] Men often reject the professional services suggested by their wives in favour of counselling with an imam. Several women expressed their frustrations with the assistance provided by imams:

> The biggest thing is when imams say they're marriage counsellors, yet they have no skills in counselling at all. So, I'd often be in sessions with these imams, me and my husband and the imam, and it would just be a back and forth yelling or screaming. It was never counselling at all. So that was probably the biggest thing that probably affected the events that occurred later because there was no space for the two of us to express how we felt or what was going on for us and come to some sort of understanding. And the purpose of the imam in that situation should have been to facilitate our ability to understand each other and that never occurred. It was either the imam sitting there giving us like half an hour to yell at each other and then going, *Okay, you both need to be patient* and then he'd just basically, just be really directive about things … he would just basically give us your five steps as to how to have a happy marriage but not translate that into … what's relevant for us or personalising that for us … I didn't understand how he could just step into someone's home and sort of tell them what to do rather than trying to understand what's happening for these two people and support these two people to get through what they're going through. And there was never any of that mediation process with the imams.[46]

[43] Interview 28 (Sydney, August 2016).
[44] Bano (n 20) 203; Interview 55 (Melbourne, January 2020).
[45] Bano (n 20) 201–02.
[46] Interview 9 (Melbourne, April 2016).

Several interviewees raised similar concerns about the qualifications of imams as community workers. In the words of one social worker:

> You wouldn't go and see a physiotherapist for a skin condition, and the same with the community sector. [They have] to be trained, qualified professionals with a base minimum. So, for me, [if you're dealing with domestic violence], you have to have a minimum of either a social work degree or equivalent of … 8 to 10 years' experience in the community sector.[47]

On the other hand, professionals working with women in this field recognise the imams as 'a very very strong help-seeking mechanism for so many in the community'.[48] They acknowledge that people are not going to stop seeking their advice on matters pertaining to marriage and divorce. Therefore many of the professionals interviewed believed that imams should be qualified to deal with the issues brought before them rather than attempt to redirect couples to other avenues of support: '[I]t's extremely important for imams to in fact have counselling training so that they understand strategies as well as pathways by which they can in fact bring about reconciliation'.[49]

This concern was echoed by another interviewee through comparison with other clergy members:

> Muslims … go and seek help from the imam[s] but the imams are not qualified. They are not qualified. Unlike other clergy, Catholic clergy, who have to do compulsory pastoral care units in their training. Imams don't have that; they're just expected to be the counsellor. Anyway, there's a lot of problems in this particular space.[50]

Several references were made to clergy members of other religions, who play a similar role to imams, and suggestions made as to how imams might be trained. As one psychologist noted, people may feel that there is a stigma attached to seeing a psychologist, and thus they continue to see an imam to fulfil this role.[51] This stigma around counselling is often in relation to mainstream (non-religious) counselling services, where many in Muslim communities feel that attending religious-based services is more appropriate.[52] These issues are discussed further in chapter six with respect to opportunities for improvement.

C. A Lack of Transparency

Another key theme that arose prominently in many interviews was the issue of transparency, both around the advice women are given, as well as around the procedures associated with sharia processes.

[47] Interview 66, Sydney, February 2016.
[48] Interview 38, Sydney, September 2016.
[49] Interview 37, Sydney, August 2016.
[50] Interview 12 (Melbourne, April 2016).
[51] Interview 35 (Sydney, August 2016).
[52] Buckley (n 23) 333–34.

According to one social worker in our sample, imams do not clearly communicate how they come to the decisions they issue. As a result, women may be left confused about the rationale for the advice they are given, particularly in relation to financial matters. This can leave women feeling like the process was unfair. In instances like this, where women feel that their contributions have not been valued in the settlement process, they may turn to the legal system.[53]

The following comment by one woman expressed frustration with the processes and procedures due to a lack of transparency:

> Like being aware of what to expect, like what the process is going to look like, what are the timeframes like? … I want to get on with my life. I can't just keep being … left hanging. I know that the other party needs to be there, [but] if it could be streamlined.[54]

This is a common criticism of religious bodies and processes in other jurisdictions such as the UK, with recommendations often noting the need for clearer, more transparent processes.[55]

One psychologist suggested that imams be required to provide written documentation of the decision issued and the logic for that decision so that the woman could refer to it, even after the completion of the session. This would enable the woman to reflect on the process and better understand it later when they are arguably less distressed. This would also increase transparency.[56]

D. Responding to Domestic Violence

Across Australian communities, domestic violence is one of the key reasons for marital and relationship breakdown.[57] As mentioned in chapter two, imams reported that if a woman told them her husband had committed domestic violence against her, they would encourage her to call the police. However, this is not always the case within religious processes. In interviews, women and professionals highlighted that, in some cases, religious advisers try to explain away or dismiss the woman's experiences of violence and abuse.[58]

Legal systems generally find it difficult to respond to, recognise, investigate and prosecute non-physical family violence.[59] Similarly, comparative studies have illustrated how sharia processes often fail to recognise non-physical forms of violence,

[53] Interview 37 (Sydney, August 2016).
[54] Interview 9 (Melbourne, April 2016).
[55] Parveen (n 22) 161.
[56] Interview 37 (Sydney, August 2016).
[57] See House of Representatives Standing Committee on Legal and Constitutional Affairs, *To Have and To Hold: a Report of the Inquiry into Aspects of Family Services* (Canberra 1998) 67.
[58] Gohir and Akhtar-Sheikh (n 36) 174.
[59] M McMahon and P McGorrery, 'Criminalising Controlling and Coercive Behaviour: The Next Step in the Prosecution of Family Violence?' (2016) 4(2) *Alternative Law Journal* 98.

even where documented by legal evidence or court orders.[60] Professionals reported, as did women themselves, that the imams generally understood domestic violence to be limited to physical abuse and so only sought or considered evidence of physical violence. Where they observed this approach to domestic violence, social workers and psychologists did not feel that imams were sympathetic to women's struggles, unless the situation became physically violent.

The inability to fully understand the power dynamics of domestic violence, where parties do not have equal power, leads imams to diminish the trauma of women. This is particularly so in instances where women seek to report non-physical kinds of abuse. One young woman, recalling her experience seeking mediation with an imam a first few months after her wedding observed:

> I felt like the sheikh gave him ammunition and like when I look back now, I felt like he boosted his [my husband's] ego, that everything that he was saying, he was telling me, he goes, *Yeah, but sister, there's more wrong out there. At least your husband is not on drugs, at least this* – and I was like, *how does that, what does that serve me?* Like now when I think of it – at the time, no, I felt I was in the wrong. I really did. I walked out of there … I was scared … I felt intimidated by both of them … I feel that they don't take the psychological abuse as seriously as physical and as verbal.[61]

A number of professionals identified this as a common problem among imams. As one told us: 'Although emotional and psychological abuse [can be] extreme … it's much more difficult to measure and it's less visible. So, they're the ones saying, *Oh, he's verbally [abusive], but he didn't hit you. But he didn't hit you.* Women get the message that *I'm over-reacting*'.[62]

As the example below demonstrates, the inability to recognise abuse makes it nearly impossible for imams to provide the support that women require. It can also exacerbate the abuse because the imam may become complicit in the husband's manipulation. As one psychologist explained:

> [T]hey're caught up in a domestic violence circle or … they're colluding with the perpetrator, or the perpetrator denies everything, or the perpetrator … flip[s] it and blame[s] the victim: she made me angry. And then, *How did she make you angry? – Well my dinner wasn't ready, or she said this …* And *oh, well, I can sort of see your point. I can see why you got angry. I don't [justify] the violence but I can see why you got angry.* And … they don't realise they're legitimising that anger is the responsibility of the wife, as in she caused it not knowing that there's no connection [between the violence and the woman's behaviour].[63]

Women interviewees also shared how their experiences of violence were reduced to questions about their role in 'enraging' or 'provoking' such behaviour from their husband. This typically resulted in suggestions on how they might change their

[60] Walker (n 22) 166–67.
[61] Interview 28 (Sydney, August 2016).
[62] Interview 38 (Sydney, September 2016).
[63] Interview 12 (Melbourne, April 2016).

behaviour (derived from religious understandings of a wife's responsibilities) to fix their marriage and 'invite different treatment from their husbands'.[64] The following example from a woman interviewee illustrates this point:

> Well, it was like – so say – it sounds really trivial but like if I would be like, *Oh, I'm really tired* so I couldn't cook dinner that night and then, so my husband would get really aggressive and then they would, if I would give that example to a sheikh, they would say something like, *Oh, well you should be cooking dinner, so he doesn't get aggressive.* So, it was always like *you're doing something for him to be acting the way he was acting.* So, there was no acknowledgement that people have responsibility for their own actions, especially when it comes to your partner. So, it was often the excuses made for the partner but no understanding for the female in the situation.[65]

A lack of understanding of the intricacies of domestic violence can also have unintended outcomes for women, any children involved and the imams themselves. Take for example the instance where an imam and his wife, thinking that they were being helpful to a couple, breached an intervention order:

> I know of quite a horrendous case where I was working with a woman who was a victim of domestic violence, incredibly disgusting domestic violence, like really horrendous. The guy was in jail. He was on remand at this time. The imams often also moonlight as chaplains in prisons. And this guy, her partner, had convinced the imam he hadn't done anything, that his wife was really unwell, and she had mental health issues, and he was incredibly persuasive and well-spoken, and he convinced the imam to contact his wife. Now there was an existing restraining order, and the imam did. The imam rang her up and said, 'can my wife and I meet you? We want to see if we can help you.' And when they had her in front of them, they then said, *So, here are some messages from your husband. He wants to reconcile.* I was like, '*oh my God*'; he's just assisted in a breach of an order. Do they even know that?[66]

The interviewee did not suggest anything sinister in the intentions of the imam or his wife in this case. But, their lack of qualifications and knowledge of domestic violence meant that they did not understand how domestic violence manifests or how control is exercised over the victim. Importantly, they could not see how they themselves were being manipulated for the perpetrator's own agenda.

Interviewees underscored the need for a better response to domestic violence among imams. One interviewee who had engaged with sharia processes to gain a religious divorce observed:

> I see a lot of imams washing their hands away from this matter. Especially when there is violence, a lot of them are not taking enough responsibility on this matter. They still see family relationships breakdown as an internal matter and that has to change.[67]

[64] ibid.
[65] Interview 9 (Melbourne, April 2016).
[66] Interview 12 (Melbourne, April 2016).
[67] Interview 52 (Sydney, November 2019).

Another interviewee, this time a community worker, explained:

> [A] lot of women are too embarrassed to talk about it … When it gets to the point that she wants to do something about it, she'll say it to the imam, but the imams don't see it as a big, major issue not like us ladies will see it as a major issue, unfortunately. I think the imams themselves, they need an awareness program about how bad it is.[68]

Chapter six will describe changes and improvements that have been made to some Australian sharia processes to better respond to domestic violence.

E. Acknowledgement of Injustice

Women sought out imams not only for direction and guidance but also to feel heard and achieve a sense of justice. In large part, where women felt aggrieved, they believed that the role of the imam was to vindicate this and remind their partner of their marital responsibilities. Interviewees explained how they felt injustices committed against them by their husbands were not adequately acknowledged by imams:

> I just wanted them to really explain to him what he's done, like, and I said to them because I was really upset the day of the divorce and I said to them, *Look, I'll divorce him, that's fine, I'm happy with it but I hope you guys can actually explain to him the extent of what he's done.* I don't think they did, yeah.[69]

> He just got away with murder and everything that I had said that he did was disregarded. They didn't even talk to him about what he did to me … there was no reprimand. There was no like, *Listen, you can't do this to a woman, its wrong.*[70]

These expectations should be understood against the context of how the process unfolds from the women's perspective. Women are first required to fill out a form providing information about the length of their marriage and their reasons for wanting a divorce. The panel of imams then decides on the validity of these reasons as grounds for a divorce. Women often experienced this process as lengthy,[71] intrusive and interrogative, as they were asked to disclose intimate details of their marriage to a panel of men. In the course of the process, most women revealed abuse which they may have kept hidden from their family and friends. They may have disclosed infidelity on the part of their spouse. Given this context, the women, at the end of the process, had greater expectations than simply being granted a divorce. Disappointments about these expectations may have been heightened by the fact that their husbands, in many cases, did not even appear before the panel.

Although some imams engaged with such issues when giving religious advice, other imams tended to take a theologically orientated approach to resolving

[68] Interview 46 (Melbourne, September 2016).
[69] Interview 18 (Melbourne, April 2016).
[70] Interview 28 (Sydney, August 2016).
[71] Interview 55 (Melbourne, January 2020).

disputes and overlooked other issues in doing so.[72] It may be reasonably argued that it is not the role of the imam to acknowledge injustice. However, as highlighted in the sections above, at a minimum, it is arguably necessary for imams to be properly qualified in order to identify the occurrence and dynamics of abusive behaviour and acknowledge it, where they see it.

F. Gender Imbalance on Panels

Women recognised the need to have other women participate in processes of Islamic divorce. Both mental health professionals and women involved in sharia processes identified gender bias in panels and boards which decide on religious divorces. This is a key concern often raised in relation to sharia bodies and community processes across various jurisdictions. Scholars have argued that there is a prevalence of patriarchal attitudes amongst the imams in these dispute resolution roles.[73] Reflecting these concerns, several women in our study believed that male imams identified more closely with their husbands and sympathised with them. Further, interviewees suggested that panels needed to be balanced with, ideally, at least half the panel being women.[74] Explaining this suggestion in more depth, one psychologist suggested:

> [T]he panel needs to be, I would say, ideally gender balanced because then the woman would be able to ask the right questions that she feels the woman would want to talk about, convey, double check on things and she may not be … feel intimidated by disclosing that information. But in terms of hierarchy, I don't think there, on the panel itself, I think there should be a gender balance because more often than not, especially with domestic violence which is probably a lot of the times the reason why, or family violence, a reason why situations get really bad and they need to go to divorce courts or whether it's gambling, drug addiction. A lot of perpetrators are male so having gender balance is actually very important because the gender and the patriarchy thing where *the woman needs to be patient*, *she's softer than the guy* and *she should be able to withstand*, that's also a very stereotypical understanding of females as well.[75]

The participation of women in sharia decision-making is particularly pertinent given the type of information women are expected to divulge about their marriage during the processes. It can be humiliating for women to speak openly of these experiences in the presence of an all-male panel. This is particularly true where issues around sex and intimacy are concerned as the following experiences illustrate:

> [I]t was awful, there was no emotional support … being there the only female amongst five imams … You get emotional (talking about violence and cheating) but it was like a real mechanical process.[76]

[72] Interview 8 (Melbourne, April 2016).
[73] Bano (n 20) 188.
[74] Interview 11 (Melbourne, April 2016).
[75] Interview 37 (Sydney, August 2016).
[76] Interview 18 (Melbourne, April 2016).

> Sometimes there are issues you can't discuss with a man, things that happen in the bedroom ... I can't sit in front a strange man and discuss these issues and it might be an important part of what I have to say.[77]

Concerns around discussing sensitive or traumatic issues with male imams (who are essentially strangers to women in many cases) are compounded by issues with privacy discussed below.

G. Re-traumatisation, Privacy and Forum-shopping

Women observed that they were often traumatised by the experience of trying to seek an Islamic divorce. The male-dominated nature of these processes makes women, particularly those in vulnerable positions, feel frustrated and unheard.[78] One social worker described the experience of women she sees as:

> debilitating, very disempowering. They're already making a very big decision, and we know with DV [domestic violence] especially ... we know it takes several attempts to leave. So again, the amount of trauma and draining, the draining process this woman would have had to go through to finally either make the decision to leave and seek help and then we're putting her through – I don't think there's any words that can do justice to how crippling that experience [with imams] is, and unfair, really unfair.[79]

A psychologist explained that the reality of having to present very humiliating stories of abuse, violence and rape within a marriage can be re-traumatising for women and that the women have little assurance of privacy:

> [H]aving to present and talk about what the problem is, is really quite humiliating for a lot of women and most women won't actually say the truth. So the idea of having the board is supposed to sort of give more formality and governance and protect the imams but it actually means you've got a women speaking to three people. Sometimes she'll have a conduit so one imam will speak on her behalf but her information is still travelling to men that she doesn't know. And if you're waiting to go in to be heard – and you can wait up to three to four hours – you're hearing everybody else's issues so there's absolutely no privacy and it's just really, really humiliating.

She further explained her attempts to help this woman, who had been repeatedly raped by her husband, secure a divorce:

> [The abuse] went on and on and on until we got to a year and I finally said to her, There's one way you can get a divorce on the spot but the repercussions of that are quite high and she said, 'What is it?' And I said, you're going to have to say that he sodomised you

[77] Interview 45 (Melbourne, September 2016).

[78] G Krayem and F Ahmed, 'Islamic Community Processes in Australia' in S Bano, *Gender and Justice in Family Law Disputes: Women, Mediation, and Religious Arbitration* (Waltham MA, Brandeis University Press, 2017) 257.

[79] Interview 38 (Sydney, September 2016).

> because he had, repeatedly in fact. And a lot of the rapes were sodomy … she did it but in her mind, she still, up to this day, doesn't know who might have heard her outside … but the imams gave her the divorce like that, on the spot, and she'd been waiting [about] a year.[80]

In this instance, the woman was not only concerned and distressed by the fact that she was presenting this evidence to a panel of men, but also the fact that others waiting outside might have heard the proceedings. Women noted that people walked by the office in which the proceedings were taking place or waited outside for their turn, making privacy impossible. One psychologist explained of her clients:

> Women need to be able to be comfortable to disclose information and my clients have told me that they can't be open with sheikhs, they can't disclose a lot of information, they don't feel comfortable doing so, they feel as if they're going to be judged, there's no rapport that's being developed for them to be comfortable to disclose information.[81]

Although some imams claimed to understand women's discomfort in sharing private information during divorce proceedings, ultimately the spaces within which these proceedings take place were not considered to be safe spaces by women using them.

Professionals working in this field stress the significance of preventing the further traumatisation of women in these circumstances. For this reason, some community workers and psychologists encourage a process that has come to be known as 'imam shopping'[82] or '*fatwa* shopping'. This process encourages women to find imams who have a reputation for understanding the dynamics of domestic violence and for protecting and acknowledging the rights and perspectives of women through the process. However, not all imams approve of 'imam shopping'. In fact, the shift towards more collective religious authorities (ie, imams coming together to form groups of religious authorities) was in part intended to curb imam shopping.[83]

Women who 'imam shopped' were unlikely to do so during the marriage or when they were seeking a mediator, but rather for their divorce proceedings. For example, one woman stated:

> I guess we tried to do mediation through our family first and then we went through the different imams or sheikhs that were recommended to us and they were either not helpful or they didn't want to help either. And so it got to a point where things were just not going anywhere and my partner didn't want to give me a divorce so I ended up just having to leave the home that we were living at and I went back to my parents' house and still asked for a divorce. It was happening so I had to go through … I think it's the Imam's Council of Victoria.[84]

[80] Interview 47 (Melbourne, October 2016).
[81] Interview 37 (Sydney, August 2016).
[82] Interview 12 (Melbourne, April 2016).
[83] Interview 24, Sydney, May 2016.
[84] Interview 9, Melbourne, April 2016.

One reason motivating 'imam shopping' is to ensure that women receive their financial rights in addition to receiving a divorce. As one psychologist put it:

> Well, [if] you're not happy with that opinion, go and get another one. Just even I know definitely … communities some people who just go overseas, just go to Canada, bypass Australia completely, go online, find an imam that has openly said I will divorce you, come to me and I will divorce you and I'll give it to you.[85]

While some imams complained that this wasted their time and created 'tensions' between imams,[86] from the perspective of the women this is often necessary for the preservation of their mental health, as well as to secure their substantive divorce rights.

H. Impact on Faith

Some women turned to their faith for strength during the difficult process of divorce:

> It [my faith] helped a lot especially during my mental health rehabilitation phase and I felt that when someone has rock bottom the only way to go after that is to go upwards so my faith played a long way to heal and recover from my traumatic experience and it has only grown strong after that period.[87]

However, some women described how the divorce process left them questioning their faith. One woman reported removing her headscarf following her experience of the Islamic divorce process. Another described this crisis of faith in the following way: 'I couldn't step foot in a mosque … for a long time I just didn't want anything to do with Islam. I was just hurt'.[88] This impact of sharia processes on women's faith is significant, as it is rarely acknowledged, yet may be a potential motivator for community organisations to improve these processes.

V. Conclusion

Our interviews with women who experienced sharia processes revealed the complex and important reasons why they used these processes and why the availability of these processes was important to them. These reasons ranged from emotional (wanting to end manipulation and gain closure) to pragmatic (wanting to avoid community gossip) to spiritual.

This chapter also adds nuance and depth to common concerns raised about sharia processes based on interviews with women with lived experience of sharia

[85] Interview 12, Melbourne, April 2016.
[86] Interview 24, Sydney, May 2016.
[87] Interview 52 (Sydney, November 2019).
[88] Interview 28 (Sydney, August 2016).

processes and professionals working in the area of family dispute resolution. Interviewees highlighted that there are currently no requirements for imams to have formal qualifications (that is, as mediators or counsellors) and that there was a lack of transparency in religious decision-making as well as sharia processes in general. Further, there is an illustrated failure by some imams to adequately acknowledge and/or respond to domestic violence and other injustices. These latter issues do not exist in isolation but are logically related to, and flow from, the lack of adequate training and transparency. Such issues have led some women to 'imam shop' to protect their mental health and secure better outcomes for themselves.

A failure to acknowledge women's perspectives and recognise abuse is arguably compounded by current gender imbalance on panels and boards. The fact that decision-making is largely determined by all-male panels also means that many women did not feel comfortable discussing sensitive topics, especially sexual violence. In addition, in some cases, where imams' decision-making is informed by gender bias and a lack of education on issues such as domestic violence, this can lead to the re-traumatisation of women. Lastly, women did not feel comfortable disclosing certain information due to sharia processes not being sufficiently private. For these reasons, information critical to a woman's case may not be shared, or may be excluded from consideration, which may affect the substantive outcomes of her case.

At the same time, our study reveals the subtler aspects of women's experiences with these processes. Some of the women we interviewed described how their experiences with sharia processes affected their ability to practice and stay connected with their faith. Other women were deeply affected by imams' apparent failure to informally acknowledge the injustice done to them or rebuke their husbands. Supplementing these findings, the next chapter focuses on imams' perspectives on sharia processes. It shows that some women positively experienced sharia processes, describing imams as their advocates and as playing a familial support role.

4

Imams' Roles and Perspectives

I. Introduction

In this chapter, we draw on interviews with imams to provide further insight into sharia processes through a study of imams' understandings of their roles and responsibilities in reconciliation and divorce processes. In the second part of this chapter, we consider imams' perspectives on some of the issues and concerns raised about sharia processes in chapter three. In particular, we focus on imams' views on the need for up-skilling and training, better responses to domestic violence, and the need for women's perspectives to be incorporated into sharia processes by including women as scholars and decision-makers in divorce proceedings.

While the analysis in this chapter focuses on new research on imams in Australia drawn from our fieldwork, we also draw on research of sharia processes in the UK and Canada which provide valuable points of comparison. Overall, the data reveals several serious challenges faced by imams administering sharia processes. These challenges will be taken into account in our recommendations for change to sharia processes and the Australian family law system in chapter six.

II. Imams' Understanding of their Role in Reconciliation

The focus of many imams on reconciliation stems from religious principles derived from the Quran where parties are encouraged to arbitrate disputes with the view to reconcile.[1] One imam explained:

> We, as Muslim leaders, the first thing as an imam, Islamically I'm required to try and reconcile between the two. So if there's – my responsibility is to try and amend or try and reconcile between the two parties and try and bring them to terms with they could go back to their normal marital life and continue with conditions that they might put over each other after we do some mediation or after we do some counselling and so on … So, most of the time, it's our religious obligation, our moral obligation to try and

[1] Abdullah Yusuf Ali, *The Holy Qu'ran* (Ware, Wordsworth Editions Ltd, 2001) 4:35.

> reconcile between the parties or between the couple that there is a dispute between them. We listen to their sides. Usually, it depends on the situation. So, it goes by each case. We assess each case. If it's a case that we could bring them both at once and try and reconcile it once, we'll do it.[2]

As a result, many Islamic processes guiding divorce, in Australia and abroad, consider that a key condition before any divorce certificate may be granted is that the parties attempt to reconcile, unless there is an Apprehended Violence Order (AVO) in place.[3] The process carried out by imams, therefore, typically begins with reaching out to each party to hear their side of the story.[4] One imam outlined the most common issues faced by couples who come to him:

> Most of the cases, it's family violence, drugs and alcohol and all this stuff although when I speak with the men or with the husband, they totally deny it ... in most other occasions ... [conflict is] because of not understanding each other's values and [respect for] each other's values. For example, then they'll start arguing about [how they] accept[ed] each other before when he or she was someone else and now because the real life has come ... The other thing is the interference of family members, in-laws so mother-in-law, father-in-law. In most of the cases, mother-in-law unfortunately and sisters-in-law in most of the cases. Sometimes father-in-law but in most of the family issues, it's unfortunately the sisters and the people that they mix with ... The other thing is that sometimes it is also cultural differences ... So if they marry from another part of the world ... it is difficult for them to continue because of the cultural differences ... So in most of the cases, *alhamdulillah* [Arabic phrase meaning 'praise be to God'] I find the root cause of the problem and then, *alhamdulillah*, the couple starts living together happily.[5]

Imams generally view the divorce process as one driven by emotion and believe that overall most couples will return to one another given space and time. This is the reason one imam allows the process to draw out:

> I will say to them, *Call me next week. Okay, I'll meet up with you the week after that.* I just give it at least two or three weeks for them to go back to their senses ... So, it's our responsibility to always push them towards the lines of reconciling, and many times it does work. If it doesn't work, then we start listening to them and our principle, our policy amongst the imams is that it will take at least two months, give them at least two months.[6]

This imam took the view that this space is necessary to see if the couples might consider reconciling on their own. It gives them the necessary time apart without rushing into decisions.

[2] Interview 24 (Sydney, May 2016).

[3] S Bano, *Muslim Women and Shari'ah Councils: Transcending the Boundaries of Community and Law* (Basingstoke, Palgrave Macmillan, 2012) 185; P Patel, 'Faith in the State? Asian Women's Struggles for Human Rights in the U.K.' (2008) 16 *Feminist Legal Studies* 9, 29–30; Interview 16, 1.

[4] G Krayem, *Islamic Family Law in Australia: To Recognise or Not to Recognise* (Melbourne, Melbourne University Publishing, 2014) 99.

[5] Interview 47 (Melbourne, October 2016).

[6] Interview 24 (Sydney, May 2016).

Some imams reported that they did not divorce couples and only dealt with reconciliation, instead referring them to other imams to undergo divorce processes.[7] Another imam stated that he does not even discuss divorce during reconciliation processes. He focuses instead on understanding the circumstances from each side's perspective. Echoing the concerns raised by professionals in chapter three, he stated that: 'it's extremely important for imams to in fact have counselling training so that they understand strategies as well as pathways by which they can in fact bring about reconciliation'.[8]

During this reconciliation phase, most imams will remind the couple of their rights and responsibilities. As one imam explains, it is '[t]he role of the imam, the role of people of influence in the community, parents as well … to advise both and say, *as husband and wife, these are your rights and these are your responsibilities*'.[9] One imam further explains that this is about education and that part of the role of imams is to provide an 'understanding [of] what marriage is about, understanding each one's rights and responsibilities. That's a problem. A lot of them don't understand'.[10] Another imam highlights that breaking up a family is unfortunate, but that this often stems from parties not taking responsibility. He stated:

> It's unfortunate to see the family breaking up. I don't know whether that is supported statistically or not. I heard that the divorce rate in the Muslim community is between 40 and 60 per cent which is very, very high if that is true. I think people don't know their religion, that's one, because the problems we see when they make application to us and they want, they are fighting, it's just very, very, what I can I say, very trivial things they are fighting over. People, men that are not taking their responsibility seriously. You find someone coming home 1 am, 3 am, and say, *where have you been [man]? You have a home, you have a family, to know whether they had a good sleep* – They say, *Well, I went out for chatting*, for things like that and their wives complain that these men don't even do their basic duties of the house, of the home. It's really difficult. What we read in the literature and what people talk about are quite distinct. So, when we get the application, usually it's the wife that makes the complaint. We have very rare cases where men make the complaint. For example, last Saturday we had one case where the man was complaining about mental health, his wife had mental health [issues] and she was affecting the children. So that's a very, very uncommon thing; the majority is the other way.[11]

One imam reminds couples that 'marriage is not fun … marriage is not entertainment. Marriage means responsibility; mutual understanding; children when they're, when they're bad, when they're smiling, when there's tears; life'.[12]

[7] Interview 23 (Sydney, May 2016).
[8] Interview 27 (Sydney, September 2016).
[9] ibid.
[10] Interview 40 (Melbourne, September 2016).
[11] Interview 16 (Melbourne, May 2016).
[12] Interview 50 (Sydney, October 2016).

In order to help couples and to avoid divorce, some imams will require the couple to undertake a session with a family counsellor, rather than with the imams. As one Victoria-based imam explains:

> We have a counsellor here once a week, every Wednesday … She's a family therapist, counsellor and she's a professional. She's got that title and she – we try to refer to her, for them to at least sit down with the, have a counselling session … The problem is with us, the imams, like when they come to the Board of imams, they normally come at the end of, right at the end of it all. They've sort of gone through all the process with the families, so they've come right to the end and they've come to us and that's one of the issues that we have, to be honest. We would like for there to be more support in place where we can have more sort of counselling. We can sort of, in a way, not just encourage but sort of push the parties [to do that].[13]

However, counselling does not usually yield positive results, as by the time couples get to this process, they are beyond the point of reconciliation. Imams acknowledge that it is important to seek mediation before couples feel their differences are irreconcilable.

Our interviews highlighted the potential for the imams to have conflicting or incompatible roles as they navigate their way through offering reconciliation support as a primary focus before considering the question of religious divorce. One potential conflict is between their role in offering reconciliation and their role in facilitating or providing religious divorce. Imams' preference for reconciliation may create barriers for women seeking divorce. Some imams will tell the woman to be patient with their husbands and to wait.[14] As mentioned earlier, some imams, whose focus is on reconciliation, will tell a woman that they only offer services in relation to marriage, but not divorce.[15] One of the few imams who specialise in marriage counselling and reconciliation arguably avoids the tension between the different roles of imams by making it clear to the couples that if they want a divorce, then he is not the right person to see.[16] His approach is based on getting each individual to focus on their relationship with God, and through that lens he offers a program that runs over about six months, meeting fortnightly with phone support throughout. The imam acknowledges that he cannot see everyone who wants to access this service, which is supported by a Muslim women's organisation.[17]

One psychologist we interviewed suggested another tension in the imams' roles: a tension between imams' desire to reconcile the couple and the best interest of any children involved:

> [T]he family unit is very important so measures must be in place to have the skills to negotiate whether there's a possibility of reconciliation or whether it's in the best

[13] Interview 40 (Melbourne, September 2016).
[14] Interview 12 (Melbourne, April 2016).
[15] ibid.
[16] Interview 23 (Sydney, May 2016).
[17] ibid.

> interests of the children and the couple to separate. And I think that's one of the problems, is that the Sheikhs will hesitate to consider breaking up a family because they hold onto that principle of do whatever needs to be done to keep the family together but they also don't have an understanding of the concept of what's in the best interests of the child.[18]

III. Imams' Understanding of their Role in Divorce

A. Role as Service-Providers and Advocates for Women

When a husband refuses to pronounce a *talaq* divorce, some – but not all – Muslim women consider the involvement of imams essential to effectively secure an Islamic divorce. Given their role in securing religious divorces for women, the imams we interviewed emphasised that they consider sharia processes to be principally a service for women, as they secure religious divorces for those who otherwise would not be able to obtain them. One imam said: 'Our bread and butter are the women. From the beginning, in 1984, the Board of Imams was established and from the beginning it was the women who came to seek divorce'.[19] Another imam stated that it is 'very uncommon' for men to 'make the complaint';[20] it's generally 'the wife that makes the complaint'.[21]

Imams also saw themselves as issuing religious divorces for women which are recognised in countries that may not recognise an Australian civil divorce:

> Particularly some countries within the Arab world they think if there is a divorce that is issued by an Australian court that divorce will not be recognised within that Arab country so therefore a man may have this lady prevented from that particular country on the basis that she is his wife and he has the right to do so and she may even be locked up and sectioned even though she may be divorced according to the Australian law. So when we as a body, as a religiously recognised authority, issue a divorce for this woman, this will then be relied upon within these Arab countries and if we were absent from the scene then we may have situations in which women will continue to be oppressed because the husband will try and use his 'Islamic rights' to keep her as a wife.[22]

Imams recognised that some men withhold *talaq* divorce to punish women or avoid their financial responsibilities and obligations (like *mahr*, the marriage-gift received by the wife).[23] Men often use the religious process to get outcomes that

[18] Interview 37 (Sydney, August 2016).
[19] Interview 14 (Melbourne, April 2016).
[20] Interview 16 (Melbourne, May 2016).
[21] ibid.
[22] Interview 36 (Sydney, August 2016).
[23] T Walker, *Shari'a Councils and Muslim Women in Britain: Rethinking the Role of Power and Authority* (Leiden, Brill, 2017) 113–14.

they want.[24] This is often accompanied by evasion tactics, like not responding to requests to attend conciliation meetings.[25] Imams thus often deal with challenging and difficult behaviour from the parties, especially the husbands, while facilitating divorces.

Against this background, our research identified that imams saw one of their roles as being an advocate for women. One imam noted how preservation of the rights of women from a religious perspective requires an understanding of the Australian legal system. He gave the example of a couple who had been married for 30 years:

> [Y]ou should know the law here, it's very important. And second what's the right for the wife, what's the right for the husband according to the law because the main problem, where they come to the divorce, is about financial issues, about the custody of the children. If you don't know the law, how can you sit with them? … [L]adies who stay with their husband for 30 years and she helps him to become rich and houses and all of this and now he doesn't like to give her anything and if you don't know the law here, I think you may make the lady, she loses everything.[26]

Such advocacy was also identified by a number of women interviewees. One woman described the imams as her 'advocates' and felt her concerns were taken seriously by them.[27] A second one noted 'it was really good having an imam who would just listen to me without making any judgments, that was very important'.[28] It is understandable that imams are characterised as advocates for women if we consider that they release women from unwanted religious marriages. There is the potential, as seen in other jurisdictions, that intervention by imams can offer women a space to not only speak up and seek protection for their own interests (financial and otherwise) but also challenge cultural practices (including familial or community pressure to reconcile).[29] Ultimately, imams can be vital to the successful resolution of marital disputes, allowing room for parties (and their families) to resolve complex matters, including the *mahr*.[30]

B. Backlash for Carrying Out Roles in Divorce Proceedings

Imams' ruling on issues such as divorce do not necessarily make imams popular with the husbands and former husbands who feel they have been disadvantaged.

[24] A Buckley, *Not 'Completely' Divorced: Muslim Women in Australia Navigating Muslim Family Laws* (Melbourne, Melbourne University Press 2019) 281.
[25] Walker (n 23) 154.
[26] Interview 50 (Sydney, October 2016).
[27] Interview 4 (Sydney, April 2016).
[28] Interview 13 (Melbourne, April 2016).
[29] Bano (n 3) 203.
[30] ibid 204.

These men will often challenge imams on their decisions in the divorce proceedings. They often accuse imams of 'favouring the women',[31] and these accusations may involve the use of physical and violent threats.[32] As one imam told us:

> sometimes you're really dealing with thugs, drug dealers, gangsters, death threats, everything, and we have no protection. Like when someone says to me, *If you divorce my wife from me, I will come back and shoot you*, you know? And when it comes from someone you know they are capable of doing it …[33]

As a result, some centres where imams conduct divorce proceedings have hired security guards to patrol the premises and ensure imams are not attacked at their place of work.[34] These threats have sometimes extended to the families of imams.

For this reason, imams recognise that it is important to make divorce decisions as a panel:

> [F]or example, I have given a judgment against the husband and he meets me in the masjid [Arabic term for mosque] and says, *Sheikh you did wrong*. Look, we have a group of imams, I am not the only one and my job is to be there and discuss the matter and we all have seen, not in two eyes but much more than one head, but five heads, six heads, and they feel that this is where it should be and this is the judgment.[35]

This serves to protect imams from harm but also helps cement the decisions they come to, making it more difficult for men to discredit the divorce. It also works to 'centralise' the decisions in a way, moving towards a more collective religious authority approach.[36]

Imams' privacy and home life is also an issue. People tend not to understand that imams are not available to them at all hours of the day and night. Imams have had people turn up on their doorstep when they have been at home with their families. This is concerning both for their mental health and their physical safety, as well as that of their families. One imam explains as follows:

> Sometimes your mobile won't stop, because sometimes, maybe at night, [there's] no privacy for you. This affects your life, your relationship with your family, with the children and with the relatives, with the friends, with the people around you. Sometimes, you need sometimes to go to a counsellor or a psychologist, to talk with him because always you see, you see the negative image of life. People who are fighting … who are screaming.[37]

[31] Interview 14 (Melbourne, April 2016).
[32] Interview 31 (Sydney, August 2016).
[33] Interview 63 (Sydney, May 2020).
[34] Interview 16 (Melbourne, May 2016).
[35] Interview 14 (Melbourne, April 2016).
[36] Buckley (n 24) 198.
[37] Interview 50 (Sydney, October 2016).

IV. Responding to the Concerns of Women and Professionals

A. The Need for Training and Resources

Imams unanimously recognise that they need training beyond simply understanding the specifics of marriage and divorce in Islam. Increasingly, imams feel that they are not equipped with the tools they need to navigate the complexity of relationship issues that are presented to them. In particular, many imams recognise that they do not properly understand domestic violence and have asked for more training than they have presently received.[38] Additionally, they are interested in mediation training in Family Dispute Resolution (FDR), which is the mediation process recognised by the Family Law Act 1975 (Cth).[39] One imam stated that their aim was to 'get an imam to be a qualified mediation practitioner so that … they can come from the court to us – and we've been getting a lot of enquiries about that'.[40] Another imam clearly noted that 'good intention[s are] not enough'. You need 'good intention[s] and wisdom'.[41] He believes that this can come about through continued study and upskilling in the area of mediation:

> We need internal and external resources. Internal resources such as counsellors, psychologists, lawyers, extra services for women, like someone that can speak on behalf of females rather than her coming to stand in front of four or five men. These are the sort of resources that we want. External resources such as, like housing, other legal advices or other legal consultants, resources that will work closely with the government, any resource that can at least develop the whole program together.[42]

Another imam acknowledged that before discussions about reconciliation could proceed, he attempted to determine whether there were other underlying issues that needed to be addressed pertaining to mental health or other medical issues that may have previously gone unaddressed. In such cases, he would refer them to a relevant medical practitioner prior to commencing any discussion around reconciliation for the couple. So, while this imam was not skilled in the area of mental health, he recognised the need to work with other practitioners to achieve a more holistic and long lasting outcome; even if the situation resulted in divorce, the underlying issues would be addressed.[43] This seems to be a growing trend, where imams recognise that other services need to work together with Islamic processes to ensure that couples and families are assisted in the most effective way.[44]

[38] Interview 14 (Melbourne, April 2016).
[39] Interview 24 (Sydney, May 2016).
[40] Interview 40 (Melbourne, September 2016).
[41] Interview 50 (Sydney, October 2016).
[42] Interview 24 (Sydney, May 2016).
[43] Interview 34 (Sydney, August 2016).
[44] Interview 50 (Sydney, October 2016).

Other imams suggested that they would like more resources to run pre-marriage courses which would prevent the kind of issues that they are currently facing, as couples would understand their responsibilities in marriage and upon divorce.[45] One imam stated:

> [W]e can sometimes make pre-marriage courses, how to select the proper husband and the proper wife. And the, how can we make anger management courses before marriage, the duties and rights of both, and we can make some anger management courses for the people who are going to marry together and we teach them the rights and the duties in an Islamic perspective and in the same way, how can they live together in peace and security in Australian custom and traditions. We try to make this, especially the people who come from overseas.[46]

In addition to the above-mentioned challenges, imams also faced significant time restraints. For some interviewed women this meant that imams appeared insensitive to their concerns. One woman described it as 'an awful experience … [with] no emotional support', labelling the process 'mechanical' and highlighting how disappointed she was that nothing she disclosed seemed to 'shock' the panel of imams. Explaining: '[Y]ou get emotional and like, again, it didn't shock them, the violence didn't shock them, the cheating didn't shock them'.[47] A second woman likened the process to a 'bulk billing clinic' where they were trying to get through as many cases as quickly as possible. She explains:

> they just wanted quick fix solutions … and it's not a one size fits all … [M]arriage is a very big issue, divorce as well is a very big issue, and every family deserves this time and every person in that family needs to be heard.[48]

However, from the imams' perspective they hear many of these cases each day and they find the content challenging to deal with. This makes it difficult to hear many cases in one sitting. 'We try to make no more than five, because mentally we can't cope'.[49] As we will discuss in chapter six, a diversification of the panels with a range of professionals would be better equipped to respond to the needs of the women addressing the panels, given the various pressures on imams.

B. Responding to Domestic Violence

The previous chapter detailed women's views on how imams dealt inadequately or inappropriately with their disclosures of domestic violence. Some interviews with imams also suggested that they do not always appreciate that women may have

[45] Interview 40 (Melbourne, September 2016).
[46] Interview 50 (Sydney, October 2016).
[47] Interview 18 (Melbourne, April 2016).
[48] Interview 45 (Melbourne, September 2016).
[49] Interview 31 (Sydney, August 2016).

difficulties in reporting and proving violence. One imam encouraged women to get an intervention order because he felt that he could not 'rely on people's allegations. We ask for evidence, say, *Have you reported to the police? Have you got any medical evidence to show how much the beating or domestic violence was?*'.[50] Another imam drew inferences about the veracity of women's claims based on her willingness to report violence to the authorities:

> [I]f you're saying that you don't want to get a restraining order to protect yourself from him, how can you be in serious threat of violence? It doesn't make sense.
>
> …
>
> Once you start talking about getting police involved, getting restraining orders involved and all that, they start to be a bit more honest because every woman wants to say that she's been beaten up … she's in a violent relationship, he's a monster.[51]

Yet even when women obtained intervention orders, one imam suggested that an intervention order was not proof that violence had *occurred* because intervention orders were sometimes issued by the judiciary in order to 'prevent any violence or any *risk* of violence [in the future]'.[52] Significantly, one imam did not appear to appreciate the typical cycle of abuse or cycle of violence:

> 'I'm dealing with a woman now who's a victim of domestic violence and she's in that process now of when he beats her up she hates him and then after a week or two, she loves him and she wants him back.'[53]

Other interviewees indicated that the advice of imams was often to remain patient and to return to the situation to preserve the family unit. As one community worker explains, 'That's a classic one that's known in community. If you go to an imam, the only medicine he's going to give you is *sabr* [patience]'.[54]

However, in recent years many imams have increasingly undertaken training in recognising the signs of domestic violence, including the more nuanced signs of psychological and financial abuse. Many imams understand their role to include supporting those who disclose domestic violence and reporting such cases to domestic violence services and, when necessary, to the police. As one imam noted:

> I'm one of those persons that I do not advise the sister to have patience in the case of … family violence. I always, my advice to the sisters is that you have a right, that you seek divorce and seek separation from that man who is not willing and who is not respecting you. And to those imams that advise for *sabr* [patience] and for patience in the face of family violence, my advice is that they need to read again the text of Islam about treating a woman, about how a woman, particularly a wife, should be treated in the light of Islamic teachings.[55]

[50] Interview 16 (Melbourne, May 2016).
[51] Interview 8 (Melbourne, April 2016).
[52] Interview 40 (Melbourne, September 2016).
[53] Interview 8 (Melbourne, April 2016).
[54] Interview 12 (Melbourne, April 2016).
[55] Interview 47 (Melbourne, October 2016).

This particular imam went further arguing that a *khulah* divorce is not an appropriate option in situations where violence has occurred.[56] Fundamentally, a *khulah* divorce requires the consent of the husband to the divorce, so where there are claims of violence this avenue is not a viable option, and thus there is a need to turn to *faskh* or *tafriq*.[57] As discussed in the next chapter, this is pertinent because of the ramifications it has for the wife's financial entitlement regarding the *mahr*.

As part of their domestic violence training, some imams are now 'being trained to assess risks and also manage risks'[58] in regard to domestic violence, including producing resources and providing further information sessions for other imams to educate them about domestic violence. Importantly, our data revealed that imams generally seemed to recognise the implications of an intervention order and thus where one existed, imams generally did not attempt to bring together the couple for reconciliation.[59]

Imams reported to us that where family violence occurs, they explain that this is not permissible in Islam and emphasise that Islam supports a woman leaving a violent relationship. One imam stated that if he identified a situation of domestic violence: 'Straight away we'll advise her to report him to the police. And secondly, we'll make sure that she's away from him and, thirdly, we'll speed up the [divorce] process'.[60] Further, where a woman reports violence to the imams but has not reported it previously to the police, imams will encourage her to report to the police, saying 'we empower women to do that because it [reporting violence to the police] is not against the religion, it is [sanctioned] by the religion. Whenever someone is suffering, someone is facing a difficulty, to go wherever help may come from'.[61] This was reiterated by other imams interviewed: 'we highly encourage them for them [women] to report it to the police'.[62] One group of imams made it clear that they would file a police report if they find domestic violence is present in the relationship and if women 'are in danger or at risk … we should deal with the situation a legal way'.[63] This is made clear up front so women can decide if they would like to proceed with this particular group of imams without feeling pressured into reporting an issue that they may not wish to report.

One imam takes it upon himself to report violence to the police because he feels this is his responsibility.[64] 'If you return back home, I can't really help you but

[56] ibid.
[57] R Parveen, 'Do Sharia Councils Meet the Needs of Muslim Women?' in S Bano (ed), *Gender and Justice in Family Law Disputes: Women, Mediation, and Religious Arbitration* (Waltham MA, Brandeis University Press, 2017) 148.
[58] Interview 14 (Melbourne, April 2016).
[59] ibid.
[60] Interview 24 (Sydney, May 2016).
[61] Interview 16 (Melbourne, May 2016).
[62] Interview 24 (Sydney, May 2016).
[63] Interview 50 (Sydney, October 2016).
[64] Interview 27 (Sydney, September 2016).

if you go back to your parents, then we can actually work from there to reconcile and whatever else needs to be done from there'.[65] Another imam said that while he would encourage women to report ongoing abuse to the police, he recognised that an intervention order could also escalate the situation.[66]

When the issue of women returning to unsafe environments was raised, imams stated that they would never advise a victim of domestic violence to go back to her husband, but it would ultimately be her decision:

> So we'll give that advice and we'll say, *look, it's unsafe for you*, and it's happened many times … I'll find her to be unsafe so it's our responsibility, religious responsibility before anything else, and a moral responsibility before anything else that if we see someone going back home to an unsafe environment, we need to advise them.[67]

The same imam noted that this is a bigger issue for recently arrived migrants who do not have the support of their families, making it more challenging for them to leave.[68]

Only one imam said that he did not see cases of current domestic violence and for this reason did not have a specific process for addressing the issue. The imam did say that if the woman spoke of domestic violence in her past, she would be encouraged to seek counselling but was not concurrently encouraged to contact the police.[69] He urged however that there was no 'patience with hitting … Hitting, it's danger. It is something that hurts the woman and maybe the children, and some people are very violent and if, I mean, she has the right to protect herself'.[70]

The majority of imams now seem to have a clear process for raising and dealing with domestic violence. However, as discussed in the previous chapter, imams did not clearly recognise other kinds of abuse such as psychological or financial abuse. While this question was not raised directly with imams, interviews with women, health professionals and community workers discussed in chapter three highlighted the lack of understanding about these issues more generally.

Importantly, recent initiatives have been taken by community bodies to address this lack of understanding about domestic violence. Intensive domestic violence training programs have been provided for imams and community leaders. These programs focus on the prevention, intervention, recovery and post-trauma phases of domestic violence and the relevant Australian laws such as protection orders.[71] In addition, both the Board of Imams Victoria (BOIV) and the Australian National Islamic Council's Centre for Arbitration and the Resolution Disputes Ltd (ANIC-CARD) have implemented specific domestic violence policy and administrative procedures. BOIV has also employed a trained and skilled family violence

[65] ibid.
[66] Interview 40 (Melbourne, September 2016).
[67] Interview 24 (Sydney, May 2016).
[68] ibid.
[69] Interview 34 (Sydney, August 2016).
[70] ibid.
[71] Interview 62 (Sydney, May 2020).

practitioner to work with women experiencing domestic violence. Recognising the need to work with men on this issue, BOIV is developing programs for men to address this issue. These improvements will be addressed in greater detail in chapter six.

C. Gender Imbalance in Sharia Processes

As flagged in chapter three, the majority of people involved in granting a religious divorce are men. While some organisations have taken active steps to recruit women to assist with processing applications and provide emotional support to applicants, final decisions about divorce generally rest with a panel of male imams, with the exception being the recent appointment of a woman to the decision-making panel of the BOIV. While significant steps have been taken by community organisations to improve female representation in the divorce process, the situation remains difficult for women seeking a divorce. As one woman noted:

> [T]here could be a woman on the panel. I mean we have a lot of Muslim scholars around these days … [Y]ou can't discuss with a man things that happen in the bedroom. I can't sit in front of a strange man and discuss these issues, and it might be a really important part that they would say, *okay your divorce is valid* but there wasn't a woman at my time and, you know, I could say to her, *Look, can I talk to you about this subject and you can relay it to the men*, or something.[72]

Most of the imams interviewed were able to identify that a predominately male panel would potentially create discomfort for women when sharing sensitive or private details of their marriage. They also acknowledged that disclosing the inner workings of a woman's marriage, for example details relating to sexual intimacy, could also be intimidating and humiliating:

> She's sitting in front of a panel of men, so shyness and embarrassment also plays a big role in that. So, we do believe that more services need to cater for women than men and these are the sort of things that we need to manage and just overcome over time.[73]

Several panels of imams recognised this limitation and have now involved female counsellors, social workers, community workers or psychologists in the process. One imam reported that he works closely with a female psychologist. He explained that while he feels that he can deal with men, '[w]ith the females, when it comes to very private matters and some things can be very, very private … they might probably not even want to say that out of their tongue'.[74] He further recommended that an all-female board, including psychologists, would improve the process as the current system does not account for the further trauma these processes can create for women.

[72] Interview 45 (Melbourne, September 2016).
[73] Interview 24 (Sydney, May 2016).
[74] Interview 27 (Sydney, September 2016).

Overall, the data revealed that the inclusion of women in sharia processes is generally limited to care roles that value women's emotional intelligence. While caring roles are important, limiting women's participation in sharia processes only to care roles overlooks the qualifications and expertise that women (that is, scholars) can bring if they were able to be involved in the decision-making process alongside imams.[75] In particular, imams do not generally recognise that gender affects perspective. Rather, they see themselves as neutral arbiters, applying the law without acknowledging that there is always room for interpretation.

Although most imams agreed that there was a need to include more women in sharia processes, some imams considered the existing process to be successful, saying that women 'are very comfortable'.[76] For example, some imams 'consider [themselves to be] carrying out sometimes a doctor's work because what you say to the doctor physically or whatever, you'll tell to the imam … because they have that trust'.[77] Although, in ordinary circumstances, women may not always be comfortable sharing intimate details with a man, even a male doctor. Further, imams who did not see the need for more female involvement were also those who tended to stress that confidentiality was maintained throughout the process, despite evidence from many women and professionals indicating otherwise (as outlined in chapter three).

Despite some imams not recognising the problems that arise for women due to a lack of gender representation in sharia processes, in Australia, both ANIC and BOIV have made positive steps to address these issues for women through recent changes to the constitution of their divorce panels. The BOIV divorce panel has two women already involved in the process, and importantly, one of these women is a panel member making decisions alongside the male imams. The imams insist this makes women feel more comfortable.[78] Imams also said they would like to see more women trained with the Islamic knowledge to sit on these panels as their knowledgeable equals.[79] The appointment of a female Islamic scholar to the ANIC and BOIV divorce panels is a major achievement. The importance of having women on these divorce panels will be discussed further in chapter six.

V. Conclusion

Imams first and foremost see themselves as duty-bound to reconcile parties before facilitating divorce. If reconciliation fails, imams perceive themselves as providing a service and advocacy for women who wish to secure a religious divorce, despite facing backlash from husbands and sometimes their communities.

[75] Buckley (n 23) 336.
[76] Interview 14 (Melbourne, April 2016).
[77] ibid.
[78] Interview 50 (Sydney, October 2016).
[79] ibid.

Further, imams recognise that they are under-resourced and in need of training in a number of areas relevant to their work in sharia processes, in particular domestic violence. While the previous chapter highlighted women's accounts of inadequate or inappropriate responses to reports of domestic violence, this chapter identified that the approaches of some imams towards domestic violence have improved after receiving training on this topic.

Some imams were also responsive to the concerns of women and professionals raised in the previous chapter regarding gender representation. While at least one female scholar has been appointed to ANIC-CARD and BOIV panels, as we explained in this chapter, many imams interviewed displayed limited understanding about the importance of substantive gender representation in sharia decision-making. Stereotypical thinking about women's roles in administering sharia processes, limiting women's roles to administrative or care-orientated roles, remained persistent.

5

Outcomes of Sharia Processes

I. Introduction

Chapters three and four explored the experiences and perspectives of women and other stakeholders in sharia processes. This chapter will look at the outcomes of these processes. We use 'outcomes' in a broad sense here as including decisions from panels (for example, whether a woman will receive her divorce); decisions on financial questions (for example, how much of her *mahr* a woman must forego); and advice on the religious position on, for example, the appropriate division of property or custody arrangements. This chapter will consider different divorce outcomes and their implications for women as well as financial outcomes including: *mahr*, *iddah*, *mutah* (defined in Section III below), child support and repayment of other financial contributions made by the wife during the course of the marriage. The chapter also captures imams' reluctance to substantively deal with property and child custody issues, and their preference to refer women to mediation or the Australian legal system on these matters. Significantly, this chapter will show how imams variously support, co-operate with, rely on and defer to state law, in striking contrast to tropes about Muslims seeking a separate system of sharia which supplants or undermines state law.

II. Divorce Outcomes

Discussions of sharia processes often raise concerns that women face difficulty securing a religious divorce or that these processes take a long time, leading to 'limping marriages' (where women have a civil divorce but the husband refuses to grant them a religious divorce).[1] Our interviews indicate that women who sought an Islamic divorce via sharia processes were able to obtain a religious divorce (of some type). Imams generally understood their roles as either service providers of religious divorce for women, or even as advocates for women throughout the divorce process (notwithstanding the challenges that women faced within sharia processes as outlined in the previous chapters). Thus, sharia divorce processes

[1] A Buckley, *Not 'Completely' Divorced: Muslim Women in Australia Navigating Muslim Family Laws* (Melbourne, Melbourne University Press, 2019) 13–14.

tended to be orientated towards facilitating religious divorce for women. While in some instances the divorce process was prolonged due to husbands' non-compliance or non-engagement with sharia processes, imams were willing to use a range of mechanisms to secure a religious divorce, including referral of cases to the Grand Mufti (under the Australian National Imams Council's Centre for Arbitration and the Resolution Disputes Ltd (ANIC-CARD) processes) after a set time period.[2]

While, overwhelmingly, women who apply for a religious divorce will receive one,[3] the type of divorce differs between cases, which impacts women's financial rights upon divorce under Islamic jurisprudence. Although a divorce may be granted, a secondary – yet significant – matter is what *type* of Islamic divorce is granted (*talaq*, *khulah*, *tafriq* or *faskh* divorce). These types of divorce (introduced earlier in chapter one) will be briefly summarised before discussing their differential impacts on women's Islamic financial rights, in particular *mahr* and *mutah* (which are explained in detail below and in Appendix F).

A. Summary of the Types of Islamic Divorce

The first type of divorce is the *talaq*, which all five *sunni* Islamic schools of thought recognise as the right held by a husband to issue a unilateral divorce to his wife.[4] There are various types of *talaq*, and they span a broad range of arrangements; however, ultimately, the divorce is either pronounced by the husband; exercised by the wife (where the right of *talaq* is delegated to her, discussed below as *talaq tafweedh*); or the separation is mutual.

As mentioned in chapter two, women typically seek a religious divorce via sharia processes if their husband refuses to grant a *talaq* divorce. In such a case, a panel of imams may use one of the following methods to religiously divorce the couple. The first option is a *khulah* – in this kind of divorce, a woman releases herself from the marriage, and the husband consents to the wife's request for a divorce.[5] Generally, *khulah* involves the wife returning or forfeiting the husband's wedding gift or *mahr*.[6] As mentioned previously, this is often used as a bargaining chip where the payment of *mahr* has been delayed (that is, the husband has not yet paid the *mahr* either in part or in full).

[2] As outlined in ch 2.

[3] See J Macfarlane, *Islamic Divorce in North America: A Shari'a Path in a Secular Society* (Oxford, Oxford University Press, 2012) 172 – only 20 per cent of cases fail to obtain a religious divorce, indicating that a majority of Muslims seeking religious divorce receive closure/finalisation on this matter.

[4] SN Shah-Kazemi, *Untying the Knot: Muslim Women, Divorce, and the Shariah* (Signal Press 2001) 7 <www.nuffieldfoundation.org/project/untying-the-knot-muslim-women-divorce-and-the-shariah> accessed 1 November 2020.

[5] R Parveen, 'Do Sharia Councils Meet the Needs of Muslim Women?' in S Bano (ed), *Gender and Justice in Family Law Disputes* (Waltham MA, Brandeis University Press, 2017) 148.

[6] G Krayem, *Islamic Family Law in Australia: To Recognise or Not to Recognise* (Melbourne, Melbourne University Publishing, 2014) 210.

The other type of divorce available is a *tafriq* or *faskh* – where divorce is granted by a religious 'court'. This type of divorce is used when the husband is considered to be at fault, for example, due to mistreatment of his wife. In this instance, the wife, her family (and according to some schools of thought, the husband) may request that the marriage be annulled due to it being 'defective'. The reasons that a marriage may be labelled as such range from the husband's impotence or insanity to the husband being missing or having deserted the wife. However, Islamic jurists vary in their position on the extent to which these grounds, amongst others, are sufficient to issue *tafriq* or *faskh*.[7]

Further, a woman can gain the right to effect a *talaq* divorce if her husband delegates his power of *talaq* (known as *talaq tafweedh*).[8] The option to delegate divorce rights is largely accepted in the *sunni* schools of Islamic law, though it is understood in different ways.[9] For instance, some believe this right only exists at specific moments in time, and once that passes *talaq* can no longer be delegated; whilst other schools of thought see *talaq* delegation as being attached to a particular condition (ie, husband taking a second wife), or only remaining in force until it is cancelled by the husband or vitiated by the couple reconciling and having sex.[10]

One imam summarised the ways in which these types of divorce are generally understood by imams in Australia:

> *Talaq* is in the hands of the husband. He can … pronounce *talaq*. And then a wife can ask [for] *khulah, faskh* … So *khulah* is asking the husband to release her in return for her delayed *mahr*, usually that is what happens … *Faskh* … is when they have reasons for it [that is, seeking the divorce] … like domestic violence is one of those reasons, absence of the person, sending him to [jail] or a failure to consummate the marriage, these type of things, then we will give [*faskh*].[11]

Appendix F offers a more detailed summary of some key types of Islamic divorce.

In considering the findings below, it is important to keep in mind that women understand, and/or are informed about, the differences between types of divorce to varying degrees. Our research indicated that women who were more educated and had greater Islamic knowledge navigated sharia processes more confidently, but very few women had sufficient religious knowledge to understand the different types of divorce available to them; women generally relied on the advice of imams with respect to their options and rights relating to divorce.[12]

[7] See Appendix F; JE Tucker, *Women, Family and Gender in Islamic Law* (Cambridge, Cambridge University Press, 2008) 92–93. See also Shah-Kazemi (n 4) 8.

[8] Tucker (n 7) 91.

[9] See Appendix F.

[10] Tucker (n 7) 91–92.

[11] Interview 14 (Melbourne, April 2016).

[12] Interview 59 (Melbourne, January 2020).

B. Divorce Outcomes from Sharia Processes

This section focuses on women's experiences within sharia processes and the practical impacts that the different types of Islamic divorce have for outcomes for women.

i. Khulah *or* Talaq *versus* Tafriq *and* Faskh

In Australia, Canada and the UK, the consent of the husband plays a pivotal role in determining the type of divorce granted. For instance, when husbands are brought before the imams and agree, in some cases reluctantly, to the divorce, the outcome is likely to be *khulah*. On the other hand, when husbands are unwilling to participate and their refusal to grant consent is overruled by the imam, the process plays out more like *tafriq or faskh*.[13]

Our early interviews revealed that imams generally seemed to favour *talaq*. Where possible, imams noted that they tried to get men to issue the *talaq* divorce. One imam said this was particularly true where the couple had been separated for longer than six months: '[i]f he has no logical reason then we'll give him maybe a last notice, one week, and we'll tell him that we'll finish it if the divorce will not come from him'.[14] Given this preference for *talaq* divorce, one of the great challenges imams faced in their role – in Australia, the UK and Canada – was ensuring that men turned up to scheduled appointments with the imams; it was common for men to not respond to requests to attend.[15] An imam interviewed suggested that men who avoid the process or ignore the calls of the imams are often attempting to maintain control of their wives.[16]

Where *talaq* was not an option, imams seemed to favour *khulah* in most cases and advised the parties accordingly. Our research found that many women felt they had no choice but to forgo their rights and agree to a *khulah* divorce.[17] Some interviewees felt that the imams encouraged them to go down this path to make the divorce process easier. In many cases, this meant that women would opt for *khulah* simply to have the divorce finalised as quickly as possible and, in doing so, forgo their rights to *mahr. Talaq* or *khulah* forms of divorce may be attractive to imams as this relegates the authority/responsibility for the divorce to the parties and away from the imams themselves.[18]

[13] Macfarlane (n 3) 168.

[14] Interview 34 (Sydney, August 2016).

[15] T Walker, *Sharia Councils and Muslim Women in Britain: Rethinking the Role of Power and Authority* (Leiden, Brill, 2017) 45, 154. See also JR Bowen, *On British Islam: Religion, Law, and Everyday Practice in Sharia Councils* (Princeton NJ, Princeton University Press, 2016) 84; Macfarlane (n 3) 168, 174.

[16] Interview 16 (Melbourne, May 2016).

[17] While this is the case for the initial research period, as outlined in ch 6, there have been a number of relevant changes to the process, including more scope for women to access other types of Islamic divorce.

[18] Interview 6 (Sydney, April 2016); Interview 31 (Sydney, August 2016).

At the same time, imams recognised that the husband may try to pressure his wife into seeking *khulah* divorce because he believes that she will be required to give up her *mahr* in order to receive the divorce. As one imam states:

> I don't like hearing of situations where, because the husband wasn't giving the divorce to the wife and he was clearly in the wrong and clearly is in the wrong, then she's forced to do a khulah … and in doing so the imam says that 'he owes you $50,000 or whatever. You give it up so he can divorce you' … where's the justice in that.[19]

However, this interpretation of *khulah* is contested. Some imams believe that *khulah* should only be issued where there is no fault on the part of the husband and the wife simply wants to be released from the marriage. Despite this, many women interviewed claimed that, although they disclosed that they were in abusive relationships, they were not informed of the option to seek anything other than *khulah*, such as *tafriq* or *faskh* divorces. As one woman explained:

> They let me do *khulah* on my own terms. I didn't know that if he didn't come the third time and they tried … that I could keep whatever he had given me at the time [that is, *mahr*] because he wasn't willing to co-operate. I had no idea. They didn't tell me that. I ended up doing *khulah* … I ended up doing *khulah* over the phone with him and what do they call it when you … relinquish all rights.[20]

More recent interviews with imams have indicated a change in this practice. Imams from both the Board of Imams Victoria (BOIV) and the Centre for Arbitration and the Resolution Disputes Ltd (CARD) stated that they only issue *khulah* divorce in situations where the wife states that the husband is not at fault and she simply wishes to leave. Where harm is found, especially in situations of abuse (of any kind) the imams will do their best to ensure that the husband grants the woman a *talaq* divorce (so she is not required to forgo *mahr*) or, alternatively, the imams grant her a *tafriq* or *faskh* divorce.

> Divorce, this is the right of the husband, and after divorce there is some … rights for the lady, *mahr* and the dowry and the, all of this. *Khulah*, when the lady comes, *The man is okay but I can't stay with him*, at that time, we can go to the *khulah* … if the lady comes and she comes after physical abuse, verbal abuse, emotional abuse, sexual abuse, any kind of abuse, bashing, smashing, beating, all of this, there is harm and we ask him to divorce. If not, we go to the termination, terminating the contract … We tell him, *Okay, if you don't come, if you don't apply, if you don't co-operate and co-ordinate with us, at that time we should go to terminating the contract*. And I will tell you maybe 40 per cent of the cases that come to us at the Imams Council, we go to terminating the contract [that is, by *tafriq* or *faskh*].[21]

Some imams in Australia are reluctant to enforce *tafriq* or *faskh* type divorces as they are uncomfortable referring to the panel they have assembled as

[19] Interview 23 (Sydney, May 2016).
[20] Interview 28 (Sydney, August 2016).
[21] Interview 50 (Sydney, October 2016).

a 'court'.[22] As one imam we interviewed described granting a divorce: '[i]t's a big responsibility ... no one is confident enough ... [t]o play the role [of judge] and say: *Your contract is finished*'.[23] However, many of the women interviewed in this research would have qualified for *tafriq* or *faskh* had it been presented as an option, given the levels of mistreatment perpetrated by their husbands against them in each case. As the next chapter indicates, by the time our fieldwork had concluded, both BOIV and CARD were facilitating *tafriq* or *faskh* when the conditions for this type of divorce were satisfied.

ii. Divorce through Talaq Tafweedh

Existing research established that there had previously been a reluctance amongst Australian imams to accept *talaq tafweedh* (delegated divorce), with one imam noting that this did not fall within the ambit of permissible religious divorce options. He stated that 'if Allah wanted the divorce to be in the hands of the woman, he would have allowed it. It's not something a woman should ask for'.[24] However, our research shows that in order to overcome the difficulties associated with husbands who refuse to divorce their wives, some imams in Australia have begun including a right of delegated divorce for women in the Islamic marriage contract. As one imam understood it:

> [T]he way out for the Muslim is to have a prenuptial as you would agree and a conditional marriage. Then they are agreeing on marriage things and then they put a condition. Now what we did, we did a certificate in which the woman can easily overcome these types of problems. In that we have this certificate, we have terms and conditions.
>
> The husband has agreed to relinquish his exclusive right to pronounce *talaq* to the wife provided that she shall exercise this authority in accordance with the provisions of Islamic sharia and shall seek advice from the Council of Islamic Family Arbitration or Board or any other competent panel of imams, not one imam ... this is a very good tool for the woman to escape unworkable marriages.[25]

Ultimately, a delegated right in the Islamic marriage contract would (depending on its terms and conditions) enable a woman to divorce her husband without his consent:

> Yeah, I've seen that. It's very good. [But] this is part of the problem, so many women don't know about the marital contract at all and then don't enact it even if they do know about it because they want to be nice. So it's a culture change. Knowing about it was one thing and then enacting it ...[26]

[22] Interview 34 (Sydney, August 2016).
[23] Interview 31 (Sydney, August 2016).
[24] Interview 8 (Melbourne, April 2016). See also Buckley (n 1) 377.
[25] Interview 14 (Melbourne, April 2016).
[26] Interview 12 (Melbourne, April 2016).

According to imams, in the standard marriage contract offered by BOIV, the clause granting the woman the right to a delegated divorce still requires the woman to come before a panel of imams to officiate the divorce and finalise it.[27] The advantage for women is that the divorce process is more straightforward as she possesses a right to divorce and the panel can enforce that right. In such circumstances, depending on the terms of the delegation, the wife can retain her *mahr* without demonstrating that the husband was at fault. The marriage contract, with a right to *talaq tafweedh*, used by BOIV is reproduced in Appendix B.

iii. The Impact of Civil Divorce on Religious Divorce Outcomes

The Australian legal system recognises no-fault divorce, so obtaining a civil divorce is relatively straightforward. As a result, many Muslim women will pursue both a civil and religious divorce simultaneously. However, in some Muslim communities in Australia, such as the Turkish community, our research found that many women sought only a civil, and not a religious divorce. However one interviewee with a Turkish background did seek a religious divorce following her civil divorce. She explained that she obtained both a civil and then religious divorce. She sought advice on the religious divorce through a Turkish imam.

> [Her husband said] *you're not my wife anymore*, yeah, three times and [*talaq*], and it's Turkish and that's it. And I said *Okay*, you know, *that's it, it's finished* … And after I asked from my imam … at the mosque … and he said, *Yeah, if your husband said it three times then you're finished.*[28]

As we indicated earlier, some Islamic scholars – particularly in Europe – have expressed the view that a civil divorce (regardless of who initiates it and whether the husband consents to it) counts as an Islamic divorce.[29] Our research supports previous findings that some Muslim women in Australia, relying on this ruling, understood themselves to be Islamically divorced by virtue of having obtained a civil divorce.[30] These women do not typically use sharia processes.

Imams in Australia generally do not accept the position that civil divorce (regardless of who initiates it and whether the husband consents to it) counts as an Islamic divorce. However, they will use an Australian civil divorce as a basis for granting a religious divorce *if it was initiated by the husband or there was some*

[27] Interview 14 (Melbourne, April 2016).

[28] Interview 26 (Sydney, September 2016).

[29] Buckley (n 1) 159–61; M Jaraba, 'The Practice of *Khulʿ* in Germany: Pragmatism versus Conservatism' (2019) 26 *Islamic Law and Society* 83, 87. Unfortunately, the full text of the European Council for Fatwa and Research fatwa is no longer available online. However, relevant sections are available from V Sisler, 'European Courts' Authority Contested? The Case of Marriage and Divorce Fatwas On-Line' (2009) 3 *Masaryk University Journal of Law and Technology* 51. This fatwa is also discussed in L Larsen, *How Muftis Think: Islamic Legal Thought and Muslim Women in Western Europe* (Leiden, Brill, 2018) 92.

[30] Buckley (n 1) 222; Interview 52 (Sydney, November 2020).

evidence of his consent. The imams we interviewed adopted a policy of effectively recognising civil divorces which were initiated by husbands (or where the husband had indicated his consent) as a *talaq* divorce. Imams adopted this policy to prevent men from 'withhold[ing] the right of *talaq* as a tool to bargain in property and custody, to prevent the woman [from] remarry[ing], to force the woman to rescind the deferred *mahr*'.[31] Therefore, amongst women who do use sharia processes, obtaining a civil divorce can facilitate securing an Islamic divorce. In other words, sharia processes, at least sometimes, give religious effect to civil divorces. For example, ANIC-CARD and BOIV will typically finalise an Islamic divorce as a matter of course once a civil divorce *sought by the husband* has been finalised. Imams associated with Lebanese Muslim Association accept that if a man agrees to a civil divorce through the courts by signing or attending hearings, then they can grant an Islamic divorce on the ground that his action constitutes consent to a *talaq* divorce.[32]

One interviewee spoke of how the imams facilitated the religious divorce once she had obtained the civil divorce:

> I just did the Australian one. They said that we will go through the process but you have to have the Australian one first … he said all's you need to do is to get the Australian divorce and then we can come and see you and the four of us will sign it.[33]

Another interviewee reported a similar experience: 'The sheik said to me he'll give me the paper as soon as I can get my Australian divorce'.[34] Official divorce papers help imams identify who initiated the civil law divorce. To be clear, this easy and quick route to Islamic divorce is only available if the husband filed for civil divorce, as the imams can use this as an indication of his consent.[35] A similar policy is seen in sharia processes in other jurisdictions. In the Islamic Sharia Council (ISC) in the UK, scholars may also infer a *talaq* divorce from the husband's civil actions of divorce.[36] The ISC and Sharia Council of Birmingham fast-track women's religious divorce applications if the husband does not contest the civil divorce.[37]

Moreover, many imams in Australia do not issue a religious divorce certificate without the civil divorce also having been finalised. This is to ensure that the parties do not feel that they can remarry without finalising a civil divorce. Similar recognition for civil divorce is observed in the UK. The ISC explains to women seeking Islamic divorce that they need to begin the civil divorce procedure before they can start the Islamic divorce procedure.[38] The Birmingham sharia council

[31] Interview 14 (Melbourne, April 2016).
[32] Interview 40 (Melbourne, September 2016).
[33] Interview 53 (Sydney, November 2019).
[34] Interview 4 (Sydney, April 2016).
[35] ibid.
[36] Bowen (n 15) 91.
[37] ibid 254; John Bowen's research noted that the Islamic Sharia Council has continued to take this approach to fast-track women's religious divorce applications, as well as the Sharia Council of Birmingham, as long as the husband did not contest the civil divorce. Bowen (n 15) 217.
[38] ibid 75.

makes obtaining a civil divorce a prerequisite to granting an Islamic divorce.[39] In fact, the issuing of religious divorce certificates often appears to be a formality recognising the conclusion and attainment of a civil divorce by the parties.[40]

However, our research indicates that not all women favour this policy of withholding a religious divorce until the civil divorce has been finalised. Some see the process of getting a civil divorce as protracted and anxiety-inducing. As one woman interviewed explains, 'I would have wanted the religious divorce before the Australian divorce. It would have given me anxiety to still be married to him'.[41] While some imams will issue an Islamic divorce prior to the receipt of a civil divorce, they will urge women not to remarry until both have been finalised.[42]

III. Financial Outcomes

As mentioned above with respect to *mahr*, in Islamic jurisprudence, different financial entitlements attach to different kinds of divorce. In general, financial entitlements tend to depend on whether a particular type of divorce allows for reconciliation once the divorce has been finalised. Five types of potential financial entitlements of the wife under Islamic jurisprudence should be noted, in order to appreciate our findings discussed below.

(a) As discussed earlier, *mahr* is a gift paid or promised to the wife by the husband at the time of marriage, which is an essential component of an Islamic marriage contract.[43] The *mahr* is sometimes described as the dowry paid by the husband. It is important to understand that the *mahr* might be paid at the time of marriage ('prompt *mahr*'), at a later time ('deferred *mahr*'), or may be partly prompt and partly deferred.[44] As a result, at the time of divorce, the husband may still owe the wife, part or all of the dowry. In these cases, the *mahr* is described as 'a debt owed to the wife'[45] by the husband. Whether the wife is entitled to receive the outstanding *mahr* at the time of divorce depends on the type of divorce that is being sought or issued. The *mahr* is owed in the case of *talaq* or *tafriq* divorces, but if the woman has sought *khulah*, the *mahr* is often forfeited, and the husband is often thought to no longer owe her the remainder.

(b) Depending on the type of divorce, women may be entitled to maintenance during the period of separation (*iddah*) whilst the divorce is being finalised.

[39] G Douglas et al, *Social Cohesion and Civil Law: Marriage, Divorce and Religious Courts* (Cardiff, Cardiff University, 2011) 47–48; Walker (n 15) 48.
[40] Walker (n 15) 128.
[41] Interview 68 (Sydney, February 2016).
[42] Interview 50 (Sydney, October 2016).
[43] Krayem (n 6) 143.
[44] ibid 144.
[45] ibid 181.

This entitlement is related to the kind of divorce that is being requested and whether that type of divorce allows a couple to remarry in the event of a reconciliation after the divorce has been finalised. Thus, where the couple were divorced by *talaq*, this entitlement accrues since the couple may still remarry,[46] while the entitlement does not accrue when divorce is by *khulah* or *tafweedh* (that is, where the wife has exercised her delegated right of divorce) because the couple cannot remarry once the divorce is finalised.

(c) *Mutah* – another potential entitlement – is a post-divorce financial settlement made by the husband to the wife, seen by some as a 'gift of consolation paid to divorced women'.[47] A woman is entitled to *mutah* if the husband has initiated the divorce or if it has been ordered by the court due to some fault of the husband, as in a *tafriq* or *faskh* divorce. A woman is entitled to a say in the value of her *mutah*, in the same way that she is able to negotiate the value of her *mahr*. The *mutah* is generally understood to be either highly recommended or obligatory by Islamic jurists and Qur'anic commentators.[48]

(d) The woman also has the right in Islamic jurisprudence to reclaim the financial contributions to the family unit that she made during the course of her marriage. There is also a basis in Islamic jurisprudence for compensating women for their non-financial contributions to the family unit such as nursing and caring for a young child, and even housework in certain circumstances.

(e) In Islamic jurisprudence, the woman has a right to claim child support from the father of her children.

Our research revealed that imams play, at most, a limited advisory role in financial matters relating to religious divorce. While they have a direct role in the facilitation or granting of religious divorce as an outcome, their role in financial outcomes is often indirect and tenuous. Set against the background of women's limited knowledge of their religious entitlements, we discuss imams' limited advisory role below, as well as the advice that they provide on potential Islamic financial entitlements. Since the imams' role in financial matters is so limited, and they have no power to enforce their advice, women's financial entitlements under Australian law become particularly significant. We explore the experiences of women who seek to enforce these entitlements through the state system, as well as imams' views on financial entitlements protected under civil law and the appropriateness of claiming them.

A. Imams' Limited Advisory Role in Financial Matters

Over the research period we observed that imams' practices shifted away from offering advice relating to property, finances and children. Our research indicates that many imams – including those working with BOIV and ANIC-CARD – do

[46] Interview 16 (Melbourne, May 2016).
[47] Krayem (n 6) 182.
[48] ibid 183.

not generally get involved in financial decision-making, beyond *mahr*, between the couple. (This is also observed in studies of sharia councils in the UK – most sharia councils are reluctant to get involved in financial or property settlement matters and will refer those to the civil courts.)[49]

While many imams acknowledged that women were entitled to more than just *mahr* under sharia (for example, *iddah* maintenance for her and the children, part of the property if she contributed towards it, or a financial gift given at divorce), these broader issues fall outside the scope of the imam panel determinations. One imam specified: 'we don't get involved in assets; we just focus on the *mahr*'.[50] An imam noted, in relation to ANIC-CARD practice, 'the termination, when it's issued by the Grand Mufti … does not indulge in parenting and in finance'.[51] Another imam said, 'We don't deal with property, property division'.[52]

One reason for the limited role imams take with respect to finances may be that some imams view divorce as straightforward but the division of property and custody as complex:

> [I]t becomes very complicated when it comes to money. Sometimes it's just a dowry and sometimes because if she's got rights in the dowry or not, we know Islamically that is she is the one that seeks divorce, she loses the dowry. And then you've got the other thing: sometimes she is a business partner. That's becoming very common, especially now with the second and third generation. She was his business partner, or she helped him in business, and she's entitled to a sum of money, and so on. Sometimes there are assets which are shared in between. So, the more finance that's involved, the more complicated it becomes. It's less complicated when it comes to divorce, okay? If he doesn't want a divorce, we'll divorce her. It's so easy. It just gets complicated when it comes to money.[53]

Despite imams having a limited official role in determining issues relating to property and finance, imams state that sometimes people still seek Islamic advice. Even when imams stress that couples should see a lawyer about financial matters such as property, they may give general advice about what each party is entitled to in line with their interpretation of Islamic principles. In these cases, some emphasised that they underscored that their advice was religious, and not about their legal entitlements:

> We disclose to everyone that this is only religious advice [regarding children and property], nothing legally binding, and it's very important for us as imams that we make that disclosure. We just give them that religious advice for them to take up or not. It's up to them if they want to adhere to it or they don't want to adhere to it. If they want to continue and proceed with the court or not, that goes back to them.[54]

[49] Walker (n 15) 120.
[50] Interview 40 (Melbourne, September 2016).
[51] Interview 63 (Sydney, May 2020).
[52] Interview 16 (Melbourne, May 2016).
[53] Interview 24 (Sydney, May 2016).
[54] ibid.

i. Advice on Mahr

While the imams' role on financial settlements is limited, they do play a role in advising on entitlement to the *mahr*. When a *khulah* divorce – which is initiated by the wife – is issued, imams note that 'a portion of the *mahr* would be returned and so there are financial consequences'.[55] Usually, a woman will not be asked to return the *mahr* that has already been paid but may be asked to return expensive gifts given by the husband, in particular gold and jewellery that were part of the *mahr*. However, some imams do not accept that a woman who initiates a divorce must forgo part or all of her *mahr*. As one imam stated, the *mahr* is not related to the person who initiates or asks for the divorce rather it 'is related to the one who causes the marriage to be broken'.[56] Imams who take this position examine the situation to see who is at fault or if there has been a 'breach' of marital rights and obligations in order to determine financial entitlements. Another interviewee noted: '[I]f the man is in breach he forgoes that right' to the return of the *mahr*.[57]

While imams repeatedly stated this principle in interviews, women's reports of sharia processes in practice did not align with this principle. A number of women attest to the fact that they were asked to return gifts given by their husbands or forfeit the *mahr* in order to receive their *khulah* divorce. Similar practice is observed in the UK: in issuing a *khulah*, imams at the ISC ask the wife to return any *mahr* she has received and will even offer to pass it on to the husband on her behalf. If the husband does not claim it, they return it to the wife or donate it to a charity if she so chooses.[58] Thus, a *khulah* divorce can have a significant financial impact on a woman, depending on the *mahr* and her general financial position. As one of our interviewees commented:

> They were gifts as well as stuff that I had like added into it. And then all of my Tupperware, my plates, cutlery, bedding so the quilt covers, everything like that. I had purchased a single bed and a single bed drawer set as well that was in the house and – so I had bought that out of my own money. That was still in there, he kept that. He kept absolutely everything besides the clothes that were on my back basically.[59]

The divergence between stated principle and observed practice we found in Australia is reflected in the divergence in practices relating to *mahr* in Canada. Comparatively, settlement of *mahr* during the Islamic divorce process in Canada is highly inconsistent. While some imams request husbands to pay the *mahr* if they are at fault in the divorce, others routinely ask women to pay the *mahr* despite the circumstances surrounding the divorce and who is at fault.[60] This lack of

[55] Interview 27 (Sydney, September 2016).
[56] Interview 34 (Sydney, August 2016).
[57] Interview 27 (Sydney, September 2016).
[58] Bowen (n 15) 74, also 83.
[59] Interview 68 (Sydney, February 2016).
[60] Macfarlane (n 3) 171.

consistency has often meant that the issue of *mahr* is not discussed by the imam, and women are confined to seeking only the divorce without any decision made with respect to *mahr*. In past instances, even when some of these women felt that it was their religious right to claim *mahr*, they did not gain much support from the imams, who said it was up to the husband's 'sense of religious obligation' to decide whether to grant it or not.[61]

According to researchers in Canada, such haphazard practices have meant that less than half of the women who were owed their *mahr* received it, or even the court-ordered support that they considered a substitute for the *mahr*.[62] These numbers are worse in the case of women who have been married for less than five years, with only one-third of such women receiving a deferred *mahr*, either in full or part. Twenty per cent of these women did not pursue it since they had initiated the divorce through *khulah* and had been advised beforehand by imams that they would automatically forgo their deferred *mahr* if they initiated *khulah*, even in situations where abuse was involved.[63] If they sought to pursue the *mahr* in court, however, they were almost always unsuccessful, similar to those in shorter marriages.[64]

Notably, among the women we interviewed there was considerable lack of knowledge about their rights concerning *mahr* and other financial entitlements upon divorce. There was also sometimes confusion about the precise amount of *mahr* and whether it should (or how much should) be given up in a *khulah* divorce.[65] On the other hand, many imams acknowledged that women were entitled to more than just *mahr* during divorce settlements, although some women thought that receiving *mahr* was the extent of their final property settlement. As mentioned above, women were also largely unaware of the different types of divorce, and therefore unaware of the different implications for *mahr*. The lack of awareness of alternatives to *khulah* – alternatives where women would not need to forfeit some (or all) of their *mahr* – is particularly noteworthy. The importance of greater education and transparency around types of divorce is discussed further in chapter six.

ii. Advice on Wife's Financial Contributions: Loan or Gift?

Some imams will recognise the wife's right to be compensated for financial contributions to the family unit through home loan repayments, bill payments etc. Many imams will try to determine whether the financial contribution made by the

[61] ibid 172.
[62] ibid 188.
[63] ibid 200.
[64] ibid 205.
[65] S Bano, *Muslim Women and Shari'ah Councils: Transcending the Boundaries of Community and Law* (Basingstoke, Palgrave Macmillan, 2012) 187.

woman was a 'loan' or a 'gift'. They generally characterise the wife's contribution as a loan when she sees the financial responsibility of the household as lying with the husband but has paid a bill or made a home loan repayment in order to assist him. If the wife's contribution is characterised as a loan, then this amount is still owed to her and should be repaid at some point by the husband. If, however, it is characterised as a gift, it is not an outstanding debt that the husband must repay. This distinction is important at the time of divorce. In general, however, it can cause a woman to feel disadvantaged if at the time of divorce none of her 'gifts' are taken into account. Thus, one imam acknowledged that it is important to specifically think of the woman's contribution as exactly that, a contribution rather than attempting to delineate between a gift and a loan:

> I see it as a contribution to the family unit, and when this family unit breaks up, this contribution needs to be taken into regard. It cannot be look at as a gift – why do we have to say it's a gift or a loan? Why [is there no] third element to say no, that's called a contribution to the family unit and when that unit breaks up each takes his own share of this unit that we built together.[66]

This approach may well make it easier for women to claim this contribution back as it would not require her to prove that she intended it as a loan – an intention that might be difficult to express during the subsistence of the marriage and prove at its dissolution.

iii. *Advice on Wife's Non-Financial Contributions*

A growing number of imams recognise that the non-financial contributions of women are valuable and deserve financial compensation.

> I mean how many husbands who say … run a business but the wife is doing a free accounting job for them, for example? That actually has a value, without a doubt, and this can be taken into account … So, in Australia we understand that there is something called non-monetary contribution which can be transformed or transferred into a monetary value; this is something we have to take into account. Islam has no problem accepting that.[67]

What complicates the process for the women is that imams have different interpretations on women's financial entitlements. Our findings are similar to those in Canada where some imams claim that post-divorce support for wives ends when the *iddah* period ends and other imams argue that upon divorce, the husband should compensate his wife for housework and childcare, and this extends beyond the *iddah* period.[68]

[66] Interview 31 (Sydney, August 2016).
[67] Interview 27 Sydney (September 2016).
[68] Macfarlane (n 3) 189.

Our interviews reveal there may be other reasons – besides difference of opinion on Islamic jurisprudence – why imams do not discuss non-financial contributions. One imam explained:

> If you're not trained in a specialised manner to understand how those things actually are understood – for example, if you look at the hours that people actually spend, how do we convert this into monetary value? That will require specialist training and that's the reason why the legal, the Australian law has to deal with that.[69]

So, while there is scope for accounting for non-financial contributions in Islam, imams claim that it requires a specialist kind of training to understand how to do so and not all imams are trained in this way. This may also be a reason why imams do not get involved in property settlements beyond giving the couple general (non-binding, religious) advice if asked.

iv. Advice on Child Support, Iddah and Mutah

In instances where children are involved, assuming that the children will remain with the mother, imams believe that '[where] there are children … the woman should get more [financial settlement]. But if there are no children, it's just the couple, that's where we say, *Okay 50/50*'.[70] Distribution of finances 50/50 assumes that the woman has been contributing financially to the relationship. If not, then imams will advise allocation of a smaller portion.

Many imams acknowledged that women are entitled to *iddah* maintenance for them and the children during the separation period (the *iddah* period can be defined as a three-month waiting period observed following separation to ensure that the wife is not pregnant).[71] But, as discussed above, some imams focus mainly on the *mahr* and not on other entitlements such as *iddah*. Further, as with *mahr*, whether a wife receives maintenance during the *iddah* period depends on the type of divorce granted:

> So, we empower women to do that [seek a financial settlement through Australian law]] because it is not against the religion, it is [sanctioned] by the religion. Whenever someone is suffering, someone is facing a difficulty, to go wherever help may come from. Advise that she gets this maintenance while she is … in the waiting period if that is a first or second divorce.
>
> *Is that for all types of divorce, the maintenance?*
>
> For *tafweedh*, no because in *tafweedh* everything is finished. He cannot take her back so there is no obligation there.

[69] Interview 27 (Sydney, September 2016).
[70] Interview 16 (Melbourne, May 2016).
[71] ibid.

> But in the *talaq*, it's an area, that's where we say she is entitled to maintenance because ... There is a probability that he may take [her] back.
>
> *And* khulah, *does she get* [iddah]? No.[72]

In addition to *mahr*, Islamic jurisprudence recognises an additional contribution for the woman called *mutah* (post-divorce gift). It is important to note that while this principle exists in Islamic law, it does not play out in the Australian context. That is, we did not see any evidence of this being referred to by the imams or by the women experiencing the divorce process. This could be for a number of reasons, including that the imams do not want to make decisions about the financial entitlements of women beyond *mahr* because there is no way to enforce the *mutah* payment or that the imams do not appreciate its potential importance to women.

v. *Advice on State Processes and Legal Entitlements – Property Settlement, Financial Entitlement and Children*

In many cases where imams are dealing with divorces involving religious and civil laws, they will encourage parties to seek legal advice or refer parties to the courts to settle matters around finances and children.[73] Particularly where some imams feel a woman is being treated unfairly by her husband, they have been known to refer women to a lawyer for further advice.[74] While giving religious advice, ANIC-CARD imams will encourage women to seek legal counsel with respect to property settlement as well as custody of children, as these matters are dealt with by the civil courts. Similar to the ANIC imams, BOIV imams make a point of not getting involved in issues of custody or property because there is nothing to make their decision on such issues binding.[75] This is further explained by one respondent:

> Ninety percent of the cases they're already finalised or [they're in court], which ... if there's a dispute, we will pull away. We will tell them, *Look, we're not going to deal with the money and children because you've already got lawyers, let them deal with it, we're happy to help.* If it is a matter in court, it's a big no-no. We've got nothing to do with it, we focus on the Islamic divorce.[76]

Similar practice is seen in the UK.[77] The Birmingham sharia council does not get involved with financial matters arising from marital breakdown, and instead

[72] That is, there is no maintenance for the *iddah* period following khulah. Interview 16 (Melbourne, May 2016).
[73] Walker (n 15) 120 and 130.
[74] Krayem (n 6) 210.
[75] Interview 16 (Melbourne, May 2016).
[76] Interview 63 (Sydney, May 2020).
[77] Bowen (n 15) 86, 107.

refers financial and property matters to the civil courts;[78] it demarcates the bounds of its 'authority' in dealing with divorce matters, encouraging parties to deal with financial and child custody matters via the civil framework.[79] By contrast, at least in theory, the Muslim Arbitration Tribunal (MAT) offers the possibility of resolving financial and property disputes arising from a divorce – this is through state-recognised binding arbitration under the terms of the Arbitration Act 1996[80] where the parties wish to have financial matters dealt with by the MAT.[81] In the Canadian context, some couples may have a blend of Islamic and civil law principles guiding their financial settlements.[82] Some imams may advise couples on financial matters; however, others do not consider matters such as property division at all and will refer parties to lawyers.[83] Approximately half of the imams interviewed in a North American study of Islamic divorce processes stated that they did not see their role as going beyond granting (or refusing) a religious divorce – that is, they do not consider other matters around child custody and support, or financial and property settlements and would refer parties to the courts and family lawyers.[84]

Our research suggests by referring women to legal or family dispute professionals, imams demonstrate a degree of deference to state systems and laws. Such deference is aided by the view, supported by some imams with knowledge of Australian family law, that financial settlement under sharia processes is very similar to the Australian legal framework – namely a contributions-based system that accounts for both financial and non-financial contributions.[85] Such deference is also seen in the Islamic Social Services and Resources Association (ISSRA) in Canada. While mediating, imams at ISSRA ask parties what financial amounts they are happy with rather than suggesting a 50/50 split of assets, even though they advise that the default norm of a 50/50 split is Islamic.[86] ISSRA's high level of integration with the civil law system may be discerned from the fact that the ISSRA imams claim to advise their clients that the Canadian legal system is in many ways Islamic, as it also seeks justice.[87]

Apart from the substantive content of family law, imams consider the focus on mediation in the Australian legal framework to align well with Islamic principles. In most instances, imams agree that in the area of family law 'Australian law

[78] Walker (n 15) 120.
[79] ibid 181.
[80] Bowen (n 15) 182; see also Muslim Arbitration Tribunal <www.matribunal.com/adr.php> accessed 1 November 2020.
[81] Bowen (n 15) 187.
[82] Macfarlane (n 3) 187.
[83] ibid 192.
[84] ibid 158.
[85] Krayem (n 6) 239.
[86] C Cutting, 'Sharia and Constraint: Practices, Policies, and Responses to Faith-Based Arbitration in Ontario' (Waterloo, UWSpace 2013) 212, 215.
[87] ibid 213.

accommodates more sharia in this field than anywhere else'.[88] When pressed on this issue one imam stated this was 'because the [secular] court doesn't make [a] decision on property and … custody of the children unless they go through the mediation process. In the mediation process, you can sit down, think informally, in a … less pressured [environment] … That is Islam'.[89] This focus on mediation is seen at BOIV, where imams may refer the couple to a family relationship centre for mediation. Further, BOIV imams strongly encourage couples to come to a mutual agreement related to property and not 'squander money' getting themselves into a legal dispute.[90]

Attitudes toward women using the legal systems to secure their property rights vary across the community. While, as discussed, some imams encourage utilising the Australian legal system for certain matters, there are others who do not approve of this choice if it appears Muslim women are 'forum shopping' for the best possible outcomes (particularly in terms of financial settlements).[91] Given the backlog of divorce cases in sharia processes, imams become frustrated when their offered advice is then rejected by either or both divorcing parties.

> [S]ome people, if they feel that [the Islamic advice] is not falling into their best interests then they'll go towards the legal system … [They] come to you and say, *you know what, I don't like your judgment. I'm going with someone else* … If they see it's coming in their favour … they'll continue with it. If it's not in their favour, they'll go somewhere else, which it was very upsetting because it's very much time consuming.[92]

Besides concern that forum shopping wastes imams' time, a minority of imams felt that the civil legal system was used to pursue outcomes to which parties were not Islamically entitled. For a minority of imams, even where the husband failed to give the wife her full Islamic entitlements, pursuing her financial rights in the civil courts would not make this situation right.[93] This suggestion that it is wrong to use the legal system to resolve financial matters may disadvantage women. The guilt that can accompany a woman's decision to go to court might mean that she avoids the legal process to her detriment. This is seen in Canada where research shows that some women refused court-ordered support or fifty per cent of the matrimonial assets as they believed they were not Islamically entitled to them.[94] These women were willing to accept a lower financial entitlement under civil laws, but pursued their entitlements under Islamic laws (*mahr*, *iddah* maintenance,

[88] Interview 14 (Melbourne, April 2016).
[89] ibid.
[90] Interview 16 (Melbourne, May 2016).
[91] G Krayem and F Ahmed, 'Islamic Community Processes in Australia: An Introduction' in S Bano (ed), *Gender and Justice in Family Law Disputes* (Waltham MA, Brandeis University Press 2012) 264–65.
[92] Interview 24 (Sydney, May 2016).
[93] Interview 16 (Melbourne, May 2016).
[94] Macfarlane (n 3) 207.

and child support) as they felt strongly that they were doing the right thing according to God's laws.[95]

vi. Women's Experience of the State System for Financial Entitlements

Our research shows that women who use sharia processes generally also approach state courts to enforce financial entitlements. Our research uncovers the experience of these women who are navigating the two normative systems at the same time. Where women are unhappy with the outcomes that emerge within the religious divorce process, particularly in terms of property settlements, they will often turn to the courts for legal relief.

In the interviews discussed above, some imams seemed to imply that women sought civil law recourse because they were 'forum shopping' for a different opinion. However, women may also be unhappy with sharia processes due to a lack of formality, clarity, or enforceability and not necessarily because of the substantive content of the imams' advice. For example, women revealed that some former husbands concealed the full amount of their income, refused to pay child support and hid assets.[96] In such situations, imams have little (if any) power to investigate financial circumstances or enforce decisions in order to protect women's interests. In other words, regardless of the Islamic perspective on issues of property and finance, at the time of a divorce, there is no way to implement this advice and make it legally binding. Therefore, taking the matter to the civil court might benefit women.

The Australian family law framework is set up to ensure 'just' and 'equitable' outcomes for parties, with legal force behind its decisions.[97] Civil courts take into account retrospective *and* prospective factors that will influence parties' financial situations, and thus the level of compensation they should receive within the property settlement.[98] The Family Law Act 1975 also accounts for non-financial contributions, with specific mention of contributions made 'in the capacity of a homemaker or parent'.[99] Many women, once married, still take on the majority of domestic labour and childrearing; therefore, recognising non-financial contributions benefits women.

However, when engaging with the civil legal system, a woman could encounter lengthy delays and be burdened with financial costs she cannot afford.

[95] ibid 207.

[96] Interview 6 (Sydney, April 2016); Interview 13 (Melbourne April 2016); Interview 45 (Melbourne, September 2016); Interview 51 (Sydney, October 2019); Interview 53 (Sydney, November 2019).

[97] *Family Law Act 1975* (Cth), s 79(2).

[98] RJ Bailey, 'Principles of Property Distribution on Divorce – Compensation, Need or Community' (1980) 54 *Australian Law Journal* 190.

[99] Lisa Young and Jo Goodie, 'Is There a Need for More Certainty in Discretionary Decision-Making in Australian Family Property Law?' (2018) 32 *Australian Journal of Family Law* 166.

The following comments from one woman we interviewed, illustrates the benefits and costs for some women who used the civil court system:

> Divorce and property and children, it took over 12 months. There wasn't much property because he had taken most of everything overseas anyway but the one particular thing that he thought that I would never touch, the judge went out of his way and got a federal body involved – and I didn't even ask for that. So, the judge was just so great. I mean, yes, I had to appoint a barrister and yes, it cost me a bit of money but the process, as much as courtrooms are intimidating whether it's for you or against you, it was a just process ... the judge even had me stand up and talk and he said, *Because it's an informal setting, you don't have to lift the veil off your face, I'll let you have it down* ... There was so much respect for our religion in that courtroom with that judge in particular and the judge even allowed – in his notes he talks about sharia law.[100]

One of our interviewees, a social worker working with women, reported that women find it very empowering and inclusive to be able to choose between sharia processes and the Australian state system. Having both options allows women to pursue a path that best suits them. But, the interviewee reported, they find the way sharia processes presently operate means that women:

> ... don't feel that it's very inclusive and they feel very intimidated by the whole process and actually prefer having an Australian law decide things for them. They feel a lot more confident with the outcomes and that justice will be served accordingly.[101]

> ... 99 per cent of women will still pursue the Australian law courts for custody. Regardless of what the sheikh says ... [because] that's the system they have the most faith in and that's the one I have the most faith in, to be honest, right now based on the [sharia] system that we currently have in place.[102]

Within the framework provided by civil courts and religious divorce panels, some Muslim women navigated marital dispute resolution in a pragmatic fashion, weighing up the costs and benefits of each system.[103] Using such avenues to achieve either or both a civil and religious divorce, women acted as 'skilful legal navigators'.[104]

That said, some women did prefer sharia processes as they found the civil system overwhelming. They did not know the system or where to go for assistance and felt intimidated by the courts and lawyers.[105] But even where an interviewee felt the imams' advice favoured her, the lack of enforceability of that advice

[100] Interview 45 (Melbourne, September 2016).

[101] Interview 38 (Sydney, September 2016).

[102] ibid.

[103] P Fournier, 'Please Divorce Me! Subversive Agency, Resistance and Gendered Religious Scripts' in E Giunchi, *Muslim Family Law in Western Courts* (Abingdon, Routledge, 2014); Walker (n 15) 81–82.

[104] G Krayem, 'Australian Muslim Women: Skilful Legal Navigators in a Plural World' in A Saeed and H McCue (eds), *Family Law and Australian Muslim Women* (Melbourne, Melbourne University Press, 2013).

[105] Interview 52 (Sydney, November 2019); Interview 56 (Melbourne, January 2020); Interview 49 (Melbourne, October 2016).

remained a problem. In that case, a number of imams had agreed that because she was the main breadwinner in the household, she ought to be entitled to a large portion of the asset pool. Despite this advice from the imams, she believed she did not receive her financial entitlements from her husband because he was able to pursue a property settlement in the civil law system rather than abide by the imams' advice.[106] She believed that her husband hid many of his finances and declared only a fraction of his income so that he did not have to pay child support.[107] She reported that the divorce, the maintenance of two young children, and the legal fees left her in dire financial circumstances, since she lost years of potential income from child support.[108]

When imams can see that men are likely to evade financial responsibility in the future, they may suggest that women are entitled to more of the asset pool to help her care for the children in her custody. Here, however, imams acknowledge '[t]here aren't laws in place where we can guarantee this, it's only what the judicial system would obligate him with … child support'.[109] This lack of Islamic legal protection was also an issue raised by women as reported by a social worker interviewee:

> Once they get the divorce from the sheikh, they just go through the legal process of getting the children's custody, child protection … payments and all the other, and the property settlement and all of this. They go through that but let me tell you, there's been a few women who've been saying to me, *We wish that our mashaikh* [plural of *shaikh*, an imam or religious scholar] *could deal with all of that to relieve us, release us from the legal system*. Really, I've had that. You know, if only they had proper structure, proper processes, then that could easily, they could deal with that no problem because it is about an amicable resolution at the end of the day.[110]

IV. Child Custody

As with property and financial matters, imams do not generally deal with child custody.[111] Imams interviewed unanimously declared that they avoided getting involved in any of the custody discussions between parents. However, they may sometimes advise parties if asked their opinion. For the same reasons discussed above, this could influence how parties resolve their disputes, especially if they reach an agreement without going to court. Generally, imams encouraged parents to have an 'agreement without going to court',[112] believing that while this clarified

[106] Interview 6 (Sydney, April 2016).
[107] ibid.
[108] ibid.
[109] Interview 40 (Melbourne, September 2016).
[110] Interview 60 (Sydney, March 2020).
[111] Interview 16 (Melbourne, May 2016).
[112] Interview 34 (Sydney, August 2016).

the arrangement to both parents and children it ensured the least disruption to the lives of the children.

All imams emphasised that, unless there were extenuating circumstances, the non-binding Islamic advice they offer is – in their view – similar to that of the legal system (on the assumption that children usually remain with their mothers).

> [T]here's complications … especially when it comes to money and children but obviously when it comes to the custody of children, to us, there's not much that we can do. We can give advice and the Islamic advice is very close, it corresponds with the Australian legal system.[113]

This advice aligns with traditional views on children within Islamic jurisprudence: that children under the age of discretion (that is, seven years of age) will remain with the mother, after which time the children have an option as to which parent they live with.[114] In the view of imams, the father has the right to see his children, he must organise time with his children in advance, and he is responsible for transporting them to and from their mother's home.[115] However, it is worth noting that the Australian legal system has introduced a presumption of 'shared parental responsibility' which, if applied, requires courts to consider an equal time arrangement between parents;[116] parents are encouraged to work out a 'co-operative parenting' arrangement (unless there is family violence, or it is otherwise not in the best interests of the child).[117]

Several imams also explained that they do not interfere with the legal processes around child custody because they had no way of guaranteeing the safety of children:

> [W]e don't interfere too much in children because there are somethings, or, usually we need some authority in it to deal with it, because some cases we cannot guarantee the safety of children. And for that reason we cannot be involved in this matter.[118]

The desire to keep out of custody arrangements also stemmed from a lack of resources and inability to really investigate the family context and the parental-child relationship to make a decision in the best interests of the child/ren.[119]

> For example, the area of money, who takes the house, who takes what … the children and their guardianship because it can be you know, there's a lot of processes that the Family Court consider which is the mental health of the parents, the drug abuse, if there

[113] Interview 24 (Sydney, May 2016).

[114] S Farrar and G Krayem, *Accommodating Muslims under Common Law: A Comparative Analysis* (Abingdon, Routledge, 2017) 86.

[115] Interview 24 (Sydney, May 2016).

[116] Family Law Amendment (Shared Responsibility Act) 2006 (Cth).

[117] Rae Kaspiew et al., *Evaluation of the 2006 Family Law Reforms* (Melbourne, Australian Institute of Family Studies, December 2009).

[118] Interview 34 (Sydney, August 2016).

[119] *Family Law Act 1975* (Cth), s 61DA; see also Farrar and Krayem (n 114) 88.

> is, the domestic abuse, the financial. We don't have the resources, even if we have, it will only remain a recommendation.[120]

Another imam emphasised that the Islamic perspective on custody, like the legal system in Australia, focuses on the best interest of the child.

> [S]ome schools, they say, okay, if a husband and wife divorce, the girl, the woman gets the children. Okay, what about if she gets married? Because she gets married, she needs to look after her husband, she doesn't have time to after her children and she passes them onto her mother? What's it got to do with her mother? Because her mother is the grandmother so she, automatically she's going to look after them because the husband, he's at work and won't change nappies. But what about if the husband stays at home, and says, *Okay, I'm going to – I know how to change nappies, I know how to look after babies, my job is, for example in childcare, okay, can I take the children?* So here, it just, you'll find in reality, it's the best interests of the children: who can baby them? … So, it's not … clear cut … It's the approach of the greater good.[121]

Imams had no issue with leaving child custody to be arranged by agreement between the parents or entirely by the legal system. This indicates that imams recognise the significance of making these arrangements in the best interests of the child as well as their inability to enforce religious advice on these matters. Imams recognise that while they can 'provide advice and any recommendations … they must go to a lawyer' to get information about the implications of custodial arrangements.[122]

All our interviews with women who had children corroborated the approach described by imams, which is that although fathers had access to their children, women were deemed the primary caregivers. Although these custody arrangements caused tension and anxiety for some women whose husbands used these arrangements to continue to torment or control them, the interviews contain no evidence of women being asked to give up custody of their children.

> [O]bviously when it comes to the custody of the children, to us, there's not much that we can do. We can give an advice and the Islamic advice is very close, it corresponds with the Australian legal system. He's entitled to see them: *They are your children, you take custody of the children but if the father wants to see them, he needs to arrange and organise a few days or nights that he comes and sees his kids. He takes them and brings them back.* With the custody, sometimes it can be complicated when the man wants full custody of the children which is something that we can't help Islamically or legally but, because of that, it just becomes more spitefulness.[123]

Women generally seemed to comply with the advice that their children see their father regularly. However, not all fathers were consistently involved in the lives

[120] Interview 31 (Sydney, August 2016).
[121] ibid.
[122] Interview 27 (Sydney, September 2016).
[123] Interview 24 (Sydney, May 2016).

of their children, with some not communicating with them for months at a time. In one situation the child reported threats that the father had made to the child resulting in an end to a shared custody arrangement.

> The second time [in a shared custody arrangement] – yeah, he returned him, but he abused him. He did not hit him. He abused him in a way that he asked him to be punished like that, stand like that, hold his hands straight *until I say to put them down.* And when he got tired, when [my son] got tired, then [my son] started crying and because [my son] knew that he was going to hit him, and mummy is not here, and he felt the danger, so he didn't say anything.
>
> After that, [my son] told me that, After that, mamma, he made a little aeroplane with paper and he put the bin far away and he asked me, 'If you put this aeroplane in the bin, then I will take you to your mum otherwise not.' He threatened my son in that way. And [my son] said, Mamma, I did, and he then brought me. He didn't give him juice, drink, he didn't give him any food.[124]

In this case eventually the shared arrangement was terminated by the court.

In our interviews, women seemed satisfied overall with religious advice given in relation to their children. This may be because the advice did not disadvantage women and was consistent from imam to imam and also across both sharia and legal processes.

The Australian sharia processes we studied contrast with British and Canadian processes, with respect to child custody, in two ways. First, child custody in other jurisdictions is a part of the negotiation about divorce or financial settlements, in a way that we do not observe in Australia. Many women in Canada reported concern that Islamic custody rulings would be used to leverage other financial negotiations. In two cases, Macfarlane found that husbands did indeed make their wives accept a compromised financial outcome in return for custody of the children.[125] During the reconciliation process in some British sharia processes, negotiations involved increasing the rights of fathers in accessing children (sometimes with the promise of the husband issuing a *talaq* to simplify the divorce process), even where child custody arrangements had already been settled within the civil law framework.[126] When a wife seeks a divorce, if the husband has mentioned difficulties visiting his children, the Islamic Sharia Council, for instance, requires the wife to sign an affidavit confirming that the father may see his children 'in part to converge with what they think a family court would do in these circumstances, and in part because they consider it to be an Islamic norm that both parties be able to see their children',[127] even though the Council realises that such an affidavit cannot act as a formal custody arrangement, as these are determined by civil courts.[128] We found

[124] Interview 2 (Sydney, April 2016).
[125] Macfarlane (n 3) 196.
[126] Bowen (n 15) 77.
[127] ibid 83.
[128] ibid 107.

no evidence that child custody plays a role in negotiations for divorce or financial outcomes in Australian sharia processes.

A second point of contrast is legal recognition. Imams neither seek nor receive any legal recognition or enforcement for any religious advice they offer on child custody in Australia. By contrast, the Muslim Law Sharia Council in the UK offers a more formal arrangement by setting up arbitrations to draw up contracts regarding access to children or property settlement. Nevertheless, imams acknowledge that this rarely happens as no one takes such a contract to civil court for enforcement.[129] In the Canadian context, while many of the parties seek child maintenance and custody arrangements through courts rather than imams, there are others who negotiate agreements with an imam and submit them to the courts as a consent order. Despite the method undertaken, it has been observed that, by and large, Muslims seek 'financial and legal outcomes which are a blend of both Islamic and civil law principles'.[130] Moreover, custody arrangements involve a certain amount of improvisation on the part of imams who have stated that they generally do not advise or apply classical Islamic rulings on custody. Rather, the advice they provide follows family court guidelines of 'best interests' which they believe reflect Islamic guidelines of fairness and flexibility.[131]

V. Conclusion

This chapter has demonstrated the complexity of two key issues involved in the outcomes of an Islamic divorce, namely the type of divorce granted, and the financial settlement associated with that divorce. We have identified that most women do not have significant religious knowledge concerning Islamic divorce, and we found that many women felt they had no choice but to forgo their rights and agree to a *khulah* divorce with its financial disadvantages, in particular the forfeiting or return of the *mahr*. More recently, Australian sharia processes have moved towards offering *faskh* or *tafriq* divorces which do not require forfeiting or returning the *mahr*. We found that beyond the *mahr*, while many Islamic financial entitlements for women were recognised, these did not play a major role in sharia processes. Instead, imams tended to refer those using sharia processes to mediation or the state legal system for financial and child custody matters. We reflected on imams' attitudes towards using the state system for these matters and women's experiences seeking outcomes from both sharia and state processes at the same time. We note that while the women we interviewed were largely satisfied with any advice they received on child custody from sharia processes, their experience in Australia may differ from practices in British and Canadian sharia processes.

[129] ibid 86.
[130] Macfarlane (n 3) 187.
[131] ibid 194.

Aspects of the findings in this chapter unsettle common tropes about sharia processes and their supposed antipathy to state law. We found that many imams accorded respect and religious significance to civil divorces, took care to distinguish their religious advice from legal advice, often encouraged parties to seek legal advice, supported mediation through state-supported processes, expressed the view that financial settlement under the sharia processes is very similar to the Australian legal position, deferred to the state legal system on custody and most financial issues, and did not seek any legal recognition or enforcement for any religious advice they offer on child custody in Australia.

Muslim communities are often thought to favour the legal recognition of decisions and settlements reached in sharia processes.[132] So, our interviews with imams are significant in that they revealed practically no interest in state recognition for sharia processes. Instead, we found evidence that imams deferred to the Australian legal system and largely viewed it as congruent with Islamic beliefs and practice.

[132] J Hole, 'Muslim Group Wants Sharia Law in Australia', *ABC News*, May 17, 2011; N Berkovic, 'Hyder Gulam Calls for Australia to Embrace Legal Pluralism', *The Australian*, 28 September 2012. For instance, the submission by the Australian Federation of Islamic Councils (AFIC) to the Parliamentary Joint Standing Committee on Migration asks for 'legal pluralism', possibly suggesting greater recognition of Islamic decision-makers (Australian Federation of Islamic Councils, 2011).

6

Evolution and Change

Sharia processes are often characterised as immutable and unchanging.[1] This chapter challenges that characterisation. We have observed a number of important changes in sharia processes through staggered interviews, over a five year period, with imams, women engaging with sharia processes, and the professionals supporting women. Imams associated with bodies like the Australian National Imams Council's Centre for Arbitration and the Resolution Disputes Ltd (ANIC-CARD) and the Board of Imams in Victoria (BOIV) have made a number of changes in order to improve their processes. In this chapter, we document the changes that we observed and also offer suggestions aimed at the Australian legal system, the relevant communities and providers of sharia processes in order to improve the experiences of women engaging with these processes. These suggestions also draw on the comparative experience of sharia processes in the UK and Canada and may be salient for those jurisdictions.

I. Improving Sharia Processes

When we first began our research, there was widespread concern about 'limping marriages' – where women had a civil divorce but not a religious one. There were reports of women being unable to obtain a religious divorce.[2] However, over the time period of our fieldwork we found that women who sought a religious divorce would ultimately receive it. Since the concern relating to whether a religious divorce would be granted *at all* has largely abated, we focus on other changes, and proposed changes, to sharia processes.

[1] A Emon, 'Islamic Law and the Canadian Mosaic: Politics, Jurisprudence, and Multicultural Accommodation' (2009) 37 *Canadian Bar Review* 391, 395; A El Shamsy and NJ Coulson, 'Sharīʿah', *Encyclopædia Britannica*, 25 August 2020 <www.britannica.com/topic/Shariah> accessed 1 November 2020; AA Engineer, 'Is Sharia Immutable?' *Dawn*, 1 February 2003 <www.dawn.com/news/782766/is-sharia-immutable> accessed 1 November 2020.

[2] See A Buckley, *Not 'Completely' Divorced: Muslim Women in Australia Navigating Muslim Family Laws* (Melbourne, Melbourne University Press, 2019).

A. Pre-marriage Briefing and Counselling

Counsellors and psychologists reported that Muslim couples often only approached them when the relationship had deteriorated significantly.[3] Thus, couples missed out on many early points of intervention into problems in their relationship. It has been suggested pre-marriage counselling may help to 'take the stigma away from the whole counselling, you know, marriage counselling thing and have it seen as a more positive, proactive move rather than a signal of failure'.[4] Based on interviewee suggestions, pre-marital counselling with a relationship professional might be beneficial.

As chapter four indicates, imams sometimes provide some kind of pre-marriage counselling or information sessions. It is vital that these sessions provide accessible information on sharia processes and women's options for obtaining Islamic divorce. We acknowledge that, across cultural communities, discussing divorce at the time of marriage might be awkward or considered inappropriate. Nonetheless, the problems our research indicated for women seeking religious divorce necessitates a frank and clear briefing on religious divorce to all those who might theoretically seek it in the future.

B. Rethinking Marriage Contracts and Delegated Divorce Rights – *Talaq Tafweedh*

Pre-marriage briefing and counselling sessions would also offer an opportunity to discuss the Islamic marriage contract. As discussed in chapter five, BOIV marriage contracts now contain a clause that delegates the right to *talaq* to the wife (*talaq tafweedh*) upon application to a sharia board or panel such as BOIV or CARD (see Appendix B for this marriage contract). Interviewees noted the potential for the Islamic marriage contract to be drafted in a way that helped women obtain justice and facilitate religious divorce. One imam encouraged women to gain knowledge about clauses granting them *talaq tafweedh*:

> The lady, before marriage, she should know all of this: you can have the right to get your divorce if you write this in the contract, you have the right to do this … So, we encourage all of them to please make a course with a knowledgeable person.[5]

We recommend therefore that community organisations and imams who usually draft these marriage contracts should have them reviewed to consider how they might be drafted to best support women, and facilitate their access to religious divorce, given the issues raised by our research.

[3] See ch 3.
[4] Interview 58 (Melbourne, January 2020).
[5] Interview 50 (Sydney, October 2016).

C. Financial Agreements

Another possibility which those drafting Islamic marriage contracts should consider is whether these contracts could serve as binding financial agreements under the *Family Law Act 1975* (Cth). Our research reveals that women face hurdles enforcing property settlements, including the *mahr* (marriage-gift received by the wife), that were agreed to as part of the Islamic marriage contracts. If the marriage contracts counted as binding financial agreements, this would allow women to enforce property settlements that were agreed to before, during and after the marriage.

One solicitor we interviewed had concerns that community processes did not give parties clarity about what is required of them, particularly around divorce and property settlements, and that women were disadvantaged by the unclear requirements and interaction between the religious and legal rules. This interviewee asserted: 'every Muslim getting married should do a binding financial agreement. That would get rid of all those issues'.[6] The use of binding financial agreements by Muslims is supported in the marriage contracts of the BOIV (see Appendix B, clause 7).

For Islamic marriage contracts to count as binding financial agreements, they must meet the pre-conditions for recognition under the *Family Law Act 1975* (Cth) including:

- independent legal advice from a legal practitioner for all parties before the agreement is signed
- parties must be informed of the effects of the agreement and the advantages and disadvantages for them in entering the agreement.
- the legal practitioners need to provide each party with a signed statement noting that independent advice was given
- the signed statement from the legal practitioner (or certificate) must confirm that advice has been given (inter alia) on whether or not, at that time and in light of such circumstances at the time it is reasonably foreseeable, the provisions of the agreement were fair and reasonable.[7]

The preconditions for a valid binding financial agreement indicate an additional advantage of arranging Islamic marriage contracts so that they count as binding financial agreements: encouraging women to obtain independent legal advice is likely to familiarise them with their legal entitlements.

Having a financial agreement in place does not mean that courts will not examine whether it is valid, and binding, if challenged by a party.[8] There may be other

[6] Interview 2 (Sydney, April 2016).

[7] G Watts, 'Binding Financial Agreements: Possibilities and Pitfalls' (2001) 39 *Law Society Journal* 60, 60.

[8] B Fehlberg and B Smyth, 'Binding Pre-Nuptial Agreements in Australia: The First Year' (2002) 16 *International Journal of Law, Policy and the Family* 127, 130.

preconditions to ensure that a binding financial agreement is valid and upheld (if it comes before the courts), for example, that adequate time was given to parties to consider the agreement and advice.[9]

It may not be straightforward to arrange Islamic marriage contracts so they count as binding financial agreements. There is a concern amongst lawyers that if the agreement was later determined to be invalid or 'nonbinding',[10] then the lawyers would be liable.[11] That said, we suggest that having the Islamic marriage contract count as a binding financial agreement would present significant advantages for Muslim women entering into religious marriages, particularly if the need arises to enforce agreements made around property and *mahr*.

D. The Initial Stages of Sharia Processes

Our research found that women were poorly informed about what to expect from sharia processes. They indicated that the intake process was difficult and confusing, even when there were issues of domestic violence. Many women we interviewed did not know what to expect from sharia processes. As the previous chapters indicated, many women found the divorce process stressful and intimidating. Women also expressed great difficulty in explaining very personal matters to a room of men.[12]

During the course of our research, the intake process was improved considerably by both the BOIV and ANIC-CARD. Both now have appointed a female intake officer or secretary and have implemented administrative procedures that enable key issues such as domestic violence to be identified early on in the process.

A woman seeking the services of the BOIV Board will first complete an intake form which identifies key issues relating to divorce. She can do this on the BOIV premises or online. An appointment will be made with the relevant person within the organisation such as the domestic violence officer, counsellor or imam. The woman is provided with information in the form of a pamphlet providing relevant information. When a case is opened with either the domestic violence officer or counsellor, a confidentiality agreement is also prepared and signed. Women are provided with information on different avenues to solving their issues.

The BOIV now has three women directly involved in their intake processes. One of these women holds an administrative role and is responsible for the intake of information from new clients. She will advise women on the process and on the need to complete an application form with all the necessary details. She will

[9] K Barnett, '*Thorne v Kennedy*: A Thorn in the Side of "Binding Financial Agreements"?' (2018) 31 *Australian Journal of Family Law* 183; *Thorne v Kennedy* (2017) 263 CLR 85.

[10] Predominantly for noncompliance with s 90G of the *Family Law Act 1975* (Cth).

[11] C Brierley, 'Claims Arising Out of Binding Financial Agreements' (2011) 222 *Ethos* 16; J Wade, 'The Perils of Prenuptial Financial Agreements: Effectiveness and Professional Negligence' (2012) 22 *Australian Family Lawyer* 24; Fehlberg and Smyth (n 8).

[12] Interview 46 (Melbourne, September 2016).

ascertain whether the women are seeking counselling for the purpose of reconciliation or if they are seeking a divorce. During this process, the woman approaching BOIV has the opportunity to identify through the intake paperwork if there is any domestic violence. A second woman staff member at BOIV is an experienced family violence practitioner and assists women where domestic violence has been identified, and the third woman is a counsellor.[13]

ANIC-CARD also has a woman intake officer who conducts a preliminary interview with the woman who has approached the organisation, prepares paperwork for the imams and makes appointments for a meeting with the panel of imams.

> She will take that client and she would sit and ask her questions, everything, and she will give a summary of what happened, or she will show us the minutes and give us the minutes of what's happening. So, there is this now, this protection for that sister when she comes and she's not comfortable, we are the proactive. We come out as proactive.[14]

Sharia processes in Australia are moving towards the practices John Bowen describes in the Birmingham Central Mosque sharia council in the UK where female staff – trained as a medical doctor and an education welfare officer – engage in most of the initial discussions with clients. It is only when all the facts have been ascertained and dossiers prepared that the panel of scholars become involved to make a decision.[15]

We also observed improvements to the timeline of the processes. We indicated in earlier chapters that women experienced sharia processes as lengthy. While some imams reported the time between lodging the application and the first appointment was six to ten weeks, many women reported waiting as long as three to six months for the first meeting with the imams. Our later interviews indicated that waiting times are now around three to four months.[16] The new CARD processes involve a fixed timeline and referral of all cases to the Grand Mufti of Australia. One of the imams explained the role of the Grand Mufti since the introduction of CARD:

> One of the improvements now is that an independent person, which is the Grand Mufti of Australia … allows for the termination of marriage. And the Board just receives the application and goes through the process of the application and makes recommendations to the Grand Mufti. Usually, it becomes more of a procedural matter.[17]

Imams explained that they bring the fixed timelines to the attention of the parties:

> So what we do is we tell them, *Listen, whether you come to an agreement or not, our policy says issues of children and properties, if you both don't agree on, seek it from the court.*

[13] Interview 57 (Melbourne, January 2020).
[14] Interview 63 (Sydney, January 2020).
[15] JR Bowen, *On British Islam: Religion, Law, and Everyday Practice in Shari'a Councils* (Princeton NJ, Princeton University Press, 2016) 152.
[16] Interview 50 (Sydney, October 2016).
[17] Interview 62 (Melbourne, May 2020).

> *We don't have jurisdiction. We can help you to mediate, we can provide and facilitate, we can even, we're happy to help your lawyer and her lawyer to come to an agreement, we're happy to give all that assistance but once this four months cutoff date and you guys haven't reached an agreement the file, I can assure you, it will be moved to the Grand Mufti and you will lose all power over it. It just becomes more of a formality.*[18]

When interviewees refer to the sharia process becoming a 'procedural matter' or 'formality' this refers to the fact that although husbands may resist granting a *talaq* divorce, once imams believe there are grounds for a *faskh*, *tafriq* or *khulah* divorce then they will escalate the matter to the Grand Mufti who will issue the divorce.

It is important to acknowledge these improvements were made to the particular sharia processes associated with BOIV and ANIC-CARD. We do not have data on whether these improvements were reflected in the other sharia processes mentioned in chapter two. We therefore offer general recommendations below for improvements which some sharia processes, but not all, may already have implemented.

Women should be briefed thoroughly, verbally and in writing, on the process and timeline before they engage substantively with the sharia processes. Given the other stressors on women at this time, it is particularly important that those offering Islamic divorces offer an accurate and detailed account of the process and timeline from beginning to end. The timelines reported by women were not, in fact, long in comparison with state court processes, which generally involves at least a 12-month separation period before a divorce can be finalised. However, a reliable written and verbal briefing of what women could expect, and when they could expect it, would have allowed them to feel a greater sense of control and comfort in a difficult situation.

E. Women on Panels

Our research reveals good reasons to rethink the constitution of the panels that hear women and decide on, or facilitate, requests for religious divorce. These panels should include female religious scholars.

Previous chapters discussed how many women felt uncomfortable appearing before a panel of three to five men to describe intimate aspects of their marriages. All women noted that speaking to an all-male panel of imams was intimidating and uncomfortable. Women felt particularly humiliated in describing intimate aspects of their marriage to imams. A number of women believed that male imams identified more closely, and sympathised more, with their husbands. Interviewees also noted barriers to women accessing male panel members or imams, in a context where men and women often pray and socialise separately. While a number of the imams interviewed stated that they were available to speak to women by

[18] Interview 63 (Sydney, January 2020).

appointment and did not have a problem communicating with them directly, most women could not readily access the imams' social circles and networks.[19] This means that unless they were well-connected in the community, for instance through their families or through a community organisation, they were unlikely to know where to go or whom to speak with.

Some imams interviewed were sensitive to some of these concerns, particularly the challenge women face in addressing an all-male panel. While some organisations had taken active steps to recruit women to assist with processing applications and providing 'emotional' support and comfort, the final decision on divorce rested with a panel of male imams. Most imams considered it sufficient to have a female secretary assisting in the process.

Women noted that having a female secretary was a good move but inadequate in making them feel comfortable. Interviewees suggested that women should be on the panel of imams making the decisions, that is women should have a more authoritative role in the process. As one interviewee emphasised, it was important that women 'occup[y] the same status in that panel'.[20]

In a very significant development, the Australian National Imams Council (ANIC) has recently appointed the first female member in Australia. The appointment of this Victorian woman Islamic scholar was made on 1 March 2020 at the AGM Assembly of ANIC. This woman has also been appointed to the BOIV divorce panel. This scholar has completed Islamic studies over several decades, locally and globally, including in Dubai, Amman and Melbourne. She now sits as part of the Board of Imams Victoria. Her role on that panel is best described as follows:

> In my opinion, when it comes to family disputes where women are involved too, the presence of a female member on that panel is very essential and much needed. As a woman in that role, I can give better understanding to other women's feelings, needs and what they might be going through, and clarify it to the other party. In addition, the presence of a female member can create a comfort zone for other women to disclose their personal and confidential issues where they might be reluctant to disclose in front of male members. I know for sure that I'm adding value to my role as a woman.[21]

It might be thought that theological views that discourage the appointment of women as Islamic judges might pose an obstacle to greater inclusion of women on these panels. However, there is a range of opinions on the question of whether women can serve as Islamic judges. There are important traditional Islamic scholars who argue that women are absolutely permitted to serve as Islamic judges, with no limitations on the scope of their authority.[22] Other scholars argue that women

[19] Interview 2 (Sydney, April 2016).
[20] Interview 37 (Sydney, August 2016).
[21] Interview 54 (Melbourne, January 2020).
[22] Ibn Hajar al-Asqalani mentions in Ibn Hajar al-Asqalani, *Fath al-Bari Vol. 13* (Marefah Beirut 1959) 56, that some Maliki scholars, not only Ibn al-Qasim, took this position. This opinion is also attributed to Ibn Jarir al-Tabari who witnessed the appointment of Thamal al-Qahramana, the first female

can serve as Islamic judges, except for some areas, such as criminal law.[23] Another group of scholars take the position that women may only serve as judges when there is a need or necessity for them to serve in the public interest.[24] The first female judge known to Islamic history was Thamal al-Qahramana appointed in 918 AD during the Abbasid Empire.[25] A number of contemporary Muslim-majority countries have appointed women as judges in more recent times including Indonesia (1950s), Malaysia (1960s), Afghanistan (1960s), Iran (1970s), Syria (1980s), Libya (1990s) and Palestine (2000s).[26]

It is true, however, that scholars across a number of schools of thought regarded the appointment of women as Islamic judges as forbidden or discouraged.[27] Yet, it does not follow even from this position that women cannot serve on panels in sharia processes. This is because these panels may not technically count as an Islamic *court*, and those on the panel may not technically count as Islamic *judges*. We already noted in chapter five that some imams in Australia are uncomfortable referring to the panel they have assembled as a 'court'.[28] A similar reluctance has been observed in the United Kingdom by both scholars and panel members.[29] If panels are characterised instead as religious advisory bodies and panel members as religious scholars – a characterisation that fits with their stated self-conception[30] – the question of whether women can serve as Islamic judges does not arise.

judge in Islamic history during the Abbasid Empire (Abu al-Hasan al-Mawardi, *Al-Ahkam al-Sultania w'al-Wilayat al-Diniyya (Royal Rulings)* (Dar al-Hadith Cairo 2006) 65; Ibn Hazm, *Al-Muhallā bi'l Athār* (Dar el Fikr Beirut 2015) 9/429. Muhammad Ibn al-Hasan also took this position (Ibn Rush al-Jadd, *Al-Muqaddimat al-Mumahhidat (Preludes)*, Dar al-Gharb al-Islami, 1988 (2/258). Umar Ibn al-Khattab gave al-Shifa' Bint Abdullah the duty of market control, which was an important part of the judiciary as she was called upon regularly to solve the issues of the market (Ibn Hazm, *Al-Muhallā bi'l Athār* (Dar el Fikr Beirut 2015) 4/245).

[23] According to the opinion of Abu Hanifa, it is permissible for a woman to be a judge in specific areas involving money and matters relating to women (Al-Kasani, *Badaa'i Al-Sanayeh* (DKI Beirut 1986) 9/86). According to Abu Hanifa, the woman is not entitled to judge in legal religious punishments (*hudood*) and legal retribution (Burhan al-Din al-Marghinani, *Al-Hidayah Sharah Bidayat al-Mubtadi* (Dar I'hya' al-Turath al-Arabi Beirut 1996) 3/107.

[24] This is the opinion of some scholars belonging to the Shafi'i School (Sulayman ibn `Umar Jamal, *Hashiat al Jamal ala Sharah al-Minahaj* (Dar al-kotob al ilmiyah Beirut, 2013) 8/359.

[25] Al-Dhahabi, *Tarikh al-Islam Vol. 7* (Dar al-Gharb al-Islami Beirut 2003) 14.

[26] N Sonneveld and M Lindbekk, 'Introduction: A Historical Overview of Gender and Judicial Authority in the Muslim World,' in N Sonneveld and M Lindbekk (eds), *Women Judges in the Muslim World: A Comparative Study of Discourse and Practice* (Leiden, Brill, 2017).

[27] This is the opinion of all Hanbali scholars (Abu al-Hasan al-Mawardi, *Al-Ahkam al-Sultania w'al-Wilayat al-Diniyya (Royal Rulings)* (Dar al-Hadith Cairo 2006) 110), the Maliki school of thought except for al-Dusuqi ((Ibn Arafah Al-Dusuqi, Hashiyat Al-Dusuqi 'Ala Al-Sharh Al-Kabir (Dar el Fikr, Beirut) 6/3), and is the common opinion of the Shafi'i school (Abu Hamed al-Ghazali, *Al-Wasit fi al-Mudhhab* (Darussalam Cairo 1996) 7/289.

[28] Interview 34 (Sydney, August 2016).

[29] RC Akhtar, 'British Muslims and Transformative Processes of the Islamic Legal Traditions: Negotiating Law, Culture and Religion with Specific Reference to Islamic Family Law and Faith Based Alternative Dispute Resolution' (University of Warwick 2013), 211; Bowen (n 15) 88–99.

[30] S Bano, 'Islamic Family Arbitration, Justice and Human Rights in Britain,' (2007) 1 *Law, Social Justice and Global Development Journal* 15.

We do not therefore anticipate that theological positions will necessarily stand in the way of the appointment of more women on panels. Comparative experience of sharia processes in other jurisdictions shows women taking a leadership position on these panels. For instance, John Bowen described the decision-making panel of the Birmingham Central Mosque sharia council as including a medical doctor and a female scholar, Dr Amra Bone.[31] According to Bowen: '[s]he [Dr Bone] takes the lead role in greeting petitioners and in posing the first questions',[32] has a 'leading role' in all cases and 'requests input from the others but orchestrates the sessions'.[33]

F. Professionals on Panels

Interviews also revealed the potential benefits of including a range of professionals – lawyers, mental health professionals and social workers – on the panels which hear requests for divorce. Women have described the experience of seeking divorce as being 'awful' with 'no emotional support'.[34] As discussed in earlier chapters, women also reported feeling as though their experiences of abuse, injustice and trauma were minimised in the process. Health professionals suggested that having a panel of diverse professionals, rather than simply a board of imams, was vital for ensuring the best outcome for all parties. One psychologist explains:

> I think the sheikhs should have on their panel a multidisciplinary panel where it's the sheikhs who have the legal rulings but then it has to be additional experts, whether it's a mental health professional, a child advocate professional, just like mimicking the mainstream services, mainstream law, family law. We'll appoint a family consultant to explore the dynamics of the family and give recommendations. That's a very good model. They also have an independent lawyer for the child as well so that the lawyer can actually look at what's in the best interests of the child irrespective of what the parents' wishes are and how they engage or what not. They take it into consideration, but you know what I mean. So, and I think that that multi-professional disciplinary panel is better informed than having religious theologians because they're not experts in areas of mediation, they're not experts in family law, they're not experts in child development.[35]

This suggestion speaks directly to the primary concerns raised by professionals and community workers: that imams are not qualified to properly understand the dynamics of relationships and sometimes inadvertently exacerbate the issues. If, instead, a panel with diverse experience and expertise were appointed, imams could offer their theological reasoning without overlooking the other elements of a relationship. The panel would then have expertise not only on the theological

[31] Bowen (n 15) 131.
[32] ibid.
[33] ibid 136.
[34] Interview 18 (Melbourne, April 2016).
[35] Interview 37 (Sydney, August 2016).

understanding of rights and responsibilities of marriage but also the personal dynamics of that relationship. Practical steps for resolution could then be offered for the couple. A panel of diverse experts honours the theological understanding that imams bring, while reducing the trauma of women in the process. It allows a professional to advocate on behalf of the woman, who may be emotionally distressed and struggling in the moment. The work of interpreting or explaining the effect of the abuse is not left to the woman, but rather, to an expert qualified to adequately assess the situation and ensure the woman's interests are protected.

A broader range of professionals on the panel could ensure that women were supported, that any advice or guidance from the panel was in the best interests of children involved, and that women were aware of their options under Australian law. Diversifying panels in this way also offers avenues for the decision-making panels to be representative of the diversity of the community and independent of any individual mosque, group or organisation.

G. Education and Transparency about Divorce Options and Financial Entitlements

Our research revealed that the women seeking an Islamic divorce had little understanding of their options. Women who were more educated, especially about Islamic norms of marriage and divorce, navigated sharia processes more confidently than women who did not. It is very important that those administering sharia processes explain the types of divorce available to women in a clear and accessible manner.

Understanding divorce options is particularly important because of the implications for the *mahr*. Though women interviewed varied in age, cultural background and level of Islamic and secular education, only one received or retained her *mahr* (of AUD $10,000). This is an issue in the UK and Canada as well; in Julie Macfarlane's Canadian study, less than half of women who were owed their *mahr* received it, or court-ordered support that they considered a substitute for the *mahr*.[36] In our research, women did not receive the *mahr*, in some cases because the women wished to be rid of their ex-partner expeditiously, in others because the husband refused to pay the outstanding *mahr*. In some cases, women did not understand that there were alternatives to *khulah* forms of divorce in which they forgo the *mahr*.[37] The *mahr* was potentially financially significant for most of the women interviewed; for women, the *mahr* was in effect, their final property settlement and many were left in financially dire circumstances following divorce.

[36] J Macfarlane, *Islamic Divorce in North America: A Shari'a Path in a Secular Society* (Oxford, Oxford University Press, 2012) 189.

[37] Interview 28 (Sydney, August 2016).

As discussed in chapter five, practice at BOIV and ANIC-CARD changed over the course of our research so that the *tafriq* or *faskh* form of divorce was more readily available. But where imams still favour *khulah* over other forms of divorce (for example, *faskh* or *tafriq*) where women retain the *mahr*, there should be transparency about why they do so.

This finding resonates with empirical findings on sharia processes in the UK and Canada. In Canada, researchers find there is much confusion regarding the terms '*khulah*' and '*faskh*', which are understood inconsistently and used interchangeably by many imams.[38] At least one UK sharia council generally requires women who wish to gain a certificate of the Islamic divorce to agree to forgo or return their *mahr*, primarily because husbands are less likely to berate the council or challenge their authority in granting an Islamic divorce if they are released of the obligation to return or pay the *mahr*, or if they gain the *mahr*. Scholars of the Islamic Sharia Council (ISC) call this a 'halfway *khula*[*h*]'.[39] Members of at least one sharia council in the UK acknowledge that most of the divorces they award to women are procedurally more akin to *faskh* than *khulah*, but on their website and in discussions with women they only mention *khulah*.[40] Given the implications for the women's financial state, more transparency about the basis for the imams' advice on types of divorce is appropriate.

We also suggest that imams advise women on the full range of their Islamic financial entitlements. In the previous chapter, we saw that a range of Islamic financial entitlements – *mutah*, compensation for financial and non-financial contributions – were not emphasised by imams. There are a range of reasons for this including differences of opinion, lack of enforceability and a view that these matters are to be left to mediation or the state legal system. However, providing advice on these entitlements may empower women, some of whom may otherwise be left with the view that they are only Islamically entitled to the *mahr*.

H. Clearer Processes and Procedures

Transparency should extend to policies, processes and procedures more generally. Those providing sharia processes have acknowledged the need for clearer policies, processes and procedures – including relating to domestic violence, confidentiality and conflicts of interest – that are made known to clients.

As Muslim communities across Australia are relatively small, women expressed concerns about confidentially and local community gossip.[41] Responding to this issue some Boards have addressed this matter by appointing an imam outside of that person's ethnic or cultural group to conduct the divorce process. For example,

[38] Macfarlane (n 36) 170.
[39] Bowen (n 15) 95.
[40] ibid 141.
[41] Interview 47 (Melbourne, October 2016); Interview 55 (Melbourne, January 2020).

in the official BOIV divorce processes, an imam from outside of the couple's cultural group(s) will be appointed to oversee the divorce process. This is in order to minimise conflict between the couple and the overseeing imam and to maximise anonymity, on the assumption that outsiders to their cultural community are less likely to have prior knowledge of the couple's family and that this will lead to less gossip.[42]

BOIV files a confidentiality agreement with each client; only the domestic violence officer has access to client files. BOIV identified some procedures that aim to protect the woman:

> I've noticed if there's a code of conduct that anything that the woman says – because at the beginning they take an oath, as for any majlis, they take an oath. Anything that she says is believed whether she has evidence or not.[43]

Our research revealed that women had particular concerns about potential conflicts of interest. Some women feared that their former husbands had an unfair advantage where the imams knew them personally.[44] Members of a panel should disclose any relationships which may constitute a conflict of interest and these should be managed. Imams interviewed showed an appreciation for the importance of due process and emphasised the importance of this in the Islamic tradition. We therefore suggest that there is a need for more detailed processes around conflicts of interest.

BOIV, CARD as well as the Lebanese Muslim Association (LMA) have all indicated the need for developing further policies, processes and procedures as a priority area to be addressed. BOIV and ANIC-CARD are working on these issues and see this as an important aspect of their development as an organisation. '[W]e do have procedures but what we want to do, we want to put more meat on them, introduce more procedures'.[45] Such processes should include structured timetables, clear information for the parties, screening processes that can adequately account for parties' vulnerabilities, and better written records to document the process and final determinations.[46]

I. Acknowledgement and Response to Injustice, Abuse and Harm

It was important to women using sharia processes that their perspectives were heard. For instance, many women noted that even though they filled in an

[42] Interview 16 (Melbourne, May 2016).
[43] Interview 57 (Melbourne, January 2020).
[44] Interview 55 (Melbourne, January 2020).
[45] Interview 63 (Sydney, January 2020).
[46] R Parveen, 'Do Sharia Councils Meet the Needs of Muslim Women?' in S Bano (ed), *Gender and Justice in Family Law Disputes: Women, Mediation, and Religious Arbitration* (Waltham MA, Brandeis University Press, 2017) 161.

'Application Form', they were asked the same questions by the imams in-person. They found this frustrating and this may have contributed to the sense that they were not heard.

Moreover, women using sharia processes did not simply want a divorce, although this was vital for them to move on with their lives. They wanted justice and an authoritative acknowledgement of the injustice, abuse or harm they had endured; they expected an authoritative acknowledgement that their former husband's behaviour was un-Islamic. They expected that the imam, as a religious authority figure, would rebuke or chastise their husbands. They wanted to hear from a respected authority that, given their experiences, leaving the relationship was justified. For many women, these desires and expectations were not met by the processes.

Imams should consider whether they can do more to acknowledge injustice and harm experienced by women. It may be that imams felt unable to enforce the kind of 'justice' women sought vis-à-vis their former husbands, but it may also be that imams did not fully appreciate, or over-estimated, the type of justice women sought. Taking a few minutes to acknowledge suffering and injustice or rebuke the husbands would have been valued by these women.

J. Domestic Violence

A key issue for sharia processes is whether they are responding appropriately to domestic violence. Our interviewees sought divorces under different circumstances, but abuse was an issue in all cases. Abuse may have been physical, verbal, emotional and/or financial.

As discussed in earlier chapters, imams reported encouraging women to report domestic violence to the police and gave weight to legal processes relating to domestic violence. At the same time, some women felt they were not believed by the imams in instances of domestic violence. Some interviewees felt that the imams understood domestic violence to be physical, as they only sought evidence of beatings and some interviews revealed that imams minimised non-physical domestic violence. Some women, according to community workers, were told to 'be patient' when they described domestic violence they were experiencing and felt that the violence was attributed to their 'bad behaviour' by the imams. Some women felt that they were returned to unsafe situations by the imams and were encouraged to reconcile even in situations of domestic violence. In some cases, women felt that their spouses used the sharia process to further abuse them – psychologically, financially and emotionally. Some women reported their spouses becoming more empowered to treat them badly following intervention by the imam; the women attributed this to the imams blaming women and failing to rebuke their spouses. Professionals supporting women reported that women's experiences of domestic violence were minimised by imams.

There is therefore an urgent need for imams to receive training on how to receive disclosures of domestic violence, on the different forms of domestic violence, and on how to best support women in these situations. There have been important steps towards addressing this need in the years since our first interviews in 2016. Many imams recognise the need for a better response to domestic violence and are taking steps to improve the situation:

> So, what I'm having in my mind is to start an imams' domestic violence taskforce type of thing and then produce some materials where the women can trust the imams. So, we do want to have that document published so that every woman will have a copy: Islam does not recognise domestic violence and you shouldn't be suffering in silence and you should be able to approach an imam. So, we will have a trained imam for that purpose, and we will put up all the names in that [side]. So, in the next two years, three years, this will be a reality hopefully because one of the main issues for us is training the imams in different languages.[47]

In line with programs within the broader Australian community, the government has provided funds for community education on domestic violence protection and prevention. Muslim communities have, as part of these programs, received funds for domestic violence training for the broader Muslim community and more specifically for imams. Muslims trained in domestic violence programs undertake the training of imams and community leaders in two-day intensive domestic violence programs focusing on the prevention, intervention, recovery and post-trauma phases of domestic violence, as well as the relevant Australian laws such as protection orders.[48]

Directly addressing the problems that our early interviews uncovered with imams' (lack of) understanding of the different forms abuse can take, these training sessions introduced participants to financial, emotional, mental and in-law abuse, as well as spiritual abuse. So even if a woman is reluctant to address these things, imams are taught how to recognise different kinds of abuse in the woman's body language, her interaction, and the words that she uses.

Imams at BOIV have had training in family violence matters and they have had two intensive day workshops to date with a significant number of imams commenting on how such programs have helped them begin to understand the full nature of family violence.

> I think because with the training they've picked up on violence is not always shown externally, it could be much worse internally and that's something that the imams have picked up on. So that has been a change.[49]

These processes are relatively new, and one interviewee commented:

> I think [they probably need] to get more imams involved who will commit to actually coming. So, the problem is when new imams come, they haven't been exposed to the culture of this place, which has really changed since they took on the domestic violence projects.[50]

[47] Interview 14 (Melbourne, April 2016).
[48] Interview 62 (Melbourne, January 2020).
[49] Interview 57 (Melbourne, January 2020).
[50] Interview 58 (Melbourne, January 2020).

To respond to domestic violence, the BOIV has employed a trained and skilled family violence practitioner to work with women experiencing domestic violence. This practitioner receives a referral from the intake officer when a woman seeking divorce has identified family violence as an issue in the intake paperwork. The intake form has a column relating to domestic violence with questions such as: 'Are you being controlled? Are you being financially controlled? Are you being stalked? Are you being physically harmed?'

Alternatively, the imam may refer the woman to the family violence practitioner when this issue has been raised in the divorce proceedings. Her role is to complete the appropriate referrals to support services, risk assessments and safety plans for the clients. She may refer women to external services such as housing or financial support. Some women are on temporary visas or spousal visas and many are unaware of their rights, so the family violence practitioner will assist with referrals to immigration services or visa support.

> A lot of the cases also, the sisters [women approaching BOIV] don't know or they have no idea. And it's not just family violence against – the perpetrators are not just [against] the spouse in cases like that when she has a spousal visa. It's in-laws, sister-in-law's, all of that.[51]

As part of this process, the family violence practitioner will interview the woman and undertake a complete risk assessment using the relatively new Multi-Agency Risk Assessment Management Framework (MARAM) risk assessment tool. This tool is able to indicate whether the woman is in a high risk, within risk or low risk situation with respect to her safety in the family violence context. She will also do safety plans for them, such as how to safely respond in situations of domestic violence, address any issues relating to child protection and connect women to lawyers, where there are matters relating to property in the divorce proceedings.[52] The BOIV family violence practitioner will only close a case once all issues, including those relating to immigration and housing, have been met.

These initiatives – including referral from BOIV to external family violence services – are important because interviews with professionals who support women engaging with sharia processes indicate that these women may be concerned about the prospect of going to the Family Court, calling the police and filing for intervention orders etc. Accessing these same services – the professionals suggest – seems less daunting to them when accessed via the BOIV, for example, through the family violence officer or the imam. According to professionals supporting Muslim women, they seek these services from the BOIV because:

> a lot of clientele that come in here not wanting to go to the mainstream family violence spectrums so they want an inhouse for the Muslim community, somewhere they can trust because they see the imams as an authority figure. And they feel comfortable

[51] Interview 57 (Melbourne, January 2020).
[52] ibid.

> coming here because we give like a cultural lens, somewhere that they can culturally identify themselves with.[53]

Professionals working with women also highlighted the importance of identifying domestic violence where it occurs so that there is opportunity for their partners to be rehabilitated. They observe that whether or not the woman chooses to leave the relationship, the labelling of domestic violence is important in order for the violent partner to change. In situations where there is a belief that men can be rehabilitated and the marriage saved, 'some services have to be present for the man to give him a chance to change or give him some education because, in many cases, he can learn, he can change'.[54] BOIV expresses a commitment to working with perpetrators of domestic violence, often men who they encounter in the course of their work:

> You know, we're bandaging the wounds like which reminds me back to my school counselling days. What was the core issue? And then I find out again, it's the perpetrators. So, working with the male perpetrators. Because with the Muslim space, I feel like there's not enough [training] … and with training, you know, perpetrators, mentally he will change …[55]

The BOIV also conducts a voluntary monthly women's consultation group or a four-hour workshop called Victims' Voice. This program covers topics identified by the public or victim survivors. Its purpose is to:

> assist the women who want to reconnect, who want to find hope in their process, or those who want to give hope in their process or just want to hear other people's stories so that that can uplift them and want them to move forward from a dark space that they're in.[56]

In addition, BOIV runs trauma exercises, exercises on how to combat domestic violence and workshops on topics such as the bystander effect in domestic violence and how the wider communities' response to domestic violence affects women.[57]

These developments at BOIV are significant and represent an important step in addressing domestic violence. They provide a good blueprint for how sharia processes can better respond to domestic violence.

K. Referral and Integration of Support Services

Imams were generally open to the possibility of counselling and other support services being integrated with sharia processes, and in some cases such support was provided alongside the sharia process. Imams reported referring women

[53] Interview 57 (Melbourne, January 2020).
[54] Interview 25 (Sydney, May 2016).
[55] Interview 57 (Melbourne, January 2020).
[56] Interview 57 (Melbourne, January 2020).
[57] ibid.

to the police in cases of domestic violence, and women reported such referrals. However, there is a need for imams to be empowered to refer women to a greater range of services which are appropriate to their circumstances. Our study reveals a social set-up where, as one psychologist explains:

> [Imams] become the jack of all trades despite them not having any professional skills in relationship counselling, marriage counselling or even counselling post-separation … they don't have any mediation skills as well. [Their professional inexperience with counselling] brings additional problems to the … divorce or mediation process, because they don't know how to effectively and therapeutically engage the couple.[58]

Our research revealed instances where women may have benefitted from specialised counselling, mediation, legal aid, domestic violence services, etc; if such services are referred to, or integrated into, sharia process, this would benefit women.

Imams also need to receive support from other services to help them identify when and how they should refer women to these services. As one imam told us: '[w]e want marriage counsellors, we want psychologists, we want mediators, but, you know, I'm the sheikh, I'm the person sitting and I have to find all these people. And that's, we're out of resources'.[59]

i. *Counselling*

The research revealed that women needed to have counselling support available when seeking the services of the Board. They felt it should be an integral part of the process. One of the panels has sought to address this matter. The BOIV employs a part-time trained counsellor who works with the domestic violence officer, the intake officer and the imams. A significant role of this counselor is to mediate between the couples and seek to reconcile their marital disharmony. At other times, when there is a lot of conflict between the couples, the counsellor will separate the couples initially:

> So, I do the work with her, I do the work with him and then when they're good, then bring them together. And I find it works, having that one on one time with the man, it's different. I didn't used to do that. I used to put them together and it was like I'm a referee more than a counsellor …[60]

Referrals to the counsellor are made through the intake process or during the divorce process in the panels by the imams and the counsellor works closely with the imams:

> I will get their permission and I find out exactly what I'm allowed to tell the imam from what they've told me and whatnot. And then they sit with the imams and we go through

[58] Interviewee 37 (Sydney, August 2016).
[59] Interview 31 (Sydney, August 2016).
[60] Interview 58 (Melbourne, January 2020).

> the process. And sometimes they don't need me, and if they do need me, I'll sit with them … and introduce the process and then hand them over to … and the imams.[61]

On the panel itself, where the counsellor is in attendance, efforts are made to make a woman feel more emotionally comfortable:

> if there's some intimate details that she wants to discuss, she discusses that with our [sheikha, the female scholar panel member] and she's taken to a private space or the imams leave the room so that she's given that opportunity.[62]

The BOIV reported feedback from women engaging with the process: 'They feel like the imams are more on board. That's the feedback I've been getting over the last months'.[63]

ii. Relationship Support

In some cases, women approached imams seeking not divorce, but reconciliation. Interestingly, at least one woman interviewed felt that that the imams were too quick in issuing the divorce and instead they could have intervened more and attempted to reconcile.[64] Where appropriate, imams should consider referring women to professional services focused on family relationships such Family Relationships Online, Family Relationship Services Australia or Relationships Australia. However, it should be noted that the interviewee who was critical of the speed with which she gained her divorce was in a violent and abusive relationship.

iii. Mediation

Imams were also open to the possibility that issues around separation – apart from the issuance of the religious divorce itself – could be dealt with by mediation instead of the imams themselves. One imam responded to this suggestion as follows:

> Yeah, so this way, instead of asking what's going to change from our side, instead of saying, Look, we are not going to deal with women, with the children and this, we'll say, Yes, we'll deal with it, but we'll refer you to a mediator and we'll give a recommendation. That would be perfect. That would be perfect, if we can get mediators to do this, it would be perfect … Yeah, it would be perfect. There's no problem. Yeah, and even if the mediator, regardless of their faith, we are happy if there is a body of mediators …[65]

[61] ibid.
[62] Interview 57 (Melbourne, January 2020).
[63] Interview 58 (Melbourne, January 2020).
[64] Interview 18 (Sydney, April 2016); Interview 4 (Sydney, April 2016).
[65] Interview 31 (Sydney, August 2016).

iv. Legal Services

Besides counselling, legal services would clearly benefit women engaging in sharia processes. As discussed earlier, even where the outcomes of sharia processes yield similar or more generous post-divorce property settlements for women, these cannot be enforced by the imams. While some of the women we interviewed accessed the civil courts for property settlement, women engaged in sharia processes should be referred on to legal services for them to claim their entitlements through the family law system as a matter of course. Our research revealed mixed views amongst imams for women claiming through the family law system. Some imams suggested that the civil courts were sometimes 'unfair' to the men. But many imams acknowledged that the women were entitled to more than just the *mahr*, for instance, maintenance for her and the children, part of the property if she contributed towards it, as well as financial settlement on divorce. There is then reason to think that the financial settlements available to women through the family law system are not dissimilar to their entitlements under sharia. Indeed, as discussed earlier, one imam with knowledge of Australian law acknowledged that property settlement under sharia is very similar to the Australian legal framework – namely a contributions-based system that accounts for both financial and non-financial contributions.[66]

This suggests two related proposals to better support women. Imams should be offered training on family law, with an eye to identifying convergences between sharia and family law. Armed with this training, imams should refer women to legal services through which they can claim post-divorce entitlements.

v. Other Referrals

At the BOIV, women are also told about other services that are available. In Melbourne these included organisations and services such as Safe Steps and the National Zakat Foundation.[67] The National Zakat Foundation is Melbourne based and uses funds collected from zakat donation to provide support to people in need including women requiring emergency housing or women needing a new rental property. Financial assistance and food vouchers are also available, and the organisation provides specialist services to refugees. Other women on a spouse visa who cannot access social services such as Medicare and Centrelink are also being supported by the National Zakat Foundation.[68]

L. Sensitivity to Cultural and Linguistic Diversity

The Muslim community in Australia (as in the UK and Canada) is diverse. Our research revealed that sharia processes needed to be more sensitive to this diversity.

[66] ibid.
[67] National Zakat Foundation <www.nzf.org.au> accessed 1 November 2020.
[68] Interview 58 (Melbourne, January 2020).

For instance, women had to speak in front of imams who were speaking a language the women did not know, or in which the women were not fluent. One woman described not understanding the notes made by the imam (written in a language she did not understand) which she believed contributed to a significant misunderstanding with her husband.[69] One interviewee described imams speaking about, and in front of, her in a language she did not understand.

One interviewee described the difficulties she faced when having to explain her domestic situation to panels who had little English language.

> I guess, he didn't speak any English at all. So, there was another man that semi spoke English and the female was, she was sort of semi speaking English as well … And as I was speaking, the female was translating to the man and the man was translating to the scribe so I'm pretty sure all of my [story] … would have been lost in translation.[70]

Our research shows that the imams are aware of some of these concerns and the need to serve English-speaking Australian Muslims. CARD has separate panels and has specific days set aside for dealing with English-speaking individuals. Imams are making efforts to address this issue:

> While you're dealing with a country that everyone speaks English, I mean, most of your clients are going to want you to speak English. The other ones who don't speak English, they go to their own leaders. If he is from, for example, Pakistan speaking background, they're going to go to Rooty Hill sheikhs, or if they are Arabic or Lebanese they're going to go to like, to LMA or to … another sheikh. But we're here to represent all, and if you have to represent all you have to speak the common language which is English … And now we're at the position … where we have mainly an Arabic sitting and an English sitting which takes place on Tuesday.[71]

Imams acknowledge that one of the 'gaps' in their services is their lack of access to accredited interpreters. They generally rely instead on translations from imams who are fluent in those languages or members of the community, including people who support participants through the processes.[72]

At the BOIV, most of the women seeking a divorce either speak English or Arabic, and some are Urdu speaking as well. Some also bring their own interpreter, usually a daughter, other female relative or a friend. But the application form may be filled out in whatever language they are most familiar with. BOIV makes provisions for both English and Arabic speaking individuals.

In a situation where women are stressed and feel vulnerable to being judged, it is vital to have everyone involved speaking the same language. Moreover, it is important that the language used is accessible; for instance, technical theological terms may be inaccessible to the women seeking religious divorces. Otherwise, the scope for misunderstanding, confusion and distress for the women involved,

[69] Interview 55 (Melbourne, January 2020).
[70] Interview 9 (Melbourne, April 2016).
[71] Interview 31 (Sydney, August 2016).
[72] Interview 16 (Melbourne, May 2016).

is significant. There is also scope for unfairness or perceptions of unfairness, for instance, towards women whose husbands may be more fluent in Arabic and are able to articulate themselves to the imams better than the women.

M. Support and Resources for Religious Divorce

Chapter four explored why women seek Islamic divorces and found that women had compelling reasons and that obtaining such a divorce was important for them to be able to enter into other marriages, obtain closure and move on with their lives. Imams see themselves as serving women by allowing them to obtain these religious divorces. They see themselves as engaged in a 'women's process'. While this chapter has offered a number of proposals for how the processes could be improved, these proposals should be viewed against the extraordinary stressors and resource constraints imams face.

As discussed in chapter four, husbands implicated in sharia processes sometimes threaten imams. Imams complained of being threatened and fearing for their safety as a result of being involved in sharia processes, so much so that some imams have hired security guards during sharia processes for protection from aggressive men. Almost all imams complained of being under-resourced, unsupported, under-skilled and having to respond under serious time constraints. Imams felt they were considerably under scrutiny and criticism; as one put it, '[t]he media want to pick on us'.[73] Unsurprisingly, imams felt they were under a lot of pressure and stress.

If sharia processes are to improve, Muslim community organisations must consider how they can better support imams to provide a service which is of such importance to many Muslim women. Few of the proposals made in this chapter are workable unless imams are able to do work in conditions which are safe and well-resourced.

Our later interviews revealed the transformative effect that support and funding can have on sharia processes. Previously at the BOIV, staff were all volunteers, and the services of the panels were affected by the number of hours a volunteer is able to provide to the service. But as funds became available, one interviewee noted: 'So we're noticing that's one big shift here that everyone is now in a paid position and obviously that has an impact on everybody'.[74] The improvements in the BOIV detailed earlier in this chapter may well be a result of their better resourcing.

Equally, community organisations must consider whether women seeking Islamic divorce should have to bear the costs themselves. While women did not generally raise cost as a concern in our interviews, many were in financial difficulty.

[73] Interview 31 (Sydney, August 2016).
[74] Interview 57 (Melbourne, January 2020).

We know that cost is a concern for women approaching sharia councils in the UK.[75] We also know that in Canada receiving a religious divorce usually costs women practically nothing.[76] If community organisations could fund the panels granting divorces so that they did not have to charge women for their services, this would reduce in a small way their financial burden and, more importantly, indicate community support for these women.

N. Enhanced Role for Muslim Women's Organisations

As was observed in chapter three, some women may turn to community leaders or community organisations for advice and support as they experience marital conflict and divorce. These include key Muslim women's organisations, namely Muslim Women's Association (New South Wales), now known as Muslim Women Australia (MWA),[77] and Australian Muslim Womens Centre for Human Rights (Victoria).[78] MWA established the first refuge for Muslim Women escaping family violence over 26 years ago and now includes the Linking Hearts program, which provides family violence and homelessness support to women and families from culturally and linguistically diverse backgrounds in New South Wales. MWA is able to provide support services to many Muslim women who are undergoing a divorce. As described by one of their social workers, historically they had a central role to play:

> So, we would be there to support the woman in trying to sort of get the mashaikh [plural of *shaikh*, an imam or religious scholar] to mediate between her and her partner, her husband. And if a divorce is to be finalised, we would always … have some of our women, Muslim women, older women who would be there sitting with the woman, with the Muslim woman with the sheikh in his office, going through the process, explaining to her what are the details, and then giving her time out.[79]

This kind of community support for women facing relationship problems is vital, as concern about women's standing or reputation within a community might be important to her:

> [B]ut you still see a whole lot of women living under the same sort of situation that I was but they're too frightened to get away … just what everyone else is going to think. Like there's women who have busted their husbands cheating and women who their

[75] Secretary of State for the Home Department, *The Independent Review into the Application of Sharia Law in England and Wales* (February 2018) 14, <https://assets.publishing.service.gov.uk/government/uploads/system/uploads/attachment_data/file/678478/6.4152_HO_CPFG_Report_into_Sharia_Law_in_the_UK_WEB.pdf> accessed 1 November 2020.

[76] Macfarlane (n 36).

[77] Muslim Women Australia <https://mwa.org.au> accessed 1 November 2020.

[78] Australian Muslim Women's Centre for Human Rights <https://ausmuslimwomenscentre.org.au> accessed 1 November 2020.

[79] Interview 60 (Sydney, March 2020).

husbands don't come home but, you know, to walk away and leave them, what would the community think of them.[80]

Women interviewees confirmed they found culturally specific services helpful in navigating the divorce process. The following example illustrates this when a woman was supported by case workers in a Muslim women's refugee:

> Like I'd advise them at the time, you know, I'd just get their advice, like, *He's called today, what do you think? Should I let-* and they were very supportive in saying, *Okay, let him see the kids, go see, maybe he might*, you know, the support was there.[81]

However, in more recent times, high demand, few resources and a more streamlined panel process has meant that they have not been able to maintain this support for women in the community. Our interviews with key figures from MWA have indicated that there is a need for such a support service, particularly for their Muslim clients:

> I think it would really be very amazing and vital to have a woman have the same case worker that has been working with her, that is planning her, doing her case management plan, that's walking with her throughout her journey of conflict and, you know, whether she leaves her husband or doesn't. But we have a process that is time, that is evaluated in its efficiency and effective way for every case worker that works with the client. So we would love it if that case worker was not, was able to actually move in and still advocate on behalf of the woman inside, to the panel of *mashaikh* [plural of *shaikh*, an imam or religious scholar] because she has the full story for her. And we have, like I am of the opinion and believe that it is important for the woman to not to tell her story a million and, a million times. And it's important that our *mashaikh* recognise the experience and the expertise of Muslim women organisations who've been, you know, who have been in the field for a long time, who've advocated on behalf of women and who have the Islamic jurisprudence that can, that just gets us by where we're able to walk with the woman inside. Because I hear a lot of things about when women say they go in there and they come out they feel like they're so distraught, they're not the same.[82]

MWA is also able to support women in engaging with state legal processes,[83] who might otherwise feel judged, isolated and unsupported through these processes. Professionals working with women describe women who feel ashamed or worried they will be shunned by the community for using the legal system to get a fairer deal.[84] MWA facilitates access to legal advice for women through Legal Aid NSW, which conducts outreach through the offices of MWA. This kind of community-based access to legal services may help alleviate women's concerns that accessing legal services is going to lead to isolation or judgement from their Muslim communities.

[80] Interview 18 (Melbourne, April 2016).
[81] Interview 4 (Sydney, April 2016).
[82] Interview 60 (Sydney, March 2020).
[83] ibid.
[84] Interview 38 (Sydney, September 2016).

A greater role for Muslim women's advocacy services like MWA would see the most vulnerable women being supported in a holistic way and addressing various needs such as housing, legal advice financial support and counselling in a religiously and culturally appropriate manner.

O. Tracking the Australian Legal System

One of the key developments we observed in later interviews is how panels of imams related to divorce through the Australian legal system. As discussed in chapter five, both the BOIV and ANIC-CARD will not issue a religious divorce before a civil divorce has been issued. As one senior imam explains:

> And I reiterate that we don't make any decision until the court has made the judgment and issued and the divorce and during that time there will be an entire year for reflection and contemplation by either party where we will usually issue a revocable divorce during that time when both the man and the woman have recourse in thinking about how they will plan the rest of their future. It might be that they desire to reunite within that 12-month period.[85]

However, if there is a case of domestic violence such cases will be escalated, for example:

> In some cases, which I administered about a month ago, a sister got her application done within fourteen days because there was proven beyond doubt, and there were charges of domestic violence and fear of life ...[86]

Our interviews suggested that some women find the civil system overwhelming, as they do not know the system or where to go for assistance and feel intimidated by the courts and lawyers.[87] At BOIV, the support workers advise the women about how they will be supported when they go through the court process and are told about previous women's positive experiences.[88]

> I haven't had any complaints back of their treatment in the courts. I've even gone with clients and spent the day in the court with them while they get their IVO and seen firsthand how the social workers and [the different ... people], it's not a problem. Everybody's professional, everybody knows what they're saying. They're all looking for the comfort and safety of the woman there, and I think that that's really excellent, how they've upgraded things.[89]

However, our research revealed that women's experiences with the state family law system was not universally positive. The next section draws on these experiences

[85] Interview 36 (Sydney, August 2016).
[86] Interview 63 (Sydney, January 2020).
[87] Interview 52 (Sydney, November 2019); Interview 56 (Melbourne, January 2020); Interview 49 (Melbourne October 2016).
[88] Interview 58 (Melbourne, January 2020).
[89] ibid.

to offer some recommendations for how the state family law system might improve the experiences of the Muslim women who use them.

II. Improving the Family Law System

A. Better Enforcement of Orders against Former Partners

Women who engaged with the family law system reported frustration with the problems around enforcing court orders against their former partners. One woman reported that two court orders for her former partner to provide his financial information were not enforced. She concluded, 'I really do feel like I'm being abused, and the courts can't do anything'.[90] In a number of cases, men allegedly underreported their earnings from their personal business so as to avoid paying the necessary amount of child support. A number of women reported that they received either very little or absolutely no child support.[91] These experiences are in line with broader findings around post-separation outcomes for women, and the difficulties they have in claiming child support.[92]

B. Better Tailored Legal Aid

Most of the women interviewed emphasised the importance of receiving a religious divorce (see chapter three for their reasons). Undergoing the state family law processes in addition to the process of a religious divorce puts them under additional pressure. Our interviewees reported a feeling that there was too little time to discuss issues with legal aid lawyers. Some women also raised concerns about the effectiveness of their legal aid lawyer. One woman complained that the lawyer did not give her an opportunity to speak in court though she wanted to, and even though her husband spoke to the judge.[93] Another woman felt that her lawyer was insensitive to her history of domestic violence and was not supportive of her desire to have her ex-husband stop contacting her.[94] Our findings suggest that the additional burden on women undergoing the dual state and community

[90] Interview 6 (Sydney, April 2016).

[91] Interview 18 (Melbourne, April 2016); Interview 45 (Melbourne, September 2016); Interview 53 (Sydney, January 2020); Interview 6 (Sydney, April 2016); Interview 2 (Sydney, April 2016).

[92] B Fehlberg and C Millward, 'Family Violence and Financial Outcomes after Parental Separation' in A Hayes and D Higgins (eds), *Families, Policy and the Law: Selected Essays on Contemporary Issues for Australia* (Melbourne, Australian Institute of Family Studies 2014) 240. See also B Fehlberg and C Millward, 'Post-Separation Parenting and Financial Arrangements Over Time: Recent Qualitative Findings' (2013) 92 *Family Matters* 29.

[93] Interview 26 (Sydney, September 2016).

[94] Interview 18 (Melbourne, April 2016).

processes should be taken into consideration when allocating legal aid and legal representation.

C. Enhancing the Cultural Sensitivity of Mainstream Services

While some participants felt mainstream processes including Australian courts were respectful of their Muslim identity and culture, a number of participants described mainstream services as lacking cultural sensitivity and knowledge. Women often felt that the mainstream services they were able to access were unaware of their cultural or religious needs and therefore did not serve as the necessary support in these vulnerable moments.

Throughout these processes, particularly when undergoing mediation, some of the women interviewed felt that their husbands were still being manipulative and controlling – including in the mediation sessions – though mediators did not appreciate this due to a lack of cultural understanding.

Our interviews also reveal that women did not always feel comfortable bringing cultural or religious needs or preferences to the attention of mediators. This discomfort should be understood against the context of broader societal prejudice against Muslims and Islam in Australia. Our interviews also reveal that women did not always feel comfortable bringing cultural or religious needs or preferences to the attention of mediators. This discomfort should be understood against the context of broader societal prejudice against Muslims and Islam in Australia. Mainstream services need to be culturally sensitive and knowledgeable to serve these women well and make them feel comfortable enough to articulate their cultural needs. One community worker interviewee said: '[w]hen I talked about marriage, *mahr*, straightaway you knew the process. I guess that's where it helps … familiarity, if the counsellors are familiar with the Islamic religion, culture or religion laws. It helps them to understand the client'.[95]

This might be best achieved by facilitating greater diversity in those offering mediation, including having more qualified Muslim mediators from a range of ethnic and cultural backgrounds.

D. Legal Recognition of the *Mahr*

Only one of the women interviewed for our research received the *mahr* that was owed to them. This is partly because the type of divorce previously favoured by sharia processes in Australia – *khulah* – generally anticipates that women forfeit or return the *mahr*. (As discussed in chapter five, this preference for *khulah* is changing and raises the question of whether sharia processes should use other forms

[95] Interview 1 (Sydney, April 2016).

of Islamic divorce which allow the woman to keep or claim the *mahr*.) However, even when the payment of *mahr* is mandated by sharia processes,[96] our interviews show that there is an enforceability gap. One of the women interviewed was owed a substantial *mahr* (USD $50,000) and multiple imams supported her claim to the *mahr*. The imams were, however, powerless to enforce the payment of *mahr* by her unwilling husband. The Australian legal system might have a role to play here.

In *Mohamed v Mohamed* ('*Mohamed*'),[97] the New South Wales Supreme Court upheld the enforcement of an agreement that enforced the payment of a *mahr* of AUD $50,000 in the event that the man initiates the separation from the woman, as a contract. The Court relied on the fact that in the United States, Canada and the United Kingdom such agreements had been found to be enforceable.[98] Some courts in Canada, despite their lack of knowledge of Islamic principles and legal rulings, have recognised and upheld *mahr* agreements in *nikah* contracts (Islamic marriage contracts), as they considered them to be contracts between two consenting adults.[99] Similarly, in the UK, the case of *Uddin v Choudhry* saw the court uphold the Islamic marriage contract according to English contract law principles, recognising that the *mahr* was due to the wife upon divorce as it was specified in the contract.[100]

Greater awareness of the possibility that such agreements may be enforceable by courts might give women seeking divorce knowledge of an important option, especially as many of them face financial hardship upon divorce. Associate Justice Harrison in *Mohamed* referred the question of how such agreements should be treated to both the Australian Law Reform Commission and the New South Wales Law Reform Commission.[101] Islamic marriage contracts usually stipulate the *mahr*; those drafting them (often imams or Islamic organisations) could make the *mahr* legally enforceable, if there were greater clarity about the conditions that have to be satisfied for their enforceability. As discussed earlier, the problems around the enforceability of the *mahr* might also be addressed if the Islamic marriage contract counted as a binding financial agreement under the *Family Law Act 1975* (Cth).

E. A Muslim Family Relationship Centre/Service: A One Stop Shop for Muslim Families

The recommendations we have made in this chapter are multi-faceted. We suggest that one way of meeting them might be through a specialist Muslim Family

[96] Interview 6 (Sydney, April 2016).
[97] *Mohamed v Mohamed* [2012] NSWSC 852.
[98] ibid [33]–[47].
[99] Macfarlane (n 36) 226.
[100] JR Bowen, 'How Could English Courts Recognize Shariah?' (2010) 7(3) *University of St Thomas Law Journal* 411.
[101] *Mohamed v Mohamed* [2012] NSWSC 852 [122].

Relationship Centre or service. Our interview data and previous research indicate that many Muslims are reluctant to access mainstream dispute resolution processes, as they do not view these processes as being sensitive to their religious beliefs and needs when navigating divorce.[102] Research suggests that families from culturally or linguistically diverse backgrounds (including Muslim families) may not understand or trust mainstream services, may face communication barriers, and may be influenced by socio-cultural norms that emphasise informal community processes over 'mainstream help-seeking'.[103] As such, a specialised service for Muslim families may help to overcome these concerns, as well as shortcomings within current sharia processes, particularly the pressure on imams to be 'jack of all trades',[104] including mediators, counsellors and religious experts.

Australia has seen the emergence of government initiatives to enhance access to the legal system's services for people from culturally and linguistically diverse backgrounds,[105] including the development of culturally responsive models of dispute resolution for families from migrant background communities.[106] Since there is much common ground between Family Dispute Resolution (the form of mediation outlined in the *Family Law Act 1975* (Cth)) and Islamic dispute resolution principles, there is certainly scope for greater harmonisation between informal community processes and the existing legal framework in the form of a 'one stop shop' centre that provides a number of support services to Muslim families.

Such a service could provide information and education, from premarital through to post-divorce support. The service could offer education to women seeking knowledge about their options for religious divorce, along the lines suggested in this chapter. The service could also offer greater education and awareness (particularly to women) on the benefits of having their rights recognised in their religious marriage contracts. In particular, the service could make available template marriage contracts granting women the delegated right of divorce, which should make it easier for her to effect a religious divorce, as discussed earlier.

A specialist Muslim Family Relationship Centre could offer counselling, Family Dispute Resolution, legal services, premarital counselling and legal advice. A specialist service or centre would mean that referrals to counsellors, mediators

[102] G Krayem, *Islamic Family Law in Australia: To Recognise or Not to Recognise* (Melbourne, Melbourne University Publishing, 2014) 239.

[103] S Armstrong, P Bruce and R Butler, 'Culturally Reflexive Family Dispute Resolution: An Initiative of Anglicare and CatholicCare' (Paper presented at the Fourth National ADR Research Forum, Brisbane, 16–17 July 2010) 8–9; S Armstrong, 'Encouraging Conversations About Culture: Supporting Culturally Responsive Family Dispute Resolution' (2011) 17(3) *Journal of Family Studies* 233.

[104] Interview 37 (Sydney, August 2016).

[105] Family Law Council, *Improving the Family Law System for Clients from Culturally and Linguistically Diverse Backgrounds* (2012); Urbis, *Evaluation of the Family Relationships Services for Humanitarian Entrants Initiative* (Department for Families, Housing, Community Services and Indigenous Affairs 2007); Victoria Legal Aid, *Family Harmony Sessions for the Newly Arrived Communities* (April 2011).

[106] S Armstrong, *Enhancing Access to Family Dispute Resolution for Families from Culturally and Linguistically Diverse Backgrounds* (Australian Family Relationships Clearinghouse Briefing Paper, 18 April 2011); Family Law Council (n 105).

or religious leaders would be more readily available and accessible. This would go some way to address concerns raised by interviewees who noted that they want marriage counsellors, psychologists and mediators available, as a single sheikh or imam cannot alone address the whole spectrum of issues, particularly when there is a lack of resources.[107] It would also address imams' concerns that they cannot offer this range of services and their acknowledgement of the need for them to make appropriate referrals to specialised services.

III. Conclusion

In stark contrast to assumptions that religious norms – and sharia processes in particular – are unchanging and ossified, our research found noteworthy changes during the period of the study. These included improvements to protocols around domestic violence, intake procedures, gender representation on divorce panels and the provision of psychological and other services. While acknowledging these changes in some sharia processes, this chapter lays out a set of recommendations relating to the terms of marriage contracts; the intake process; women as decision-makers on the divorce panels; transparency and education about different types of Islamic divorce; the communication of clear procedures to users; appropriate responses to injustice, harm and domestic violence; cultural and linguistic sensitivity; and opportunities for sharia processes to refer to or integrate other services. These recommendations for improving sharia processes require action on the part of imams, community organisations, professional service-providers and funding bodies. Improvements to these processes will require resourcing. Our research tracked how better resourcing made an important difference to the sharia processes provided by the Board of Imams Victoria. Our interviewees also identified problems with the Australian state response to relationship breakdown. We explain how the state system needs to be more culturally sensitive, offer better enforcement and provide better-tailored legal aid. We also argue that there is a good case for legal recognition of the *mahr* and for a specialist Muslim family relationship centre which would provide the specific multi-faceted services needed by families facing a relationship breakdown.

[107] Interview 31 (Sydney, August 2016).

7

Conclusion

This book offers a multi-perspectival account of sharia processes, with a focus on how they are experienced by the women who use them. Drawing on new interviews with these women and the professionals who support them, it identifies the complex reasons why Muslim women use sharia processes to seek a religious divorce. These include religious and spiritual motivations; the need to end emotional manipulation; a desire for closure; and a desire to avoid stigma within their community. The book identifies the major obstacles and challenges experienced by women in the sharia processes including inadequate gender representation in the divorce process, a lack of transparency, their unmet need for injustice to be acknowledged and inadequate responses to domestic violence.

The book shifts perspective in chapter four to focus on the role and perspectives of the imams who play such a vital role in these processes. Based on our extensive interviews with imams, we reveal their self-identified role as facilitating reconciliation, acting as an advocate for women and facilitating religious divorce for women. Imams overwhelmingly conceived of sharia processes as principally services for women which free them from unwanted marriages. They identified key challenges they faced including workload pressures, threats from disaffected husbands, the need for training and skills on family dispute resolution, mediation and family violence. We also uncovered imams' views on some of the challenges for women that we discussed earlier.

While the book pays sustained attention to how women experience sharia processes as *processes*, it also includes a detailed study of their outcomes, broadly understood to include decisions (such as on divorce) and religious advice. We found that a particular type of Islamic divorce – *khulah* – was the dominant outcome, even though women might have qualified for other types of Islamic divorce that make it easier for them to retain the *mahr*. We found that there was a shift towards granting other types of divorce during the course of our study. We also found that imams were very reluctant to deal with any financial matters, besides the *mahr*. While they theoretically acknowledge that women have many other financial entitlements under Islamic jurisprudence – *iddah* payments, *mutah*, child support, compensation for financial and non-financial contributions during marriage – these do not feature prominently in sharia processes. Instead, many imams consider that financial settlements and child custody are best left to mediation and state processes.

Chapter six on evolution and change, covering the past five years of our study, details the many significant improvements that have been made to Australian sharia processes during this period. A woman scholar has been appointed to the Board of Australian National Imams Council (ANIC) and sits on a panel deciding on divorce. Sharia processes now include women in administrative, counselling and other roles. Imams have received training on identifying and responding to family violence. Those involved with sharia processes have taken steps towards clarifying their policies and procedures.

Acknowledging the changes that have already been made to sharia processes, we offer recommendations for how sharia processes should change further to better support the women who use them. We also suggest that the state system needs to be more culturally sensitive, offer better enforcement and provide better-tailored legal aid. We argue that there is a good case for legal recognition of the *mahr* and for a specialist Muslim family relationship centre which would provide the specific multi-faceted services needed by women facing a relationship breakdown, including counselling, family mediation, legal services, premarital counselling and legal advice.

The book has further and larger implications beyond these immediate findings and recommendations. There has been much media reporting, and political discussion, of 'sharia law', often understood as an ossified system of religious law which would compete with or displace state law.[1] Muslims, it is often asserted or implied, support the introduction of such a system.[2] If there was any interest in displacing or competing with state law, we would expect to find it amongst our interviewees, who included imams and community actors providing sharia processes.

None of the participants in our research called for, or exhibited any interest in, such a system of 'sharia law' which displaces or competes with state law. Instead, imams were cautious about misrepresenting their status; we discussed in chapter five how some imams in Australia are reluctant to enforce *tafriq* divorce (which

[1] P Hanson, The Senate First Speech. Commonwealth of Australia Senate, 14 September 2016; P Bibby, 'Muslim leader wants elements of sharia in Australia', *Sydney Morning Herald*, 8 March 2010 <www.smh.com.au/national/muslim-leader-wants-elements-of-sharia-in-australia-20100307-pqlo.html> accessed 1 November 2020; A Emon, 'Islamic Law and the Canadian Mosaic: Politics, Jurisprudence, and Multicultural Accommodation' (2009) 37 *Canadian Bar Review* 391, 395; A El Shamsy and NJ Coulson, 'Sharīʿah', *Encyclopædia Britannica*, 25 August 2020 <www.britannica.com/topic/Shariah> accessed 1 November 2020; AA Engineer, 'Is Sharia Immutable?' *Dawn*, 1 February 2003 <www.dawn.com/news/782766/is-sharia-immutable> accessed 1 November 2020; see K Mendecka, 'Sharia Councils in Western Society: Compromise or Surrender (With Particular Reference to the United Kingdom)' (4th International Conference – Interdisciplinary Approach to Law in Modern Social Context, 21–22 April 2016) <www.tf.vu.lt/wp-content/uploads/2016/04/Interdisciplinary-Approach-to-Law-in-Modern-Social-Context_Pranešimų-rinkinys.pdf> accessed 1 November 2020, for some of the tropes about sharia processes vis-à-vis the state legal system.

[2] J Hole, 'Muslim Group Wants Sharia Law in Australia', *ABC News*, 17 May 2011; N Berkovic, 'Hyder Gulam Calls for Australia to Embrace Legal Pluralism', *The Australian*, 28 September 2012. For instance, the submission by the Australian Federation of Islamic Councils (AFIC) to the Parliamentary Joint Standing Committee on Migration asks for 'legal pluralism', possibly suggesting greater recognition of Islamic decision-makers (Australian Federation of Islamic Councils, 2011).

requires a religious court) as they are uncomfortable referring to the decision-making panel as a 'court'. We found that interviewees supported, co-operated with, relied on and deferred to state law. The most significant organisations administering sharia processes in Australia do not issue religious divorces before the state has issued a civil divorce. They practically give religious effect to civil divorce, in some circumstances. Where they encounter domestic violence, they encourage reporting to the police. Many imams defer to state family law on important matters of custody and property and at least one major organisation supports women in approaching state courts. Further, our research uncovered that sharia processes changed significantly during the period of our research. Thus, while this book draws attention to many problems with sharia processes, its findings strongly undercut the tropes associated with 'sharia law', its incongruence with state law and its supposed immutable nature.

This study has taken a self-consciously comparative approach, situating our findings against literature on sharia processes in other countries. It is hoped that it contributes to our understanding of such processes in contemporary secular states more generally. Our findings may also be of interest to those interested in other religious bodies, particularly *batei din*[3] and ecclesiastical courts, who may deal with similar issues around religious divorce.

While the comparators for our study have been British and Canadian sharia processes, our findings may be of use beyond such jurisdictions. One-third of the world's population lives under controversial personal laws, which apply religious norms to religious groups in family matters. Some prominent reform proposals involve the replacement of personal law systems with some role for community actors who wish to provide services around religious divorce and dispute settlement.[4] This book, offering an in-depth study of women's experiences using such services, should contribute to the question of whether and how the replacement of personal laws with such actors might be justified.

This book also has valuable lessons for the many contentious conflicts that arise between norms of gender equality and non-discrimination on one hand, and religious freedom and autonomy, on the other. These include conflicts about women's access to religious sites,[5] discriminatory religious family laws,[6] women's disqualification to lead religious services or serve as priests, practices of gender-based segregation, and so on. Where these conflicts arise, some favour state intervention into religious practices – including coercive state intervention. Others favour

[3] Rabbinical tribunals.

[4] F Ahmed, 'Remedying Personal Law Systems' (2016) 30 *International Journal of Law, Policy and the Family* 248; A Shachar, *Multicultural Jurisdictions Cultural Differences and Women's Rights* (Cambridge, Cambridge University Press, 2001) 117–45.

[5] *Indian Young Lawyers' Association v State of Kerala* (2019) 11 SCC 1; Y Jobani and N Perez, *Women of the Wall: Navigating Religion in Sacred Sites* (Oxford, Oxford University Press, 2017).

[6] Y Sezgin, *Human Rights under State-Enforced Religious Family Laws in Israel, Egypt, and India* (Cambridge, Cambridge University Press, 2013); F Ahmed, *Religious Freedom under Personal Law System* (Oxford, Oxford University Press, 2016).

'internal reform',[7] envisaging that the religious community may autonomously[8] change its practices. These calls for internal reform are sometimes countered with assertions that such reform is improbable, and, in any case, would be ineffective. We, of course, take no broad position on these grand debates about gender and religion. But we hope to have contributed to these debates, particularly the feasibility and desirability of internal reform, by offering this empirically informed account of the significant changes we observed in Australian sharia processes over a relatively short time period.

This project uncovered important questions for further research. Any account of sharia processes is necessarily partial and limited. Sharia processes are diverse – a reflection of the diverse Muslim communities which use them. This book captures some of that diversity. We saw how different cultural communities approached religious divorce and family disputes differently. We saw how no single group or single interpretation of Islamic norms had a monopoly on sharia process in any Muslim community. A range of individuals, groups and institutions with unique decision-making methods and administrative procedures offer services relating to marriage, religious divorce and family disputes across Australian, British and Canadian Muslim communities. Our study is based on empirical study of these processes in Melbourne and Sydney – two Australian cities with significant Muslim populations – set alongside existing scholarship on sharia processes in Canada and in the UK. While it reflects significant cross-sections of Muslim communities, it does not purport to comprehensively capture its range of practices, for example, it focuses on the Sunni Muslim community in Australia and does not have significant data on the experiences and processes of Shia Muslims. Indeed, we hope that this study prompts further inquiries into sharia processes in other Australian regions, towns and cities, which we expect to further reveal the diversity amongst Muslim communities in Australia.

One of the important findings of this study is that – contrary to visions of sharia as medieval, ossified and unchangeable – sharia processes can and do change significantly. It was beyond the scope of this study to identify the causes of the change we observed. But this is a question worthy of further study because if triggers for change were better understood, we would be better able to suggest mechanisms by which the changes we recommend in chapter six might be brought about. For instance, state funding for response to domestic violence seemed to have prompted some of the changes we observed in Victoria. Self-reflection on the part of those administering sharia processes, based on their observations or reporting of the experiences of users of these processes, might have prompted

[7] C Choudhury, '(Mis)Appropriated Liberty: Identity, Gender Justice and Muslim Personal Law Reform in India', (2007) *Georgetown Public Law Research Paper* <ssrn.com/abstract=969020>; J Redding, 'Human Rights and Homo-Sectuals: The International Politics of Sexuality, Religion, and Law' 4 (2006) *Northwestern University Journal of International Human Rights* 436, 468.

[8] On religious community autonomy, see Denise Réaume, 'Justice Between Cultures: Autonomy and the Protection of Cultural Affiliation' (1995) 29 *University of British Columbia Law Review* 117.

some changes. Criticism from within and outside Muslim communities might have prompted others. Equally, criticism might provoke 'reactive culturalism'[9] where those administering sharia processes 'bunker down' in defence of their practices. These are speculations and further research on this would be valuable.

Our research also indicates that some sharia processes may be inadequately responsive to cultural and linguistic diversity. This raises another question in need of further study: whether cultural or linguistic biases and stereotypes (based on ethnicity, nationality or language) also influence sharia processes.

One of the primary aims of this study was to uncover women's experiences of using sharia processes. Gender stereotyping, fixed understandings of gender roles and a lack of appreciation for the nature of gender-based violence played an important part in these experiences. Some of the imams we interviewed, we said, did not demonstrate an understanding for domestic violence which did not involve physical abuse. We noted how women administering sharia processes were viewed as playing a supportive and caring, as opposed to an authoritative and intellectual, role. (The inclusion of a woman scholar on one of the panels deciding on religious divorce may challenge such perceptions.) Further research is needed to understand how gender stereotyping, gender scripts and biases influence sharia processes, and how they might be addressed.

[9] Shachar (n 4) 35.

Appendix A: Methodology and Project Phases

Phase One: Pre-Interview Stage

Identifying Key Institutions, Groups and Individuals

Our connections within the Muslim community enabled preliminary unrecorded face-to-face and phone conversations with imams and community leaders across New South Wales and Victoria in order to identify the key groups, institutions and individuals involved with sharia processes in Australia. This phase was also important in order to build trust while simultaneously underscoring for community actors, the role duality of some of the researchers who engaged with them as 'outsider' academics, even while they were community 'insiders' by virtue of being Muslim women.

Recruiting Interviewees

Interviewees were recruited via a designated secure website publicised in different ways. The project was advertised on a designated Facebook page and through various Islamic media and community organisations who were asked to publicise the project recruitment and information sheet. This sheet was also sent to organisations that support Muslim communities and individuals who might engage with sharia processes such as Migrant Resource Centres, Community Legal Centres, mediation services, Family Relationship Centres, Family Violence Services. Finally, we contacted many professionals such as lawyers, psychologists, counsellors, mediators etc. who were likely to have knowledge or experience of sharia processes. This research utilised a primary selection approach to sampling in that it sought out research participants who had intimate and direct knowledge of divorce processes being explored.[1]

[1] This is imperative for grounded theory because if the participants are only tangentially relevant, a comparison between previous data collected cannot take place. Vico Chiang, Diana Keatinge and Ann Williams, 'Challenges of Recruiting a Vulnerable Population in a Grounded Theory Study' (2001) 3 *Nursing and Health Sciences* 205–11.

Phase Two: Pilot Interviews

Of the three pilot interviews, one was with a religious leader (an imam), one with a lawyer and one with a woman who had been through the divorce process in Sydney. These interviews were in-depth and open ended, in line with grounded theory methods, allowing the researcher to take control of the guided conversation, while seeking input from the research participants.[2] These pilot interviews helped us to refine the interview questions. The pilot interviews simply asked interviewees to explain the connection they had to community divorce processes.[3] These interviews were then coded manually to understand the emerging themes and allow researchers to frame the following interviews.

Phase Three: Interviews

In recruiting the sample population, we sought to check and refine emerging categories[4] and to systematically seek multiple perspectives[5] on sharia processes. We looked firstly at the experiences of women engaging with sharia processes, usually due to a relationship breakdown, and then the perspectives of others involved in the process so as to ensure all key voices were explored. Thus the categories were expanded to include: community leaders, psychologists, social workers, imams as well as the initial categories of solicitors/lawyers and women who had experience with the process. It should be noted that while the call for participation was open to men as well as women, no men who had gone through sharia processes sought to participate in the research (that is likely because as discussed in the book it is women who make up the majority of applicants for religious divorce). The method of recruitment was, as described above, via secure website, social media sites, community media outlets, letters to various community and professional organisations that would have had clients who went through a religious divorce. At this stage 58 interviews were conducted in New South Wales and Victoria. These interviews were conducted throughout 2016. These were followed by a further 15 interviews in 2019/2020 as described below.

[2] K Charmaz and L Belgrave, 'Qualitative Interviewing and Grounded Theory Analysis' in JF Gubrium et al (eds), *The Sage Handbook of Interview Research: The Complexity of the Craft* 2nd edn (London, Sage Publications, 2012).

[3] For example, the woman interviewed was asked to relay her experience from marriage to divorce while interviewers sought specifics, in particular around marriage contracts and the different stages of divorce.

[4] K Charmaz, 'Grounded Theory' in JA Smith, R Harré and L Van Langehove (eds), *Rethinking Methods in Psychology* (London, Sage Publications, 1995) 28.

[5] A Strauss and J Corbin, 'Grounded Theory Methodology: An Overview' in NK Denzin and YS Lincoln (eds), *Handbook of Qualitative Research* (London, Sage Publications, 1994) 280.

All interviews were conducted by a small team of interviewers to ensure a consistency of approach and they were generally conducted by two interviewers to minimise any risks that may arise in the interview.

Women Who Engaged with Sharia Processes

Recruitment

These women interviewees were recruited either directly through the web page, via professionals who recommended them to us or through women's organisations trusted by the women. Some women approached us directly because they saw the research advertised and wanted to share their story.

Our Sample

The background of the women interviewees who had engaged with sharia processes varied. Some were homemakers, some were well-educated professional women, and others worked for Islamic organisations. Their ethnic background varied considerably. Interviewees had cultural backgrounds from Australia, Indigenous, South Asia, South East Asia, Middle Eastern and the Horn of Africa regions.

At this stage of the project, 13 women were interviewed (seven in New South Wales and six in Victoria). Working with women in this project required sensitivity to the challenging nature of these discussions for many of the parties involved, but in particular for the women who had engaged with sharia processes. It was necessary to ensure that they were not re-traumatised through their discussions with us about their experiences. The involvement of insider researchers, with close and trusted connections to Muslim communities, likely helped participants to feel more comfortable while discussing their experiences. Women were assured that their participation was anonymous and voluntary and that their consent could be withdrawn at any time without repercussions, in line with university ethics guidelines.

The interviews were conducted by a small team of interviewers. All of the interviews were recorded with the participant's consent and conducted in a safe and confidential environment either in the woman's home, or in a quiet and safe room in an Islamic organisation space such as a Muslim women's association. Participants were given breaks during the interview when recounting experiences that were potentially traumatic.

The interviewers ensured that they had access to a Muslim counsellor (who was familiar with Muslim clients and the nature of our project) for every interview that was conducted with the women. While no counsellor needed to be called during an interview, in at least three interviews the women were left contact details of a reputable psychologist with whom they could follow up. This was particularly important as in one instance it was revealed that the interview was the first time that the woman had spoken to anyone about the violence that had occurred in her marriage which, by the time of the interview, had ended. A member of the interview team also followed up with the women after the interview to ensure that women were supported post-interview.

Imams and Community Leaders

The interviews with the Imams were conducted in both Sydney and Melbourne after several meetings and communications with representative bodies of imams in both New South Wales and Victoria. These included the Australian National Imams Council (ANIC) and the Board of Imam Victoria (BOIV) as well as other organisations which run sharia processes, such as the Lebanese Muslim Association (LMA) in New South Wales. Interviews were also conducted with imams who worked in the field of marriage and divorce but who did not sit on any panels associated with these organisations; these imams worked in certain mosques or were well known in the community for their work in this field. We were very careful to send out information about the project to as many imams as possible through the mailing list of the representative bodies, mosque and local community organisations as well as letters to individual imams.

Our Sample

At this stage of the project, 21 imams and community leaders were interviewed (14 in New South Wales and five in Victoria). The imams came from various ethnic, cultural and linguistic backgrounds including Lebanese, Syrian, Egyptian, Sudanese, Jordanian, Pakistani, Afghan, Bangladeshi, Somali, Palestinian and Australian. They all reported having qualifications in Islamic Studies from recognised international institutions. Most of the imams were born and educated overseas but most had been living in Australia for many years. A few of the imams had undergraduate or postgraduate qualifications in Australia. A small number of imams had other qualifications such as being an accredited marriage celebrant or family dispute resolution practitioner. Two imams were qualified and practising solicitors in Australia. The imams varied in age, ranging from being in their 30s to being above 60 years. The imams varied in their ability and command of the English language. Most of them were able to speak English fluently, however one interview required the presence of a translator.

The interviews were conducted by the same team of researchers and all were attended by at least two interviewers. All the interviews were conducted in the office of the imams or the community organisation and with one exception (which required the presence of a translator) were conducted in English. It is important to note that communication was ongoing with imams and this was to ensure that we were kept informed of changes and updates to the divorce process.

Other Interviewees

Recruitment

Others interviewees involved in the research included people who worked with women who engaged with sharia processes such as community workers, psychologists, social workers, counsellors, mediators as well as lawyers. These interviewees were recruited via the webpage, community advertisements and letters to professional organisations/bodies. Prior to recruitment, they were asked about their expertise in dealing with Muslim clients who had gone through sharia processes to ensure that they had the necessary experience and understanding of these community processes.

Sample

At this stage of the study, we conducted 26 interviews with professionals (14 in New South Wales and 12 in Victoria). All of this group were professionals from a broad range of cultural backgrounds such as Australian, South Asian, South East Asian, Middle Eastern and the Horn of Africa. Whilst most were Muslim, we also interviewed two who were not Muslim but worked closely with Muslim clients. The interviews were conducted in their offices or workplaces by the same team of interviewers.

Phase Four: Compiling and Interpreting Data

Following transcription of the interviews, data was coded using the social science tool Nvivo. Once the categories of analysis were identified, we proceeded to write the data up with particular attention to women's experiences of the sharia processes. In order to comply with ethical considerations, all participants were anonymised. In some instances, key identifying information relating to women who had engaged with the processes has been left out or changed. This was to assure the participants that they are left unidentified and to minimise any harm to which they might be exposed as a result of participation.[6]

Phase Five: Recommendations

After the analysis of the data, we compiled preliminary findings, including recommended changes to sharia processes, based on our understanding of how women

[6] T Clarke, '"Over-Researched Here!": Exploring Accounts of Research Fatigue within Qualitative Research Engagements' (2008) 42(5) *Sociology* 953–70.

experienced these processes. In order to further refine our findings and recommendations, we made presentations to groups of imams both in New South Wales and Victoria and conducted further interviews.

We made two separate presentations on our tentative recommendations to groups of imams involved with sharia processes in both New South Wales and Victoria. The presentations were followed by detailed discussions with these imams. The aim of these presentations and discussions was to understand if researchers had accurately captured the processes as they currently were, given the time that had elapsed since the first set of interviews, and to receive feedback on the recommendations. We then conducted further interviews with imams and others involved in the community divorce processes to capture any recent changes to these processes that were not captured by the initial interviews. These interviews reflected the ways in which sharia processes had changed and evolved over time, which we describe in chapter six of this book.

Finally, we interviewed more women who had engaged with sharia processes more recently. This helped us understand their experience with the newer sharia processes and to assess whether the proposed recommendations would indeed improve women's experiences of sharia processes more generally.

At this final stage of project another 13 interviews were conducted in Victoria and New South Wales with the sole purpose of refining the recommendations.

Limitations of the Research

General Limitations

While the conversations and interviews for this project were extensive, there are of course limitations. The location of the researchers meant that there was a geographical limitation to where the interviews were conducted. Our focus on sharia processes in New South Wales and Victoria excluded processes that may have taken place or be evolving in other states. While the largest Muslim populations are in New South Wales and Victoria, we do not wish to suggest sharia processes may not be taking places in other parts of the country. We were informed by the imams we interviewed in New South Wales and Victoria that some women from other states accessed their services remotely. Additionally, the interviews focused on processes as they play out in urban settings – primarily Sydney and Melbourne. None of the participants were from rural or regional parts of these states.

As researchers, we made a concerted effort to circulate information about the project and call-outs to participate in the project, however we recognise that the women who took up our offers were women who had better social connections. This means that women who were less connected may not have seen the call-outs or if they did, may not have felt comfortable participating. Further research should be conducted with a focus on interviewing less-connected women and hearing their voices. Similarly, even women who did participate in the project may have censored themselves in interviews. The interviewers did their best to make the women feel heard and comfortable, highlighting how the information the women shared was vital for reforming the process, but there is no guarantee that women did not struggle telling others their story, especially where the interviewers shared community ties.

These limitations are the reason why we do not generalise our findings to suggest that all women experience these processes in this way. Rather, we have taken a more holistic approach to the process, examining it from various perspectives to highlight the issues that ought to be addressed in order to improve the process for women, who are the people who overwhelmingly access these processes. This means that although the numbers of women interviewed may be 'small' compared to the number of women in the Muslim community who seek a divorce each year, we did our best to hear from women with different cultural backgrounds, levels of religiosity, ages, class backgrounds, as well as both from women who had children and women who did not. However it ought to be acknowledged that while we had this diversity in the sample, we did not interview any women or imams who identified as shi'a Muslims. This means that the book does not address the processes or issues that may be experienced differently by these groups. However the themes that emerged were similar across these interviews and highlighted specific patterns that could be addressed. These experiences were well supported by the interviews with counsellors, social workers, psychologists, community workers and lawyers.

Men who had been through the divorce process did not approach us to be included in the interviews and neither community workers nor imams suggested divorced men for us to interview. There is certainly scope for future research to explore the participation of men in these processes and to examine how they perceive these processes, particularly in light of the fact that certain imams noted this was a women's process.

Appendix B: Board of Imams Victoria Marriage Contract

Contract of Islamic Marriage
Certificate

مجلس الأئمة لولاية فكتوريا

Board of Imams Victoria Inc.

(Affiliated with Australian National Imams Council* (ANIC) *Ltd.)

بسم الله الرحمن الرحيم

وَمِنْ آيَاتِهِ أَنْ خَلَقَ لَكُم مِّنْ أَنفُسِكُمْ أَزْوَاجًا لِّتَسْكُنُوا إِلَيْهَا وَجَعَلَ بَيْنَكُم مَّوَدَّةً وَرَحْمَةً إِنَّ فِي ذَلِكَ لَآيَاتٍ لِّقَوْمٍ يَتَفَكَّرُونَ

And one of His signs is that He created mates for you from yourselves that you may find rest in them, and He put between you love and compassion; most surely there are signs in this for a people who reflect. (Al-Quran 30:21)

عقد زواج إسلامي

ISLAMIC MARRIAGE CONTRACT

	BRIDEGROOM	**BRIDE**
Surname اسم العائلة		
Name الاسم		
Date of Birth تاريخ الميلا د		
Religion الدين		
Occupation العمل		
Nationality الجنسية		
Father's Name اسم الأب		
Mother's Name اسم الأم		
Address العنوان		

Place of Marriage اسم مكا ن الزواج		Date تاريخ الزواج	

Name of Bride's *Wali* / *Wakeel* (If any) اسم الولي أ و ا لوكيل		
Amount/ Value of *Mahr* مبلغ المهر	Amount/ Value of *Mahr* مبلغ المهر المتفق عليه	
	Paid المعجل	
	Deferred المؤخر	

*The bridegroom has agreed that the amount /value of deferred *Mahr* (Dower) will become due and payable to the bride at the dissolution of Islamic marriage (*Talaq*) or the death of the husband.

Bridegroom's signature: …………………………… Bride's signature: ………………………….........

Signature of the Wali (Guardian): ……………………………………….

Witnesses

Name : FATIH M SARI Signature:……………………………………. Date: ……/……../…………

Name: MOHIDEEN IMRAN Signature: ……………..……………………… Date: ……./……./………….

IMAM'S DECLARATION

Dated this ………………… day of ……… 2020, I, the undersigned Imam, an authorised Islamic Marriage Celebrant, declare and confirm that I have duly solemnised the Islamic marriage between the above named couple in the presence of Bride's *Wali* (Guardian) and the witnesses after verifying that all the necessary conditions for a valid Islamic marriage are fulfilled and satisfying the same to be true to the best of my knowledge.

Imam's Name: Sheikh Muhammad SALEEM Signature:……………………………

Disclaimer: This certificate is not evidence of nor has it the effect of creating a legal marriage under The Marriage Act 1961 (Cth) and should the parties wish to have their marriage recognised at law the same will need to be registered as per section 80 of The Marriage Act 1961 (Cth) . The couple must file for a legal marriage as required and pursuant to The Marriage Act 1961 (Cth)

مجلس الأئمة لولاية فكتوريا

Board of Imams Victoria Inc.

(Affiliated with Australian National Imams Council (ANIC) Ltd.)

THE AGREEMENT

WHEREAS:

Marriage in Islam is a sacred and permanent bond between a man and a women of Islamic faith and is based on kindness and mercifulness (al Mawddah wa al Rahmah). We, the Husband and Wife were married in accordance with the provisions of Islamic Law(Shariah) and wish always to adhere to the Islamic faith. We, the husband and wife together desire always that our marriage and marital relations be practiced, ruled, regulated, governed and dominated by the Islamic ethics and the Islamic Law (Shariah). Nevertheless, we wish to make provisions hereby to govern our relationship accordingly.

TERMS AND CONDITIONS

1. *Both the parties to this marriage (herein after 'We') promise to each other to be faithful and adhere to the Islamic way of life at all times to the best of our ability and refrain from any act that may cause distress, dissonance or distrust in the family relationship.*
2. *We acknowledge and respect the "Freedom of Choice" of the other in relation to education, work/employment choices, family relationships, sports, friendship, hobby, travel, medical treatment and any other activities as long as that it is perused, established and maintained for the purpose of reasonable enjoyment of life in accordance with the provisions of Islamic Law (Shariah)*
3. *We acknowledge and recognise the traditional role of each other in establishing the family relationship and share and complement each other in household responsibilities. This may include cooking, cleaning, shopping, and other tasks that is necessary to maintain a harmonious relationship in the family.*
4. *We agree to and shall treat each other with utmost respect and care and shall not cause, inflict or act in such a way that may lead to physical, mental or psychological harm to the other.*
5. *We agree and acknowledge that the Husband is the primary provider of the family and the wife is the primary carer of the family and promise each other to complement each other in maintaining the day to day affairs of the family.*
6. *We acknowledge and recognise that the welfare of the children is paramount in dealing with matters related to children. This may include 'inter alia' care and upbringing, custody, guardianship, visitation rights (if any following the dissolution of this marriage) and any other matters that may be necessary to protect the welfare of the children in this marriage.*
7. *We acknowledge and respect each other's right to earn, own property, financial freedom and other rights and agree that issues related to property and financial resources shall be resolved through "Binding Financial Agreement" as specified in S.90(B),90(C) or 90(D) of the Family Law Act 1975 (Cth)*
8. *The husband has agreed NOT to exercise his option to marry another woman without the prior written consent of the Wife while this marriage subsists.*
9. *The husband has agreed to relinquish his exclusive right to pronounce Talaq to the wife provided that she shall exercise this delegated authority in accordance with the provisions of Islamic Law (Shariah) and shall seek advice from "Council of Islamic Family Arbitration & Mediation" of the Board of Imams Victoria or any other competent panel of Imams.*
10. *Any dispute between the parties to this marriage shall be dealt with, with respect and in accordance with the provisions of Islamic Law (Shariah). This may include seeking advice and counselling, mediation, family reconciliation (Sulh) and arbitration (Tahkeem) from competent professionals, family members and or Imams.*
11. *This marriage shall become voidable if either party failed to comply with any of the above conditions. The aggrieved party shall seek advice from "Council of Islamic Family Arbitration & Mediation" of the Board of Imams Victoria or any other competent panel of Imams as to the status of this marriage.*
12. *This shall be a valid and enforceable agreement.*

Dated on this………………. (……..) day of…………… 2020

Signatures; *Bride & Groom* *Witnesses*

……………………………… ……………………………… ………………………………

……………………………… ………………………………

Disclaimer: This certificate is not evidence of nor has it the effect of creating a legal marriage under The Marriage Act 1961 (Cth) and should the parties wish to have their marriage recognised at law the same will need to be registered as per section 80 of The Marriage Act 1961 (Cth) . The couple must file for a legal marriage as required and pursuant to The Marriage Act 1961 (Cth)

Appendix C: Board of Imams Victoria Islamic Mediation/ Reconciliation Application

الإسلامى العائلي مجلس التحكيم

Council of Islamic Family Arbitration& Mediation (CiFAM)

Application for Mediation/Reconciliation
Family Counselling

Please complete this application and send to;

CiFAM
P.O. Box 137- Coburg VIC 3058
Email. info@boiv.org.au

Check List

Use the checklist to make sure you have done everything you need to do.

Tick if completed ☑

☐ 1. You have answered all the questions.

☐ 2. You have provided the correct mailing addresses and contact numbers.

☐ 3. You have attached an explanation of your reason for submitting this application.

☐ 4. You have provided a copy of your civil divorce certificate (If any)

☐ 5. You have provided personal identification (e.g., Drivers license, passport, etc…).

☐ 6. You have signed your statutory declaration in front of an authorised person.

☐ 7. You have provided a copy of the restraining order (If any)

You can expect us to:

- Contact you to confirm an appointment date and time as soon as possible.
- Undertake checks, as required, to confirm that the information and documents you have provided are truthful and accurate.
- Finalise your application as quickly as possible and in accordance with Islamic law (*Shariah*)
- Explain our decisions to you and provide a written document. (E.g. Certificate of Islamic Divorce)

We expect you to:

- Provide any documents or information we request within the specified time or tell us immediately if this is not possible
- Quote your full name when you contact us or send us documents to the address above.
- Make sure we are able to contact you. You should tell us if you change address or phone number.
- Let us know if you cannot come to an appointment, we have made with you.
- Keep your contact with us to a minimum, to allow processing of your own and other applications to proceed as quickly as possible.

Our Contact Details;

945 Sydney Road, Coburg North, VIC 3058

Phone: 03 85909329 – Mobile: 0432911 825

Email: info@boiv.org.au

www.boiv.org.au

مجلس التحكيم العائلي الإسلامى

Council of Islamic Family Arbitration & Mediation Inc.

(Inc. No. A0060341D)

Email: info@boiv.org.au OR boardofimams@gmail.com

Web: www.boiv.org.au

Application for Mediation – Reconciliation and Family Counselling

(Note: This application should be made by both the husband and wife.)

Husband		Wife
1. Surname		
2. Given Name		
3. Have you been living separately.	Yes : ☐ No ☐ If YES, Date of Separation ……./ ……../……..	7.Any intervention order? Yes☐ No ☐ (Please attach a copy of IVO)
4. Please state if there is any restriction to participate in mediation or family counselling?		
4.Postal address.		
5. Home Phone.		
6. Mobile.		
7. Email.		
8. Occupation.		
9. What language (s) do you speak?	English – Arabic – Turkish- Somali Other (Pls. Specify) :	English – Arabic – Turkish- Somali Other (Pls. Specify) :
10. Do you need an interpreter?	Yes ☐ No ☐ No	Yes ☐ No ☐
11. What is your Residential Status.	**Australian Citizen – Permanent Resident,** Spouse Visa Holder - (If other, Pls specify) Australian Citizen	**Australian Citizen – Permanent Resident,** Spouse Visa Holder - (If other, Pls specify) :
12. Do you have any children from this	Yes / NO Boys: ………………… Age (s) ……………………………………………	

marriage?	Girls: .... Age (s) ....
13. Have you participated in any family counselling? (If yes, please give details)	Yes ☐ No ☐ ....

Declaration	I declare that the above information is true to the best of knowledge	I declare that the above information is true to the best of knowledge
Signature & Date		

For office use: Date received:.............................. Comments: ....

Reasons for your application.

Commonwealth of Australia

STATUTORY DECLARATION

Statutory Declarations Act 1959

1 Insert the name, address and occupation of person making the declaration

I .... of ....
(Name) (Address)

.... VIC ....

2 Set out matter declared to in numbered paragraphs

make the following solemn declaration under the *Statutory Declarations Act 1959:*

1. I truly and sincerely declare that I am a married person with .... according to Islamic rites and seeking to resolve matrimonial disputes between me and my spouse in accordance with the provisions of Islamic law (*Shariah*).

2. I declare that I have appointed the Council of Islamic Family Arbitration and Mediation (CIFAM) on my own free will to mediate or arbitrate and resolve the marital conflicts existing between me and my spouse in accordance with the provisions of the *Shariah* whether it be the case of reconciliation (*Sulh*) or Mediation.

3. I solemnly and sincerely declare that I will co-operate fully with the Council of Islamic Family Arbitration and Mediation in its efforts to mediate or arbitrate between me and my spouse and abide by its decision.

4. I agree to pay application processing fee and any other fees to CiFAM in lieu of services provided to me in the mediation & arbitration process.

5. I acknowledge that I have read the above statement or had it read to me, explained and understood by me.

I understand that a person who intentionally makes a false statement in a statutory declaration is guilty of an offence under section 11 of the *Statutory Declarations Act 1959*, and I believe that the statements in this declaration are true in every particular.

,3 Signature of person making the declaration

3 ....

4 Place
5 Day
6 Month and year

Declared at 4 .... on 5 .... day of 6 .... 20 ....

Before me,

7 Signature of person before whom the declaration is made (see over)

7 ....

8 Full name, qualification and address of person before whom the declaration is made (in printed letters)

8 ....

Note 1 A person who intentionally makes a false statement in a statutory declaration is guilty of an offence, the punishment for which is imprisonment for a term of 4 years — see section 11 of the *Statutory Declarations Act 1959.*

Note 2 Chapter 2 of the *Criminal Code* applies to all offences against the *Statutory Declarations Act 1959* — see section 5A of the *Statutory Declarations Act 1959.*

Appendix D: Board of Imams Islamic Divorce Application

مجلس التحكيم العائلي الإسلامى

Council of Islamic Family Arbitration& Mediation
(CiFAM)

Application for Mediation/Reconciliation, Arbitration or Islamic Divorce

Please complete this application and send to;

CiFAM
P.O. Box 137- Coburg VIC 3058
Email. info@boiv.org.au

Check List

Use the checklist to make sure you have done everything you need to do.

Tick if completed ☑

☐ 1. You have answered all the questions.

☐ 2. You have provided the correct mailing addresses and contact numbers.

☐ 3. You have provided a copy of your marriage certificate (Islamic Marriage).

☐ 4. If your marriage certificate is not in Arabic or English then an N.A.A.T.I approved translation of the original document is required in English or Arabic.

☐ 5. You have attached an explanation of your reason for submitting this application.

☐ 6. You have provided a copy of your civil divorce application (If any)

☐ 7. You have provided a copy of your civil divorce certificate (If any)

☐ 8. You have provided personal identification (e.g., Drivers license, passport, etc…).

☐ 9. You have signed your statutory declaration in front of an authorised person.

☐ 10. You have provided a copy of the restraining order (If any)

You can expect us to:

- ☐ Contact you to confirm an appointment date and time as soon as possible.
- ☐ Undertake checks, as required, to confirm that the information and documents you have provided are truthful and accurate.
- ☐ Finalise your application as quickly as possible and in accordance with Islamic law (*Shariah*)
- ☐ Explain our decisions to you and provide a written document. (E.g. Certificate of Islamic Divorce)

We expect you to:

- ☐ Provide any documents or information we request within the specified time or tell us immediately if this is not possible
- ☐ Quote your full name when you contact us or send us documents to the address above.
- ☐ Make sure we are able to contact you. You should tell us if you change address or phone number.
- ☐ Let us know if you cannot come to an appointment, we have made with you.
- ☐ Keep your contact with us to a minimum, to allow processing of your own and other applications to proceed as quickly as possible.

Our Contact Details;

945 Sydney Road, Coburg North, VIC 3058

Phone: 03 85909329 – Mobile: 0432911 825

مجلس التحكيم العائلي الإسلامى

Council of Islamic Family Arbitration & Mediation Inc.

(Inc. No. A0060341D)
Email: info@boiv.org.au OR boardofimams@gmail.com
Web: www.boiv.org.au

Your application is for; Arbitration ☐ Reconciliation & Mediation ☐ Islamic Divorce ☐

Application by ; Husband ☐ Wife ☐ Both ☐

	Applicant's Details	Details of the Spouse	
1. Surname			
2. Given Name			
3. Date & Country of Birth (if born overseas)	Date: Place of Birth: ……………………	Date: Place of Birth: ……………………	
4. Date and place of Islamic Marriage.	Date: ………………………………… Place:……………………….. (Please provide copy of the Islamic marriage Certificate)	4.a. Is your marriage registered in Australia or Overseas? (If yes, please provide copy of the registration)	Yes No
5. Have you been living separately.	Yes : ☐ No ☐ If YES, Date of Separation …………………	5.Any intervention order? Yes ☐ No ☐ (Please attach a copy of IVO)	
6. What is the marriage dower – (*Mahr*) agreed upon at the time of *Nikah*	Total: …………………………………………………………………………… Paid Immediately: ……………………………………………………………………… Deferred: ………………………………………………………………………………		
7. Have you applied for 'Civil divorce' at Australian Federal Court? - Yes ☐ No ☐ (If yes, please attach the copies of the application and Certificate of Civil Divorce).			
8.Postal address.			
9. Home Phone.			
10. Mobile.			
11. Email.			
12. Occupation.			
13. What language (s) do you speak?	English – Arabic – Turkish- Somali Other (Pls. Specify) :	English – Arabic – Turkish- Somali Other (Pls. Specify) :	

14. Do you need an interpreter?	Yes ☐ No ☐		Yes ☐	No ☐
15. What is your Residential Status.	**Australian Citizen – Permanent Resident,** Spouse Visa Holder - (If other, Pls specify)	**Australian Citizen – Permanent Resident,** Spouse Visa Holder - (If other, Pls specify) :		
16. Do you have any children from this marriage?	Yes / NO Boys: ………………… Age(s) ……………………………………………… Girls: …………………… Age (s) ……………………………………………..			
17. Have you been married previously?	Yes ☐ No ☐	If YES, how many children do you have from previous marriage? Boys……………… Age(s) ……………………………………. Girls …………….. Age(s) …………………………………….		
18. Do you have child visitation & custody arrangements	Yes ☐ No ☐	If YES, please give brief details in a separate paper or attach childcare arrangement agreement.		
19. Have you participated in any counselling? (If yes, please give details)	Yes ☐ No ☐ ……………………………………………………………………………… ……………………………………………………………………………… ……………………………………………………………………………… ………………………………………………………………………………			
20. Do you think that there is a possibility to reconcile with your spouse? If no, please give reasons.				

Declaration	I declare that the above information is true to the best of knowledge	I declare that the above information is true to the best of knowledge
Signature & Date		

For office use: Date received:………………………… Comments: ……………………………….

Reasons for your application.

Commonwealth of Australia

STATUTORY DECLARATION

Statutory Declarations Act 1959

1 Insert the name, address and occupation of person making the declaration

I .... of ....
(Name) (Address)

.... VIC ....

make the following solemn declaration under the *Statutory Declarations Act 1959:*

2 Set out matter declared to in numbered paragraphs

1. I truly and sincerely declare that I am a married person with .... according to Islamic rites and seeking to resolve matrimonial disputes between me and my spouse in accordance with the provisions of Islamic law (*Shariah*).

2. I declare that I have appointed the Council of Islamic Family Arbitration and Mediation (CIFAM) on my own free will to mediate or arbitrate and resolve the marital conflicts existing between me and my spouse in accordance with the provisions of the *Shariah* whether it be the case of reconciliation (*Sulh*) or divorce by *Talaq, Khulu', Tafreeq* or *Fasakh* (separation or annulment).

3. I solemnly and sincerely declare that I will co-operate fully with the Council of Islamic Family Arbitration and Mediation in its efforts to mediate or arbitrate between me and my spouse and abide by its decision.

4. I agree to pay application processing fee and any other fees to CiFAM in lieu of services provided to me in the mediation & arbitration process.

5. I acknowledge that I have read the above statement or had it read to me, explained and understood by me.

I understand that a person who intentionally makes a false statement in a statutory declaration is guilty of an offence under section 11 of the *Statutory Declarations Act 1959*, and I believe that the statements in this declaration are true in every particular.

,3 Signature of person making the declaration

3 ....

4 Place
5 Day
6 Month and year

Declared at [4] .... on [5] .... day of [6] .... 20 ....

Before me,

7 Signature of person before whom the declaration is made (see over)

7 ....

8 Full name, qualification and address of person before whom the declaration is made (in printed letters)

8 ....

Note 1 A person who intentionally makes a false statement in a statutory declaration is guilty of an offence, the punishment for which is imprisonment for a term of 4 years — see section 11 of the *Statutory Declarations Act 1959.*

Note 2 Chapter 2 of the *Criminal Code* applies to all offences against the *Statutory Declarations Act 1959* — see section 5A of the *Statutory Declarations Act 1959.*

Appendix E: Lebanese Muslim Association Application

بسم الله الرحمن الرحيم

THE FATWA & ISLAMIC ARBITRATION MAJLIS
CENTRE FOR AUSTRALIAN MUSLIM AFFAIRS
SYDNEY, AUSTRALIA

مجلس الفتوى والتحكيم الشرعي
المركز الإسلامي العام
سيدني . أستراليا

Islamic Divorce Application

By: Husband ☐ Wife ☐ Both ☐

	Husband's Details	Wife's Details
1. **Surname**		
2. **Given Names**		
3. **Date & Place of Birth**		
4. **Occupation**		
5. **Address**		
6. **Phone & Email**		
7. **ID**		
8. **Father's Name**		
9. **Mother's Name**		

10. **Marriage Details**	☐ **Islamic Marriage:** Date	Place
	☐ **Australian Marriage:** Date	Place
	☐ **Overseas Marriage:** Date	Place

11. **What is your Residential Status (please circle):**	Australian Citizen, Permanent Resident, Spouse Visa Holder. Other (please specify):	Australian Citizen, Permanent Resident, Spouse Visa Holder. Other (please specify):

12. **What is the marriage dower – *Mahr* agreed upon the time of marriage?**	Total	
	Paid Immediately	
	Deferred	

A 71-75 Wangee Rd, Lakemba NSW 2195 | PO Box 297, Lakemba NSW 2195
P (02) 9750 6833 | **E** fatwa@lma.org.au | **W** lma.org.au

LMA

13. Previously have you been married?	YES ☐ NO ☐	If yes, ONCE ☐ TWICE ☐	How many children do you have from previous marriage(s)? How was the previous marriage(s) ended?	
14. Have you been living separately?	YES ☐	NO ☐	If yes, date of separation	
15. Have you applied for a civil divorce? (please attach a copy of the civil divorce certificate)	YES ☐	NO ☐	If yes, please provide date	Date
16. Previously have you been divorced Islamically?	YES ☐	NO ☐	If yes, please provide details:	
17. Do you have children from this marriage?	YES ☐	NO ☐	Boys: ___ Girls: ___ Age: ___ Age: ___	
18. Do you have any child visitation & custody arrangements?	YES ☐	NO ☐	If yes, please provide details:	
19. Have you participated in any counselling?	YES ☐	NO ☐	If yes, please provide details:	
20. Do you think that there is a possibility to reconcile with your spouse?	YES ☐	NO ☐	If yes, please provide details:	

Applicant Declaration: I declare that the above information is true to the best of knowledge.

Signature and Date: ______________________________

Additional Comments

Appendix F: Summary of Key *Sunni* Positions on Islamic Divorce[1]

This section summarises some key *Sunni* positions relating to Islamic divorce for ease of reference. These positions are not exhaustive of *Sunni* jurisprudence, nor do they fully capture the substantial differences of opinion *within* different schools of thought.

I. Divorce for Men – *Talaq*

This type of divorce spans a broad range of arrangements, but typically it is pronounced by the husband and requires his consent. A marriage contract may contain a clause that gives the woman the right to effectuate a *talaq* divorce; this is known as *talaq tafweedh* (discussed later).

A. Qur'anic Verses Relating to *Talaq*

> Divorced women remain in waiting for three periods, and it is not lawful for them to conceal what Allah has created in their wombs if they believe in Allah and the Last Day. And their husbands have more right to take them back in this [period] if they want reconciliation. And due to the wives is similar to what is expected of them, according to what is reasonable. But the men have a degree over them [in responsibility and authority]. And Allah is Exalted in Might and Wise. (2:228)
>
> Divorce can happen twice, and [each time] wives either be kept on in an acceptable manner or released in a good way. It is not lawful for you to take back anything that you have given [your wives], except where both fear that they cannot maintain [the marriage] within the bounds set by God: if you [arbiters] suspect that the couple may not be able to do this, then there will be no blame on either of them if the woman opts to give something for her release. (2:229)
>
> And if he has divorced her [for the third time], then she is not lawful to him afterward until [after] she marries a husband other than him. And if the latter husband divorces her [or dies], there is no blame upon the woman and her former husband for returning to each other if they think that they can keep [within] the limits of Allah. These are the limits of Allah, which He makes clear to a people who know. (2:230)

[1] We thank Anisa Buckley and Mohamed Hamed for excellent research on this compilation.

O you who have believed, when you marry believing women and then divorce them before you have touched them, then there is not for you any waiting period to count concerning them. So provide for them and give them a gracious release. (33:49)

B. Hadith Relating to *Talaq*

Divorce is that which God has permitted which He hates most.[2]

C. Difference between Revocable and Irrevocable *Talaq* Divorce

Types of *talaq* divorce	**Husband's action effectuating divorce**	**Wife's right**	**Consequences**
Talaq raj'i (revocable divorce): in this type of *talaq*, the legal and financial ramifications of divorce come into effect at the end of the wife's waiting period or *'iddah*	Husband pronounces divorce through a single pronouncement after his wife has had her period and from which time he has not had intercourse with her[3] Husband can reconcile, take the wife back (ruju') if they had consummated the marriage[4] and if she is still within her *'iddah*[5]	The wife is entitled to any deferred *mahr* The wife is entitled to maintenance and residence during her *'iddah*, including if she is pregnant[6]	Once *'iddah* has been completed, it is considered as a minor irrevocable *talaq* in that it is counted as one *talaq*, should the husband wish to resume the marriage afterwards they can without needing an intervening marriage and new marriage contract[7]
Talaq ba'in (irrevocable divorce): in this type of *talaq*, the legal and financial ramifications come into effect immediately	Husband pronounces divorce before consummation occurs, or Husband pronounces divorce once each month for three months, or Husband pronounces divorce three times at once (triple *talaq*)[8]	Wife is entitled to any deferred mahr Scholarly opinions differ on wife's entitlements to maintenance and residence during *'iddah* (see below)	This is considered a major irrevocable *talaq* whereby the marriage cannot be resumed and the couple cannot remarry each other unless certain conditions are met[9]

[2] Al-Bayhaqi, *As-Sunan al-Kubra Vol. 7* (DKI Beirut 2003) 527, no. 14894.
[3] Ibn Rushd, *The Distinguished Jurist's Primer (Bidayat Al-Mujtahid Wa Nihayat Al-Muqtasid)*, trans. Professor Imran Ahsan Khan Nyazee, vol II (Reading, Garnet Publishing Limited, 1996) 75.
[4] ibid 73.
[5] ibid 101.
[6] ibid 114.
[7] Khalid Al-Azri, 'One or Three? Exploring the Scholarly Conflict over the Question of Triple Talaq (Divorce) in Islamic Law with Particular Emphasis on Oman' (2011) 25(3) *Arab Law Quarterly* 277, 280.
[8] Ibn Rushd (n 3) 72.
[9] For re-marriage to each other, there must be an intervening marriage (*tahlil*) which is consummated. If the wife is divorced from this intervening marriage, she can then marry her first husband again with a new marriage contract. Al-Azri (n 7) 277, 280.

D. Differing Juristic Opinions on Common Issues Around *Talaq*

Issue	Shafi'i	Maliki	Hanafi	Hanbali	Other scholars
How many pronouncements should the husband make during the wife's *'iddah*?[10]		One	Three, one each month		
Does ruju' by words need to be witnessed?[11]	Yes, obligatory. But some scholars within the *Shafi'i* school say it is not obligatory[12]	Recommended		Not necessary[13]	
Can ruju' take place via intercourse alone?[14]		Yes, but only if husband intended *ruju'*	Yes even if husband did not intend *ruju'*[15]		
Is a woman divorced irrevocably entitled to residence and maintenance during her *'iddah*?[16]	Residence but not maintenance	Residence but not maintenance	Residence and maintenance	Neither	
Is a divorced wife entitled to *mutah* (post-divorce financial settlement made by the husband to the wife)?[17]	Yes, if husband initiated divorce, except for women with fixed *mahr* divorced prior to consummation	This is recommended, but not an obligation on the husband	Yes, if the woman was divorced before consummation with no fixed *mahr*	Yes, if husband initiated divorce, except for women with fixed *mahr* divorced prior to consummation	

[10] Ibn Rushd (n 3) 75.
[11] ibid 101.
[12] Kecia Ali, 'Marriage in Classical Islamic Jurisprudence: A Survey of Doctrines' in A Quraishi and FE Vogel (eds), *The Islamic Marriage Contract: Case Studies in Islamic Family Law* (Cambridge MA, Islamic Legal Studies Program, Harvard Law School, 2008) 43, note 246.
[13] ibid.
[14] Ibn Rushd (n 3) 101.
[15] ibid 102.
[16] ibid 114.
[17] ibid 118.

II. Divorce for Women – *Khulah*

This is the woman's right to release herself from the marriage.

A. Qur'anic Verses Relating to *Khulah*

> Women have the same rights against their men as men have against them. (2:228)
>
> Divorce can happen twice, and [each time] wives either be kept on in an acceptable manner or released in a good way. It is not lawful for you to take back anything that you have given [your wives], except where both fear that they cannot maintain [the marriage] within the bounds set by God: if you [arbiters] suspect that the couple may not be able to do this, then there will be no blame on either of them if the woman opts to give something for her release. (2:229)
>
> If you fear a breach between the two, appoint an arbitrator from his people and an arbitrator from her people. If they both want to set things right, Allah will bring about reconciliation between them. Allah knows all, is well aware of everything. (4:35)

B. Hadith Relating to *Khulah*

Habiba bint Sahl, wife of Thabit ibn Qais, approached the Prophet wanting a divorce, as narrated by Ibn 'Abbas: 'Oh Messenger of Allah, I do not find anything wrong with him from the religious and moral points of view, but I detest disbelief after entering the folds of Islam'. The Messenger of Allah said, 'Will you return to him his orchard [that he had given to you]?'. She said, 'Yes'. The Messenger of Allah said [to Thabit], 'Accept the orchard and divorce her through a single repudiation'.[18]

C. Differing Juristic Opinions on Common Issues around *Khulah*

i. Hadith Relating to Khulah

Habiba bint Sahl, wife of Thabit ibn Qais, approached the Prophet wanting a divorce, as narrated by Ibn 'Abbas: 'Oh Messenger of Allah, I do not find anything wrong with him from the religious and moral points of view, but I detest disbelief

[18] Badr Al-Din Al-Aini, *Umdat al-Qari Sharah Sahih al-Bukhari, Vol. 20* (Dar Ehiya al- Tourath al – Arabi, Beirut 2018) 262–63; Ibn Rushd (n 3) II, 79. Anne Sofie Roald notes that the term 'khul'' was not used by the Prophet in this hadith, and was probably coined by later jurists and hadith scholars such as Imam Ahmad ibn Hanbal and Bukhari. AS Roald, *Women in Islam: The Western Experience* (Abingdon, Routledge, 2001) 218.

after entering the folds of Islam'. The Messenger of Allah said, 'Will you return to him his orchard [that he had given to you]?'. She said, 'Yes'. The Messenger of Allah said [to Thabit], 'Accept the orchard and divorce her through a single repudiation'.[19]

ii. *Differing Juristic Opinions on Common Issues Around* Khulah

	Shafi'i	**Maliki**	**Hanafi**	**Hanbali**
Does *khulah* require the husband's consent?[20]	Yes	Unclear, they categorise *khulah* under Quranic verse 4:35, whereby the court or the arbitrators' decision shall be binding without requiring the consent of the husband or the wife[21]	Yes	Some say yes, some say no[22]
How much does the wife pay as compensation for *khulah*?[23]	When she is the cause of the divorce, she can pay more than the *mahr*, if not, an equivalent amount or less	When she is the cause of the divorce, she can pay more than the *mahr*, if not, an equivalent amount or less	Wife must consent to giving more than the *mahr*, husband must consent to accepting less than the *mahr*[24]	Husband taking more than amount of the *mahr* is reprehensible[25]
Is *khulah* irrevocable?[26]	No	Yes	Yes, akin to a single irrevocable *talaq*[27]	No

[19] Al-Din Al-Aini (n 18) 262–63; Ibn Rushd (n 3) II, 79. Anne Sofie Roald notes that the term 'khul'' was not used by the Prophet in this hadith, and was probably coined by later jurists and hadith scholars such as Imam Ahmad ibn Hanbal and Bukhari. Roald (n 18) 218.

[20] Ibn Rushd (n 3) 81.

[21] Muhammad Munir, 'The Law of Khul' in Islamic Law and the Legal System of Pakistan' (2015) 2 *LUMS Law Journal* 33, 39.

[22] ibid 50.

[23] Ibn Rushd (n 3) 79.

[24] Munir (n 21) 44.

[25] ibid 50.

[26] ibid.

[27] ibid 44.

III. Divorce for Women – Judicial Divorce (*Tafriq* or *Faskh*)

In this type of divorce the marriage is dissolved by a religious court, usually because the husband has committed a wrong, including mistreatment of the wife.

A. Qu'ranic Verses on *Tafriq/Faskh*

> And when you divorce women and they have [nearly] fulfilled their term, either retain them according to acceptable terms or release them according to acceptable terms, and do not keep them, intending harm, to transgress [against them]. And whoever does that has certainly wronged himself. And do not take the verses of Allah in jest. And remember the favor of Allah upon you and what has been revealed to you of the Book and wisdom by which He instructs you. And fear Allah and know that Allah is Knowing of all things. (2:231)
>
> If you fear a breach between the two, appoint an arbitrator from his people and an arbitrator from her people. If they both want to set things right, Allah will bring about reconciliation between them. Allah knows all, is well aware of everything. (4:35)

B. Differing Juristic Opinions on Common Issues Relating to *Tafriq/Faskh*

	Shafi'i	**Maliki**	**Hanafi**	**Hanbali**
Grounds for judicial divorce	Non-provision of maintenance after three days	Defects of husband, non-provision of maintenance, absence of husband for more than a year, harm or injury suffered by wife[28]	Impotence of husband, husband's absence for 90 years, wife exercises option of puberty[29]	Breach of conditions in the contract, sexual dysfunction, insanity, leprosy, incest[30]

[28] Ron Shaham, 'Judicial Divorce at the Wife's Initiative: The Sharia Courts of Egypt, 1920–1955' (1994) 2 *Islamic Law and Society* 222, 223–26.

[29] J Rehman, 'The Sharia, Islamic Family Laws and International Human Rights Law: Examining the Theory and Practice of Polygamy and Talaq' (2007) 21(1) *Int J Law Policy Family* 118.

[30] S Sabiq, *Fiqh us Sunnah* (Scotts Valley CA, Createspace Independent Publishing Platform, 2017); Al-Suyuti al-Rahbani, *Matalib uwli al-Nuha fi Sharah Ghayat al-Muntahaa* (Islamic Office Lebanon, 1994) 5/206; Ibn Qudamah al-Maqdisi, *Al-Mughni* (Cairo Library Egypt, 1968); Ibn Qudamah al-Maqdisi, *Al-Kaafi fi Fiqh al-Imam Ahmad Ibn Hanbal* (DKI Beirut, 1994) 3/42.

IV. Divorce for Women – *Talaq Tafweedh* and Other Stipulations

When the marriage contract contains a clause that gives the woman the right to effectuate a *talaq* divorce, delegated to her by her husband, this is known as *talaq tafweedh*.

A. Qu'ranic Verses Relating to *Talaq Tafweedh*

> O Prophet, say to your wives, 'If you should desire the worldly life and its adornment, then come, I will provide for you and give you a gracious release. But if you should desire Allah and His Messenger and the home of the Hereafter – then indeed, Allah has prepared for the doers of good among you a great reward'. (33:28–29)
>
> O you who believe, abide by your contracts. (5:1)
>
> And fulfil every engagement, for it will be enquired into. (27:34)

B. Hadith Relating to *Talaq Tafweedh*

Used to support the validity of stipulations in marriage contracts

> From among all the conditions which you have to fulfil, the conditions which make it legal for you to have sexual relations (marriage contracts) have the greatest rights to be fulfilled.[31]

Used to deny the validity of stipulations in marriage contracts.

> Any stipulation that is not in the book of Allah is invalid ...[32]

[31] Muhammad al-Bukhari, *Sahih Al-Bukhari Vol. 3 Book 50*, Hadith 882 <https://sunnah.com/bukhari/54/10>.
[32] Muhammad bin Yazid Ibn Majah al-Qazvini, *Sunan Ibn Majah Book 19*, Hadith 10 <https://sunnah.com/ibnmajah/19/10>.

C. Differing Juristic Opinions on Issues Around *Talaq Tafweedh*

	Shafi'i	Maliki	Hanafi	Hanbali
Can the wife exercise *talaq al-tafweedh* unconditionally or only on breach of conditions of the marriage contract?	Conditional, time limited[33]	The wife can exercise this type of divorce unconditionally[34]	The wife's right to exercise this type of divorce may be conditional or unconditional[35]	The wife can exercise this type of divorce unconditionally[36]
Does a *talaq al-tafweedh* constitute revocable or irrevocable divorce?[37]	Irrevocable	Irrevocable[38]	Can be revocable (if explicit) or irrevocable (if ambiguous) depending on the type of delegation granted to the wife, but is considered one *talaq*[39]	Irrevocable

[33] Al-Kasani, *Badaa'i Al-Sanayeh* (Cairo, DKI Beirut 1986) 51.

[34] Z Mir-Hosseini, 'The Delegated Right to Divorce: Law and Practice in Morocco and Iran,' in Lucy Carroll and Harsh Kapoor (eds), *Talaq-I-Tafwid: The Muslim Woman's Contractual Access to Divorce: An Information Kit* (London, Women Living Under Muslim Laws, 1996) 125.

[35] Muhammad Munir, 'Stipulations in a Muslim Marriage Contract with Special Reference to Talaq Al-Tafwid Provisions in Pakistan' (2005–06) 12 *Yearbook of Islamic and Middle Eastern Law* 235, 246.

[36] Ibn Qudamah, *Al-Moghni Vol. 7* (Cairo Library Egypt, 1968) 403.

[37] ibid 243.

[38] ibid 244.

[39] ibid 245.

Appendix G: Qatari Family Law Code

LAW NO. 22 of 2006 PROMULGATING 'THE FAMILY LAW' 22 / 2006

We, Hamad Bin Khalifa Al-Thani, Emir of the State of Qatar,

After perusal of the Constitution;

The Proposal of the Minister of Awqaf and Islamic Affairs;

The Draft Law submitted by the Council of Ministers; and

After taking the opinion of the Shura Council,

Have enacted the following Law:

…

Article 3

Unless provided by this Law, or otherwise decided by the Court, the prevailing view in the Hanbali School shall be followed. If no such prevailing opinion in the Hanbali School is to be found on a situation not specifically provided for in this Law, the judge may apply as deemed appropriate the views of the other four Sunni Schools. The judge can apply the general rules of jurisprudence in Islamic Sharia if all the above recourses, in the order stated above, are unable to reach a satisfactory outcome.

Article 4

This Law shall apply to those subjected to the Hanbali School of Thought. Others shall be subject to their provisions. Family matters of non-Muslim parties shall be subject to their own provisions. The provisions of this Law shall be applicable, in all cases, to those who request its application or are of different religions or schools.

This law shall apply to those subjected to the Hanbali School of Thought. Those subjected to other schools of thoughts and/or non-Muslim jurisprudence shall be subjected to provisions of their respective Schools of Thought and/or non-Muslim jurisprudence. The provisions of this law shall in all cases be applicable to those who request its application or are of different religions or schools.

BOOK TWO

Separation of Spouses

Part 1: General Provisions

Article 101

Separation between the spouses may be effected by:

1. By the decision of the husband and is termed divorce.
2. Agreement between the spouses, termed *Mukhala'h* or *khul'* or (redemptive divorce).
3. Judicial decree, termed *faskh* (rescission).
4. Death of one of the spouses.

Article 102

A Judge considering a separation claim shall take all provisional measures necessary to secure a temporary alimony for the wife together with Child support, custody and visitation rights.

Article 103

Judges may declare a couple separated on the ground of forbidden marriage, the conversion of the wife to Islam or the failure of one of the preconditions of the marriage contract, until passing judgment thereupon.

Article 104

If *khul'* (redemptive divorce) or separation is made with an agreed consideration paid by wife willingly, such consideration shall be satisfied before decreeing rescission or *khul'* (redemptive divorce).

Article 105

Rescission shall be considered dissolution of the marriage contract on the ground of a defect associated with its conclusion or subsequent intervention with the effect of preventing its continuance. Rescission shall be an irrevocable separation (*ba'in*), but shall not reduce the number of divorces. Every judicial separation shall be considered a rescission.

Part 2: Divorce

Article 106

Divorce, when expressed in the Islamic formula for divorce, shall be considered dissolution of a proper marriage contract.

Article 107

Divorce may take effect by:

1. Express pronouncement or writing, and in the case of inability to pronounce or write, by understandable gesture.
2. Metonymy (implication), if the husband intended divorce.

Article 108

Divorce may not take effect:

1. If it is equivocal or conditional, intended to pressure for doing or not doing something, or to believe or disbelieve in something.
2. For a wife who has consummated her marriage, during *Iddat* or menstruation cycle or during post-menstruation cleanness in which sexual intercourse occurred.
3. On breaking an oath to divorce or tahreem (to consider the wife as forbidden).
4. Repeating pronouncements of divorce or associating it with numbers, whether verbally, in writing or by gesture, shall be considered but only one divorce.

Article 109

Divorce may be effected by the husband personally or his agent having a special power of attorney to that effect, or by the wife if the husband gave her such power.

Article 110

For a divorcer to effect divorce, he must be of sound mind and act of his own free will.

Divorce by an insane person, by a person under an intellectual disability, by a person under duress, or by a person who lacks comprehension because of intoxication, anger or otherwise, shall have no effect.

Article 111

Divorce may be revocable and irrevocable:

1. A revocable divorce shall not end the marriage contract until expiration of the *Iddat* waiting period.
2. An irrevocable divorce shall end the marriage contract immediately on occurrence of the same. It shall be of two kinds in terms of effect:
3. Minor disunion or separation: The divorced woman may not remarry her ex-husband except by a new contract and dowry.
4. Major disunion or separation: The divorced woman may not remarry her ex-husband until after the expiry of her *Iddat* period by a second proper marriage actually consummated according to Sharia law.

Article 112

Every divorce shall be revocable except divorce for the third time, a divorce before consummation and a divorce stated in this Law to be irrevocable or rescinded.

Article 113

Divorce may occur by the husband formally pronouncing it before the Judge. Before ordering such pronouncement, the Judge shall attempt to reconcile between the parties.

A divorce occurring outside the court room shall be proved by Evidence or admission and shall have been communicated to the wife.

Article 114

After pronouncement of divorce, the Judge shall make an order as to the amount of alimony for the wife during her *Iddat*, Children support and the rights to Child custody and visitation. Such order shall have immediate enforceable effect.

Article 115

A divorced woman shall be entitled to enjoyment compensation if the divorce is made by the husband without any fault on her part.

A divorce for non-support due to insolvency of the husband shall be exempted from the provisions of the preceding paragraph.

Enjoyment compensation shall be assessed based on the wealth of the husband and the status of the wife and shall not exceed three Years of her alimony.

Article 116

A husband shall have the right to revoke the divorce and return to his divorcee before expiry of her *Iddat* if the divorce is revocable, and such right may not be waived.

Article 117

Revocation may occur by words or in writing and in the event of inability to speak, by understandable gestures. Revocation shall be notarized and immediately communicated to the wife.

<u>Part 3: Khul': (Redemptive Divorce)</u>

Article 118

Khul' (redemptive divorce) is a dissolution of a marriage contract by mutual consent of the husband and wife expressed in the word of *khul'* or its meaning, with consideration from the wife. It is not conditioned by post-menstruation cleanness. It shall be considered a rescission.

Article 119

For *khul'* to be valid, the wife must have the capacity to offer and give, and the husband to effect, divorce.

Article 120

Consideration for *khul'* may not be a waiver of Child custody or any Child right.

Article 121

Khul' shall be valid even where the consideration is invalid; such consideration shall be and void and the Judge shall assess the appropriate consideration.

Article 122

If the couple cannot agree on *khul* (redemptive divorce), the Court shall attempt to reconcile between them by appointing two arbitrators to conduct reconciliation within a period not exceeding six Months. If the two arbitrators cannot reach a settlement, and the wife demands *khul'* for consideration of waiving all her financial legal rights and refund of the dowry money, the Court shall order the separation between them.

Part 4: Separation by Judicial Decree

Chapter One: Separation on the ground of Defect or Illness

Article 123

Each of the spouses may request separation on the ground of a defect or chronic illness which makes marital life impossible to continue, and for which there is no cure or for which a cure can be hoped for only after an elapse of more than one Year, whether such illness is mental or physical and whether contracted before or after the marriage contract.

Article 124

The right to request separation on the ground of defect or chronic illness shall lapse if the defect or chronic illness was made known before the marriage contract, or expressly accepted after it.

Article 125

Notwithstanding the provisions of the preceding Article, the wife's right to request separation because of the husband's defects such as impotency or castration, whether congenital or accidental, shall not lapse even if she explicitly accepts such defects.

Article 126

If, by medical checkup, it is proved that impotency is incapable of being cured or that a cure can be hoped for only after an elapse of more than one Year, the Court shall separate the spouses upon the request of the wife without adjourning the decision of the claim. The court has the right to postpone divorce proceeding for a year if it can be proven that impotency can be treated in less than a year. If after adjourning the decision of divorce, it is proven that the husband has been cured; the divorce claim shall be rejected. In case of insistence the court shall separate the spouses.

Article 127

To identify defects or illnesses, the Court shall consult experienced medical experts.

Chapter Two: Separation on the ground of Not Settling Due Dowry

Article 128

A wife who has not consummated her marriage shall be granted a separation decree for not settling her due dowry in the following two cases:

1. If the husband has no ostensible property to settle the dowry.
2. If the husband's insolvency is apparent or his financial status is unknown and the period fixed by the Court expired without settling the dowry.

No separation decree shall be made for failure to settle the due dowry to a wife after consummation of marriage and the dowry shall remain a debt of the husband to be paid to the wife.

Chapter Three: Separation on the ground of Detriment (Dharar) and Breach (Shiqaq)

Article 129

The wife, before or after consummation of marriage, shall have the right to request separation on the ground of detriment which makes marital life impossible to continue for her like. The Judge shall attempt to reconcile between the spouses.

If reconciliation cannot be achieved and detriment is proved, separation shall be decreed. Detriment may be proved by Evidence including hearsay testimony.

Article 130

If detriment is not proved and breaches between the spouses continue while reconciliation by the Judge cannot be achieved, the Judge shall appoint two arbitrators from their respective relatives who are likely to have the ability to reconcile between the couple; if there are no such arbitrators from their relatives, then appointment shall be from outside their families. The Judge shall decide the duration of the arbitration.

Article 131

The arbitrators shall seek the causes of marital breaches and attempt to reconcile the couple.

The arbitrators shall make a report to the Judge of their attempts and state to what extent each of the spouses has contributed to the breaches together with their opinion.

Article 132

The Judge may adopt the report of the two arbitrators if it complies with the provisions of the preceding Article, otherwise he shall appoint other arbitrators by a substantiated decision to start reconciliation afresh, or add a third arbitrator to join the existing two arbitrators.

Article 133

The Judge may decree separation based on the two arbitrators' report in cases where reconciliation cannot be achieved and breaches continue between the spouses. If the two arbitrators do not make their report and differences between the spouses are intensifying, he shall decree their separation.

Article 134

If the Judge is of the opinion that the separation of the spouses should be decreed and that the wife is largely or wholly to blame, he shall separate between them with property to be given by the wife as determined by the Judge after perusal of the two arbitrators' report. If the husband is largely or wholly to blame, or both are to blame or blame cannot be established, he shall separate between them without property to be given by one to the other.

Article 135

If the spouses agree to separate with consideration, but differ over the amount of such consideration, the Judge shall attempt to reconcile such difference. If the Judge cannot achieve reconciliation and the difference becomes intensified, he shall decree their separation upon consideration to be determined by him.

Article 136

If a wife requests separation before consummation of marriage, and offers her dowry and all property received and waives her financial rights, and the husband refuses to divorce her upon a reasonable justification, the Judge shall attempt to reconcile between them. If the Judge cannot achieve such reconciliation and the difference becomes intensified, he shall decree their separation upon the property offered by the wife.

Chapter Four: Separation on the ground of Non-Support and Insolvency

Article 137

If a wife requests separation on the ground of lack of spending on her by her present husband, who has no ostensible property, and refuses to spend, and claims insolvency and insists not to spend, their immediate separation shall be decreed.

Article 138

If a wife requests separation on the ground of lack of spending on her by her present husband, who has no ostensible property, and refuses to spend, and claims insolvency and proves it, the Judge shall grant him a respite period not exceeding three Months; if he does not spend on his wife thereafter, the Judge shall decree their separation.

Article 139

If a wife requests separation on the ground of lack of spending on her by her present husband who has no ostensible property, and refuses to spend, and claims insolvency, but he is unable to prove it, the Judge shall fix a period for him, of not exceeding one Month, during which to spend on his wife, otherwise they shall be separated thereafter.

Article 140

If a wife requests separation on the ground of lack of spending on her by her husband, who is absent in a known place at which he can be served notice, and he has no ostensible property or left her no property to spend from, the Judge shall grant him a period of four Months during which to spend on his wife, otherwise they shall be separated.

Article 141

If the wife requests separation on the ground of lack of spending on her by her husband, who is absent in an unknown place, and he has no ostensible property, and left her no property to spend from, the Judge shall decree their separation.

Article 142

Subject to the provisions of the preceding two Articles, the Judge shall decree separation between the spouses only after proving the claim and the wife taking the judicial oath that that her maintenance has not been satisfactory.

Chapter Five: Separation on the ground of Absence, Being Missing and Imprisonment

Article 143

A wife may request separation on the ground of the absence of her husband, whose domicile or place of residence is known, for a period of one Year or more, even if he has left property from which maintenance can be satisfied. The Judge shall fix a date for him not exceeding two Months cautioning him either to come back to live with her or transfer her to him or divorce her; otherwise their separation shall be decreed.

Article 144

A wife may request separation from her husband who is missing or absent in an unknown place for a period not less than one Year. The Judge shall decree their immediate separation without adjourning, even if the husband has property.

If the missing husband returns or it transpires that he is alive, he shall take his wife, unless she has consummated marriage with another husband without knowledge of the first husband still living, in which case she shall be the second husband's wife.

Article 145

If a husband is imprisoned by a final judgment for a period of not less than two Years, the wife may request separation. However, separation may be decreed only after the elapse of one Year from the date of imprisonment.

Chapter Six: Separation on the grounds of Ilaa, Zihar, Liaan, Apostasy, and the Wife Converting to Islam

Section 1: Separation on the ground of Ilaa (Temporary Desertion)

Article 146

Ilaa occurs when the husband makes an oath to cease copulation with his wife permanently or for a period of time with a minimum four months.

Article 147

A wife may request separation on the ground of Ilaa, unless the husband breaks his oath before the elapse of four Months after Ilaa.

The Judge shall order the husband to either break his oath or divorce her; if he refuses, separation shall be decreed.

Section 2: Separation on the ground of Zihar (Permanent Desertion)

Article 148

Zihar occurs when a husband compares his wife and/or her body parts to that of another woman forbidden to him to marry.

Article 149

Zihar must be made by express articulation, not by implication, unless the husband has intended it or there is circumstantial Evidence pointing thereto.

Article 150

A wife shall be entitled to request separation on the ground of *Zihar* if the husband refuses expatiation. The Judge shall caution him to expatiate for *Zihar* within four Months from the date of such cautioning; if he refuses, separation shall be decreed.

Section 3: Separation on the ground of Liaan (Mutual Cursing)

Article 151

Li'aan shall occur by a husband testifying four times, swearing by Allah that his accusation of his wife of adultery or his denial of parentage is true and a fifth testimony that the curse of Allah shall be upon him if his accusation is false.

And the wife shall testify four times, swearing by Allah that his accusation of her of adultery or his denial of parentage is false and a fifth testimony that the wrath of Allah shall be upon her if his accusation is true.

Article 152

After completing *Li'aan*, the Judge shall decree the absolute separation between the spouses.

Section 4: Separation on the ground of Apostasy

Article 153

Separation shall occur between the spouses immediately upon one of them or both turning apostate if such apostasy occurred before consummation of marriage.

Article 154

The Judge shall separate between the spouses on apostasy of one of them after consummation of marriage after giving them time to repent and come back to Islam within a period the same as the waiting period of *Iddat*; if no such repentance occurs, he shall decree their separation.

Section 5: Separation on the ground of the Wife Converting to Islam

Article 155

If a wife, whose husband is not a Muslim, converts to Islam before or after consummation of marriage, the Judge shall give the husband time to convert to Islam within a period the same as the waiting period of *Iddat*; if no such conversion occurs, he shall decree their separation.

If spouses convert to Islam or the husband converts to Islam and the wife is Christian or Jewish, there being no forbidding causes between them, their marriage shall remain valid.

BIBLIOGRAPHY

Books, Journals, Reports

Aftab, A, 'Religious Accommodation in the Secular State: The Sharia Debates in Australia, Canada, and the United Kingdom' (2019) 79 *Studies in Law, Politics, and Society* 85

Ahmad, Nehaluddin, 'A Critical Appraisal of "Triple Divorce" in Islamic Law' (2009) 23 *International Journal of Law, Policy and the Family* 53

Ahmed, F, *Religious Freedom under Personal Law System* (Oxford, Oxford University Press, 2016)

—— 'Remedying Personal Law Systems' (2016) 30 *International Journal of Law, Policy and the Family* 248

Ahmed, F and Norton, JC, 'Religious Tribunals, Religious Freedom, and Concern for Vulnerable Women' (2012) 24 *Child and Family Law Quarterly* 383

Akhtar, RC, *British Muslims and Transformative Processes of the Islamic Legal Traditions: Negotiating Law, Culture and Religion with Specific References to Islamic Family Law and Faith Based Alternative Dispute Resolution* (PhD, University of Warwick 2013)

—— 'Non-legally Binding Muslim Marriages in England and Qatar: Circumventing the State' (2020) 8(1) *Electronic Journal of Islamic and Middle Eastern Law* 20

Al-Azri, Khalid, 'One or Three? Exploring the Scholarly Conflict over the Question of Triple Talaq (Divorce) in Islamic Law with Particular Emphasis on Oman' (2011) 25(3) *Arab Law Quarterly* 277

Al-Dhahabi, Muhammad ibn Ahmad, *Tarikh al-Islam Vol. 7* (Beirut, Dar al-Gharb al-Islami, 2003)

al-Ghazali, Abu Hamed, *Al-Wasit fi al-Mudhhab* (Cairo, Darussalam, 1996)

Al-Haddad, SH, 'Fatwa: A Civil Divorce Is Not a Valid Islamic Divorce' (2010) *Islam21c*: <www.islam21c.com/fataawa/912-fatwa-a-civil-divorce-is-not-a-valid-islamic-divorce/>

Al-Hasan al-Mawardi, A, *Al-Ahkam al-Sultania w'al-Wilayat al-Diniyya (Royal Rulings)* (Cairo, Dar al-Hadith Cairo, 2006)

al-Jadd, Ibn Rush, *Al-Muqaddimat al-Mumahhidat (Preludes)* (Beirut, Dar al-Gharb al-Islami, 1988)

Al-Kasani, *Badaa'i Al-Sanayeh* (Cairo, DKI Beirut, 1986)

al-Marghinani, Burhan al-Din, *Al-Hidayah Sharah Bidayat al-Mubtadi* (Beirut, Dar I'hya' al-Turath al-Arabi, 1996)

al-Mawardi, Abu al-Hasan, *Al-Ahkam al-Sultania w'al-Wilayat al-Diniyya (Royal Rulings)* (Cairo, Dar al-Hadith, 2006)

Ali, AY, *The Holy Qu'ran* (Ware, Wordsworth Editions Ltd, 2001)

Ali, K, 'Marriage in Classical Islamic Jurisprudence: A Survey of Doctrines' in A Quraishi and FE Vogel (eds), *The Islamic Marriage Contract: Case Studies in Islamic Family Law* (Islamic Legal Studies Program, Harvard Law School 2008)

Ali, SM, 'Why Was the Institute Formed?' <www.muslimcanada.org/sufi/mumtaz.htm?> accessed 1 November 2020

Armstrong, S, *Encouraging Conversations About Culture: Supporting Culturally Responsive Family Dispute Resolution* – A Report for Family Relationship Centres at Bankstown managed by CatholicCare Sydney and Parramatta managed by Anglicare Sydney; also available as Armstrong, S, 'Encouraging Conversations about Culture: Supporting culturally responsive family dispute resolution' (2011) 17(3) *Journal of Family Studies* 233

—— *Enhancing Access to Family Dispute Resolution for Families from Culturally and Linguistically Diverse Backgrounds* (Australian Family Relationships Clearinghouse Briefing Paper, 18 April 2011)

Armstrong, S, Bruce, P and Butler, R, 'Culturally Reflexive Family Dispute Resolution: An Initiative of Anglicare and CatholicCare' (Paper presented at the Fourth National ADR Research Forum, Brisbane, 16–17 July 2010)

Aroney, N and Ahdar, R, 'The Accommodation of the Shari'a within Western Legal Systems' (2012) 13 *Rutgers Journal of Law and Religion* 387

Australian Bureau of Statistics, *Religion in Australia: 2016 Census Data Summary* (28 June 2017) <www.abs.gov.au/ausstats/abs@.nsf/Lookup/by%20Subject/2071.0~2016~Main%20Features~Religion%20Data%20Summary~70>

Badr Al-Din Al-Aini, *Umdat al-Qari Sharah Sahih al-Bukhari, Vol. 20* (Dar Ehiya al- Tourath al – Arabi, Beirut, 2018)

Bailey, RJ, 'Principles of Property Distribution on Divorce – Compensation, Need or Community' (1980) 54 *Australian Law Journal* 190

Bakht, N, 'Family Arbitration Using Sharia Law: Examining Ontario's Arbitration Act and its Impact on Women' (2004) 1 *Muslim World Journal of Human Rights* 1

Bano, S, 'Islamic Family Arbitration, Justice and Human Rights in Britain' (2007) 1 *Law, Social Justice and Global Development Journal* 15

—— 'In Pursuit of Religious and Legal Diversity: A Response to the Archbishop of Canterbury and the "Sharia Debate" in Britain' (2008) 10 *Ecclesiastical Law Journal* 283

—— 'An Exploratory Study of Shariah Councils in England With Respect to Family Law' (Centre for Islamic and Middle Eastern Law, University of Reading 2012)

—— *Muslim Women and Shari'ah Councils: Transcending the Boundaries of Community and Laws* (Basingstoke, Palgrave Macmillan, 2012)

Bano, S (ed), *Gender and Justice in Islamic Law Disputes, Women, Mediation and Religious Arbitration* (Waltham MA, Brandeis University Press, 2017)

Barnett, K, '*Thorne v Kennedy*: A Thorn in the Side of "Binding Financial Agreements"?' (2018) 31 *Australian Journal of Family Law* 183

Berkovic, N, 'Hyder Gulam Calls for Australia to Embrace Legal Pluralism', *The Australian*, 28 September 2012

Bhatti, M, 'What Is Islamic Dispute Resolution and Why Is It Controversial in Australia?', *The Conversation*, 7 February 2019 <www.theconversation.com/what-is-islamic-dispute-resolution-and-why-is-it-controversial-in-australia-110497>

Bibby, P, 'Muslim Leader Wants Elements of Sharia in Australia', *The Sydney Morning Herald*, 8 March 2020 <www.smh.com.au/national/muslim-leader-wants-elements-of-sharia-in-australia-20100307-pqlo.html>

Birmingham Central Mosque, 'Birmingham Sharia Council' <https://centralmosque.org.uk/wp-content/uploads/2019/03/Birmingham-Shariah-Council-Prospectus-March-2019.pdf>

Black, A, 'Legal Recognition of Sharia Law: Is This the Right Direction for Family Law Matters?' (2010) 84 *Family Matters* 65

Bowen, JR, 'Private Arrangements: "Recognizing Sharia" in England', *Boston Review*, 1 March 2009, <www.bostonreview.net/john-bowen-private-arrangements-sharia-England>

—— 'How Could English Courts Recognize Shariah?' (2010) 7(3) *University of St Thomas Law Journal* 411

—— *On British Islam: Religion, Law, and Everyday Practice in Shari'a Councils* (Princeton NJ, Princeton University Press, 2016)

Boyd, M, 'Dispute Resolution in Family Law: Protecting Choice, Promoting Inclusion' (Ministry of the Attorney General 2004) <www.attorneygeneral.jus.gov.on.ca/english/about/pubs/boyd>

Brannick, T and Coghlan, D, 'In Defense of Being "Native": The Case for Insider Academic Research' (2007) 10 *Organizational Research Methods* 59

Brennan, G, 'Lessons from a Life in the Law' – Hal Wootten Lecture (UNSW 23 August 2012) <www.law.unsw.edu.au/sites/default/files/imce/files/wootten/hal_wootten_lecture_-_sir_gerard_brennan_0.pdf>

Brierley, C, 'Claims Arising Out of Binding Financial Agreements' (2011) 222 *Ethos* 16

Buckley, A, *Not 'Completely' Divorced: Muslim Women in Australia Navigating Muslim Family Laws* (Melbourne, Melbourne University Publishing, 2019)

—— 'What Are Muslim Women's Options in Religious Divorce?', *ABC Religion & Ethics*, 6 March 2020 al-Marghinani, Burhan al-Din, *Al-Hidayah Sharah Bidayat al-Mubtadi* (Beirut, Dar I'hya' al-Turath al-Arabi, 1996)

Charmaz, K, 'Grounded Theory' in JA Smith, R Harré and L Van Langehove (eds), *Rethinking Methods in Psychology* (London, Sage Publications, 1995)

Charmaz, K and Belgrave, L, 'Qualitative Interviewing and Grounded Theory Analysis' in JF Gubrium et al (eds), *The Sage Handbook of Interview Research: The Complexity of the Craft* 2nd edn (London, Sage Publications, 2012)

Chiang, V, Keatinge, D and Williams, A, 'Challenges of Recruiting a Vulnerable Population in a Grounded Theory Study' (2001) 3 *Nursing and Health Sciences* 205

Choudhury, C, '(Mis)Appropriated Liberty: Identity, Gender Justice and Muslim Personal Law Reform in India', (2007) Georgetown Public Law Research Paper, <http://ssrn.com/abstract=969020>

Clarke, T, '"Over-Researched Here!": Exploring Accounts of Research Fatigue within Qualitative Research Engagements' (2008) 42(5) *Sociology* 953

Cutting, C, 'Faith-Based Arbitration or Religious Divorce: What Was the Issue?' in AC Korteweg and JA Selby (eds), *Debating Sharia: Islam, Gender Politics, and Family Law Arbitration* (Toronto, University of Toronto Press, 2012)

—— 'Sharia and Constraint: Practices, Policies, and Responses to Faith-Based Arbitration in Ontario' (Waterloo, UWSpace 2013)

Dalph Grillo, R, *Muslim Families, Politics and the Law: A Legal Industry in Multicultural Britain* (Farnham, Ashgate, 2015)

Dekker, K, Brouwer, W and Colic-Peisker, V, *Suburbs with a Higher Concentration of Muslim Residents in Sydney and Melbourne: Spatial Concentration, Community, Liveability and Satisfaction* (Melbourne, RMIT, Social and Global Studies Centre 2019)

Douglas, G et al, *Social Cohesion and Civil Law: Marriage, Divorce and Religious Courts* (Cardiff, Cardiff University, 2011)

Edwards, M, 'Aust Imams Recommend Muslim Clerics Preach in English', *ABC Local Radio*, 18 September 2006 <www.abc.net.au/am/content/2006/s1743077.htm>

El Shamsy, A and Coulson, NJ, 'Sharīʿah', *Encyclopædia Britannica*, 25 August 2020 <www.britannica.com/topic/Shariah>

Engineer, AA, 'Is Sharia Immutable?', *Dawn*, 1 February 2003 <www.dawn.com/news/782766/is-sharia-immutable>

Emon, A, 'Islamic Law and the Canadian Mosaic: Politics, Jurisprudence, and Multicultural Accommodation' (2009) 37 *Canadian Bar Review* 391

European Council for Fatwa and Research, 'The European Council for Fatwa and Research: Renewed Leadership, Renewed Hopes' <www.e-cfr.org/blog/2018/12/16/european-council-fatwa-research/>

Family Law Council (2012) *Improving the Family Law System for Clients from Culturally and Linguistically Diverse Backgrounds*

Farrar, S and Krayem, G, *Accommodating Muslims under Common Law: A Comparative Analysis* (Abingdon, Routledge, 2017)

Fehlberg, B and Millward, C, 'Post-Separation Parenting and Financial Arrangements Over Time: Recent Qualitative Findings' (2013) 92 *Family Matters* 29

—— 'Family Violence and Financial Outcomes after Parental Separation' in A Hayes and D Higgins (eds), *Families, Policy and the Law: Selected Essays on Contemporary Issues for Australia* (Melbourne, Australian Institute of Family Studies, 2014) 240

Fehlberg, B and Smyth, B, 'Binding Pre-Nuptial Agreements in Australia: The First Year' (2002) 16 *International Journal of Law, Policy and the Family* 127

Forrest, J, 'Suburbs "Swamped" by Asians and Muslims? The Data Show a Different Story', *The Conversation*, 5 July 2017 <https://theconversation.com/suburbs-swamped-by-asians-and-muslims-the-data-show-a-different-story-79250>

Fournier, P, 'Please Divorce Me! Subversive Agency, Resistance and Gendered Religious Scripts' in E Giunchi (ed), *Muslim Family Law in Western Courts* (Abingdon, Routledge, 2014)

Glaser, BG and Strauss, AL, *The Discovery of Grounded Theory* 7th edn (Piscataway NJ, Aldine Transactions, 2012)
Gleeson, H and Baird, J, '"Now Is the Time for Change": Politicians and Advocates Call for an Urgent Review of the Islamic Divorce Process', *ABC News*, 19 April 2018
Gleeson, H, Baird, J and Malik, S, '"I'm Not His Property": Abused Muslim Women Denied Right to Divorce', *ABC News*, 18 April 2018
Gohir, S and Akhtar-Sheikh, N, 'British Muslim Women and Barriers to Obtaining a Religious Divorce' in S Bano (ed), *Gender and Justice in Family Law Disputes: Women, Mediation, and Religious Arbitration* (Waltham MA, Brandeis University Press, 2017)
Griffith, A, 'Insider/Outsider: Epistemological Privilege and Mothering Work' (1998) 21 *Human Studies* 361
Griffith-Jones, R, *Islam and English Law: Rights, Responsibilities and the Place of Shari'a* (Cambridge University Press 2013)
Hanson, P, The Senate First Speech. Commonwealth of Australia Senate, 14 September 2016
Hole, J, 'Muslim Group Wants Sharia Law in Australia', *ABC News*, 17 May 2011
House of Representatives Standing Committee on Legal and Constitutional Affairs, *To Have and To Hold: A Report of the Inquiry into Aspects of Family Services* (Canberra, 1998)
Ibn al-Asqalani H, *Fath al-Bari Vol. 13* (Beirut, Marefah, 1959)
Ibn Arafah Al-Dusuqi, *Hashiyat Al-Dusuqi 'Ala Al-Sharh Al-Kabir* (Beirut, Dar el Fikr, 2011)
Ibn Hazm, *Al-Muhallā bi'l Athār* (Beirut, Dar el Fikr, 2015)
Ibn Qudamah, *Al-Moghni Vol. 7* (Cairo, Cairo Library Egypt, 1968)
Ibn Rushd, *The Distinguished Jurist's Primer (Bidayat Al-Mujtahid Wa Nihayat Al-Muqtasid)*. Translated by Professor Imran Ahsan Khan Nyazee. Vol. II (Reading, Garnet Publishing Limited, 1996)
Immigration and Refugee Board of Canada, *Canada: Information on the Procedures for Securing a Divorce in Islam in Canada, on Whether These Procedures Are Uniform throughout Canada, and on Whether a Record of the Divorce Would Be Kept at a Mosque if the Divorce Took Place in Canada* (1 May 1997) <www.refworld.org/docid/3ae6acf360.html>
Jamal, Sulayman ibn `Umar, *Hashiat al-Jamal ala Sharah al-Minahaj* (Beirut, Dar al-kotob al ilmiyah, 2013)
Jaraba, M, 'The Practice of *Khul*ʿ in Germany: Pragmatism versus Conservatism' (2019) 26 *Islamic Law and Society* 83
Jobani, Y and Perez, N, *Women of the Wall: Navigating Religion in Sacred Sites* (Oxford, Oxford University Press, 2017)
Kaspiew, R et al, *Evaluation of the 2006 Family Law Reforms* (Australian Institute of Family Studies, December 2009)
Koen, J, Wassenaar, D and Mamotte, N, 'The "Over-Researched Community": An Ethics Analysis of Stakeholders Views at Two South African HIV Prevention Research Sites' (2017) 194 *Social Science and Medicine* 1
Korteweg, AC, 'The Sharia Debate in Ontario: Gender, Islam, and Representations of Muslim Women's Agency' (2006) 18 *ISIM Review* 50
Krayem, G, 'Australian Muslim Women: Skilful Legal Navigators in a Plural World' in A Saeed and H McCue (eds), *Family Law and Australian Muslim Women* (Melbourne, Melbourne University Press, 2013)
—— *Islamic Family Law in Australia: To Recognise or Not to Recognise* (Melbourne, Melbourne University Publishing, 2014)
Krayem, G and Ahmed, F, 'Islamic Community Processes in Australia: An Introduction' in S Bano (ed), *Gender and Justice in Family Law Disputes: Women, Mediation, and Religious Arbitration* (Waltham MA, Brandeis University Press, 2017)
Larsen, L, *How Muftis Think: Islamic Legal Thought and Muslim Women in Western* Europe (Leiden, Brill, 2018)
MacEoin, D and Green, DG, *Sharia Law or 'One Law for All'*? (London, CIVITAS: Institute for the Study of Civil Society 2009)

Macfarlane, J, *Islamic Divorce in North America: A Shari'a Path in a Secular Society* (Oxford, Oxford University Press, 2012)

—— 'Practising an "Islamic Imagination": Islamic Divorce in North America' in AC Korteweg and JA Selby (eds), *Debating Sharia: Islam, Gender Politics, and Family Law Arbitration* (Toronto, University of Toronto Press, 2012)

—— *Understanding Trends in American Muslim Divorce and Marriage: A Discussion Guide for Families and Communities* (Dearborn MI, Institute for Social Policy and Understanding, 2012)

Macklin, A, 'Multiculturalism Meets Privatization: The Case of Faith-Based Arbitration' (2013) 9 *International Journal of Law in Context* 343

Martin, VB et al, 'What Is Grounded Theory Good For?' (2018) 95 *Journalism and Mass Communication Quarterly* 11

McMahon, M and McGorrery, P, 'Criminalising Controlling and Coercive Behaviour: The Next Step in the Prosecution of Family Violence?' (2016) 4(2) *Alternative Law Journal* 98

Mendecka, K, 'Sharia Councils in Western Society: Compromise or Surrender (With Particular Reference to the United Kingdom)' (4th International Conference of PhD Students and Young Researchers, Interdisciplinary Approach to Law in Modern Social Context, 21–22 April 2016) <www.tf.vu.lt/wp-content/uploads/2016/04/Interdisciplinary-Approach-to-Law-in-Modern-Social-Context_Pranešimų-rinkinys.pdf>

Mir-Hosseini, Z, 'The Delegated Right to Divorce: Law and Practice in Morocco and Iran' in L Carroll and H Kapoor (eds), *Talaq-I-Tafwid: The Muslim Woman's Contractual Access to Divorce: An Information Kit* (London, Women Living Under Muslim Laws, 1996)

Mnookin, RH and Kornhauser, L, 'Bargaining in the Shadow of the Law: The Case of Divorce' (1979) 88 *Yale Law Journal* 950

Munir, M, 'The Law of Khul' in Islamic Law and the Legal System of Pakistan' (2015) 2 *LUMS Law Journal* 33

—— 'Stipulations in a Muslim Marriage Contract with Special Reference to Talaq Al-Tafwid Provisions in Pakistan' (2005–06) 12 *Yearbook of Islamic and Middle Eastern Law* 235

Nakamura, H, *Conditional Divorce in Indonesia* (Cambridge MA, Islamic Studies Legal Program, Harvard Law School, 2006)

Nik Badli Shah, Nik Noriani, 'Legislative Provisions and Judicial Mechanisms for the Enforcement and Termination of the Islamic Marriage Contract in Malaysia' in Asifa Quraishi and Frank E Vogel (eds) *The Islamic Marriage Contract: Case Studies in Islamic Family Law* (Cambridge MA, Islamic Legal Studies Program, Harvard Law School, 2008)

Ozalp, M, 'Do Australian Muslims want Shari'ah Law in Australia?' (2012) 221(3) *St Mark's Review* 66

Parveen, R, 'Do Sharia Councils Meet the Needs of Muslim Women?' in S Bano (ed), *Gender and Justice in Family Law Disputes: Women, Mediation, and Religious Arbitration* (Waltham MA, Brandeis University Press 2017)

Patel, P, 'Faith in the State? Asian Women's Struggles for Human Rights in the U.K.' (2008) 16 *Feminist Legal Studies* 9

Pearl, D and Menski, W, *Muslim Family* Law 3rd edn (London, Sweet & Maxwell, 1998)

Poynting, S and Briskman, L, 'Islamophobia in Australia: From Far-Right Deplorables to Respectable Liberals' (2018) 7 *Social Sciences* 213

Rahman, F, 'A Survey of Modernization of Muslim Family Law' (1980) 11(4) *International Journal of Middle East Studies* 451

Razack, S, 'The Sharia Law Debate in Ontario: The Modernity/Premodernity Distinction in Legal Efforts to Protect Women from Culture' (2007) 15 *Feminist Legal Studies* 3

Réaume, D, 'Justice Between Cultures: Autonomy and the Protection of Cultural Affiliation' 29 (1995) *University of British Columbia Law Review* 117

Redding, J, 'Human Rights and Homo-Sectuals: The International Politics of Sexuality, Religion, and Law' (2006) 4 *Northwestern University Journal of International Human Rights* 436

Rehman, J, 'The Sharia, Islamic Family Laws and International Human Rights Law: Examining the Theory and Practice of Polygamy and Talaq' (2007) 21(1) *International Journal Law Policy Family* 108

Roald, AS, *Women in Islam: The Western Experience* (Abingdon, Routledge, 2001)

Sandberg, R et al, 'Britain's Religious Tribunals: "Joint Governance" in Practice' (2013) 33 *Oxford Journal of Legal Studies* 263

Saris, A, 'Challenging Stereotypes: Gender-Sensitive Imams and the Resolution of Family Disputes Law in Canada Montreal' in F Banda and LF Joffe (eds), *Women's Rights and Religious Law* (Abingdon, Routledge, 2016) 257

Schofield King Lawyers, 'Intersections between the Law, Religion and Human Rights Project' (January 2011) <www.humanrights.gov.au/our-work/intersections-between-law-religion-and-human-rights-project-literature-review-prepared>

Secretary of State for the Home Department, *The Independent Review into the Application of Sharia Law in England and Wales* (February 2018)

Sezgin, Y, *Human Rights under State-Enforced Religious Family Laws in Israel, Egypt, and India* (Cambridge, Cambridge University Press, 2013)

Shachar, A, *Multicultural Jurisdictions: Cultural Differences and Women's Rights* (Cambridge, Cambridge University Press, 2001)

—— 'Privatizing Diversity: A Cautionary Tale From Religious Arbitration in Family Law' (2008) 9 *Theoretical Inquiries in Law* 573

Shah-Kazemi, SN, *Untying the Knot: Muslim Women, Divorce, and the Shariah* (Signal Press 2001) <www.nuffieldfoundation.org/project/untying-the-knot-muslim-women-divorce-and-the-shariah>

Shaham, R, 'Judicial Divorce at the Wife's Initiative: The Sharia Courts of Egypt, 1920–1955' (1994) 1(2) *Islamic Law and Society* 217

Siddiqui, M, Hutchinson, A-M, Momtaz, S and Sir Hedley, M, 'The Independent Review into the Application of Sharia Law in England and Wales' (Presented to Parliament by the Secretary of State for the Home Department by Command of Her Majesty, February 2018)

Sonbol, Amira El Azhary, 'A History of Marriage Contracts in Egypt' in Asifa Quraishi and Frank E Vogel (eds) *The Islamic Marriage Contract: Case Studies in Islamic Family Law* (Cambridge MA, Islamic Legal Studies Program, Harvard Law School 2008)

Sonneveld, N and Lindbekk, M, 'Introduction: A Historical Overview of Gender and Judicial Authority in the Muslim World' in N Sonneveld and M Lindbekk (eds), *Women Judges in the Muslim World: A Comparative Study of Discourse and Practice* (Leiden, Brill, 2017)

Sonneveld, N and Stiles, N, 'Khul': Local Contours of a Global Phenomenon' (2019) 26 *Islamic Law and Society* 1

Strauss, A and Corbin, J, 'Grounded Theory Methodology: An Overview' in NK Denzin and YS Lincoln (eds), *The SAGE Handbook of Qualitative Research* (London, Sage Publications, 1994)

Sisler, V, 'European Courts' Authority Contested? The Case of Marriage and Divorce Fatwas On-Line' (2009) 3 *Masaryk University Journal of Law and Technology* 51

Sukarieh, M and Tannock, S, 'On the Problem of Over-Researched Communities: The Case of the Shatila Palestinian Refugee Camp in Lebanon' (2012) 47 *Sociology* 494

The Islamic Shari'a Council, 'Prices' <www.islamic-sharia.org/services/prices/>

The Muslim Law Sharia Council UK, 'Khula (Divorce)' <www.shariahcouncil.org/khula-divorce/>

Tucker, JE, *Women, Family and Gender in Islamic Law* (Cambridge, Cambridge University Press, 2008)

Uddin, I, 'Islamic Family Law: Imams, Mosques, and Sharīʿa Councils in the UK (2020) 8 *Electronic Journal of Islamic and Middle Eastern Law* 25

—— '*Nikah*-only Marriages: Causes, Motivations, and Their Impact on Dispute Resolution and Islamic Divorce Proceedings in England and Wales' (2018) 7 *Oxford Journal of Law and Religion* 401

Unluer, S, 'Being an Insider Researcher While Conducting Case Study Research' (2012) 17 *Qualitative Report* 1

Urbis, 'Evaluation of the Family Relationships Services for Humanitarian Entrants Initiative' (Department for Families, Housing, Community Services and Indigenous Affairs 2007)

Victoria Legal Aid, Family Harmony sessions for the Newly Arrived Communities (April 2011)

Wade, J, 'The Perils of Prenuptial Financial Agreements: Effectiveness and Professional Negligence' (2012) 22 *Australian Family Lawyer* 24

Walker, T, *Shari'a Councils and Muslim Women in Britain: Rethinking the Role of Power and Authority* (Leiden, Brill, 2017)
Watts, G, 'Binding Financial Agreements: Possibilities and Pitfalls' (2001) 39 *Law Society Journal* 60
Williams, R, 'Civil and Religious Law in England: A Religious Perspective' (2008) 10 *Ecclesiastical Law Journal* 262
Women Living Under Muslim Laws, 'Knowing Our Rights: Women, Family, Laws and Customs in the Muslim World' (London, Women Living Under Muslim Laws, 2006)
Young, L and Goodie, J, 'Is There a Need for More Certainty in Discretionary Decision-Making in Australian Family Property Law?' (2018) 32 *Australian Journal of Family Law* 166
Zakaria al-Ansari, *Asnā al-Matalib fi Sharah Tareeq al-Talib Vol. 3* (dkislamiyah)

Cases

Indian Young Lawyers' Association v State of Kerala (2019) 11 SCC 1
Mohamed v Mohamed (2012) NSWSC 852
Thorne v Kennedy (2017) 263 CLR 85

Legislation

Family Law Act (1975) (Cth)
Family Law Amendment (Shared Responsibility Act) 2006 (Cth)

INDEX

NB – Page locators in *italics* refer to information in figures

accountability concerns, 4
acknowledgement of injustice:
lack of, 49–50, 107–8
Apprehended Violence Orders, 26, 42–43, 56
Australia:
Australian National Islamic Council, 23, 24, 28–30, *29*
Board of Imams Victoria, 24–27, *26*
Centre for Arbitration and Resolution Disputes, 24, 28–30, *29*
Lebanese Muslim Association, 24, 30–32, *31*
Australian Muslim Women's Centre for Human Rights (AUS), 117
Australian National Islamic Council (AUS), 23
Centre for Arbitration and Resolution Disputes, 24, 28–30, 79–80
child custody arrangements, 87
civil divorces, relationship with, 77
domestic violence policy, 66–67
gender representation, 69
property settlement, 87
referral to, 32–33, 71
sharia process, *29*
reform, 96
civil divorces, relationship with, 77, 119
clearer processes, 107
faskh more readily available, 106
intake processes, 99–101

best interests of the child, 58–59, 91–92, 94, 104–5
Board of Imams Victoria (AUS), 24–27, 79–80
child custody arrangements, 87
civil divorces, relationship with, 77, 119
divorce applications, 145–50
domestic violence policy, 66–61
gender representation, 69
marriage contract (example), 137–38
mediation/reconciliation application (example), 139–44
property settlement, 87
reform, 96
civil divorces, relationship with, 77, 119
clearer processes, 107
faskh more readily available, 106
intake processes, 99–101
sharia process, *26*

Canada:
sharia institutions:
Canadian Council of Muslim Theologians, 20
Canadian Council of Muslim Women, 20
Canadian Society of Muslims, 19
Darul Iftaa, 20–21
Institute of Islamic Civil Justice, 19
Institute of Islamic Civil Justice, 21
Islamic Social Services and Resources Association, 21
sharia procedures and practices:
civil v religious divorce, 21–23
variety, 21–22
Canadian Council of Muslim Theologians (CAN), 20
Canadian Council of Muslim Women (CAN), 20
Canadian Society of Muslims (CAN), 19
Centre for Arbitration and Resolution Disputes (AUS), *see* **Australian National Islamic Council**
child custody, 94–95
comparative law, 93–94
enforcement of sharia family law, 94
imams' advisory role, 13, 60, 80
best interests of the child, 91–92
child protection issues, 91–92
deference to state family law, 85–88, 127
fathers' right to *see* children, 91
mothers' role, 90–91
khulah divorces, 27
women's perspective, 92–93

child support, 79
iddah maintenance, 84
imams' advisory role, 84–85
mutah, 85
children, *see* **best interests of the child; child custody; child support**
choice:
khulah divorce, 73, 94
women's choice to engage with sharia processes, 1–2, 89
civil divorce, 5–6
'limping marriages', 20, 39, 70, 96
pre-religious divorce requirement, as a, 17, 18, 21–23, 30, 32, 76–78, 119, 127
recognition of, 59
religious divorce outcomes, impact on, 76–78
community mediation services, 21, 36–37
concerns surrounding sharia processes, 1–2
coercion of women, 2–3
discriminatory outcomes, 4
fairness, 4
response to family violence, 3
consent:
khulah, 5, 65, 73
talaq, 5, 77
talaq tafweedh, 75
cost of religious divorces, 23, 88–89
financial support, 116–17
United Kingdom, 18–19
counselling, 18, 25, 36, 112–13
imams, 44–45, 57–58
pre-marriage counselling, 97
cultural and linguistic diversity, 114–16, 129
recognition of, 121

Darul Iftaa (CAN), 20–21
deference to courts/state law, 14, 70, 86, 95, 127
deferred *mahr*, 77, 78, 82, 154
discrimination, 4, 127–28
divorce, *see* **civil divorce; religious divorce**
domestic violence, 3
imams' lack of training, 46–49, 66–67
recognition of, 63–67, 108–11
referral to appropriate professionals, 110–11

education, 123
financial entitlement and outcomes, 105–6
enforcement:
post-separation orders, 120, 124, 126
sharia family law, 94, 95
European Council for Fatwa and Research, 23
expectations from sharia processes, 44, 49–50, 99–101

fairness, 4, 46, 51, 94, 107, 114–15, 118
civil courts, 114
financial agreements, 98
family law improvements:
cultural sensitivity, 121
education, 123
enforcement of post-separation orders, 120
integrated services (Muslim Family Relationship Centre), 122–24
legal aid, 120–21
legal recognition of *mahr*, 121–22, 124, 126
family mediation, *see* **mediation**
***faskh*,** 5, 72
domestic violence, 64–65
financial entitlements, 106
juristic opinions, 158
mutah, 79
outcomes, 74–75
Quranic verses, 158
***fatwa*:**
divorce:
equivalence of civil and religious divorce, 23
European Council for Fatwa and Research, 23
fatwa shopping, 52–53
***fatwa* shopping,** 52–53
financial agreements, 98–99
financial assistance, 114
financial entitlement and outcomes:
child support, 79
education about options, 105–6
financial agreements, 98–99
iddah, 78–79, 84
imams' advisory role, 79–80
child custody, 85–86
child support, 84–85
deference to state systems, 85–88
financial contribution, 82–83
iddah, 84
legal entitlements, 85–88
mahr, 81–82
mutah, 85
non-financial contribution, 83–84
property entitlement, 85–87
mahr, 78, 81–82
mutah, 79, 85
reclaimed financial contributions, 79

transparency, 105–6
women's experience of state system, 88–90
formality of sharia councils:
Australia, 23
Canada, 20, 22
United Kingdom, 15–16
forum shopping, *see fatwa* **shopping; imam shopping**

gender bias of religious divorce panels, 50–51
expectations from sharia processes, 99–101
imam recognition of, 67–68
improvement:
expectations from sharia processes, 99–101
female intake officers, 99–101
inclusion of professionals on panels, 104–5
inclusion of women on panels, 101–4
timelines and delays, 100–1

iddah, 78–79, 125
child support, 84
imams' advisory role, 80, 84–85
financial entitlement and outcomes, 78–79, 84
khulah, 79, 84–85
talaq divorces, 154, 155
imam shopping, 52–53
imams, 68–69
domestic violence, 46–49
inadequacy of response, 63–67
financial matters (advisory role), 79–80
child custody, 85–86
child support, 84–85
deference to state systems, 85–88
financial contribution, 82–83
iddah, 84
legal entitlements, 85–88
mahr, 81–82
mutah, 85
non-financial contribution, 83–84
property entitlement, 85–87
gender bias of religious divorce panels, 50–51
imam recognition of, 67–68
individuals, working as, 32–33
reconciliation:
imams' conflicting roles, 58
imams' perspective, 55–59
Quranic principles, 55–56
role in religious divorces:
advocates for women, 59–60
backlash, 60–61
service providers, as, 59–60
skills/training, lack of, 44–45
recognition of, 62–63
Institute of Islamic Civil Justice (CAN), 19, 21
integrated support services, 111–12, 116–17
counselling, 112–13
financial assistance, 114
food vouchers, 114
legal services, 114
mediation, 113
medical care, 114
other referrals, 114
proposal for Muslim Family Relationship Centre, 122–24
relationship support, 113
Islamic Sharia Council (UK), 16–17, 77, 93, 106
sharia processes, *17*
Islamic Social Services and Resources Association (CAN), 21, 22, 86

khulah, 5
child custody, 27
choice, 73, 94
consent, 5, 65, 73
cost, 18–19, 27
domestic violence, 64–65
education, 105–6
Hadith, 156–57
iddah, 79, 84–85
juristic opinions, 157
mahr, 73–74, 78, 81–82, 121–22, 125, 157
return of, 27, 71, 94
outcomes, 73–74
Quranic verses, 156

Lebanese Muslim Association (AUS), 24, 30–32
divorce application, 151–52
sharia process, *31*
legal aid, 112, 118, 120–21, 124, 126
legal services, 20, 37, 114, 118, 123–24, 126
'limping marriages', 20, 39, 70, 96
linguistic diversity, 114–16, 129

mahr, 78
deferred *mahr*, 77, 78, 82, 154
education, 105–6

financial agreements, 98
financial entitlement and outcomes, 78, 81–82
imams' advisory role, 81–82
Khulah, 27, 71, 73–74, 78, 81–82, 121–22, 125, 157
legal recognition of, 121–22, 124, 126
return of, 22
Khulah divorces, 27, 71, 94
talaq, 154, 155
marriage contracts, 123, 124
Board of Imams Victoria marriage contract, 137–38
financial agreements, 98–99
talaq tafweedh, 5, 75–76, 97, 153, 159, 160
see also, *mahr;*
mediation, 3–4, 12–13, *17*, 21, 34–35, 42–44, 112, 113, 126
Board of Imams Victoria, 24–25, *26*
application, 139–44
cultural sensitivity, 121
imams, 62, 86–87
Lebanese Muslim Association, *31*
professional mediation, 36
Muslim Arbitration Tribunal (UK), 18–19
Muslim Law Sharia Council (UK), 16, 18
Muslim Women Australia (AUS), 117–19
***mutah* (divorce),** 79
child support, 85
faskh, 79
financial entitlement and outcomes, 79, *85*
imams' advisory role, 84–85, 106
talaq, 155

Ontario Arbitration Act, 19
outcomes, 94–95
child custody, 90–94
divorce outcomes, 70–71
civil divorce, impact on religious divorce, 76–78
faskh, 74–75
khulah, 73–74
talaq, 73
talaq tafweedh, 75–76
financial outcomes:
child support, 79
iddah, 78–79
imams' role, 79–90
mahr, 78
mutah, 79
reclaimed financial contributions, 79
oversight concerns, 4
pre-marriage counselling, 97
privacy concerns, 42, 51–52
procedural fairness, 4
see also fairness
professional/community mediation services, 36–37
property settlements, 13
arbitration, 18–19
Darul Iftaa, 20
financial agreements, 98–99
imams' advisory role, 79–80, 85–88
legal services, 114
state role, 88–90

reconciliation:
imams' conflicting roles, 58
imams' perspective, 55–59
prioritisation of, 42–43
Quranic principles, 55–56
women's perspective, 42–43
referral to appropriate professionals:
domestic violence, 110–11
integrated support services, 111–12
counselling, 112–13
financial assistance, 114
food vouchers, 114
legal services, 114
mediation, 113
medical care, 114
other referrals, 114
relationship support, 113
relationship support, 113
religion, importance of, 1
religious divorce:
abuse, 5
choice of, 6
costs, 23, 88–89
financial support, 116–17
United Kingdom, 18–19
faskh/tafriq, 5
khulah, 5
reasons for seeking:
avoiding stigma, 41–42
'closure'/moving on, 40–41
emotional exploitation, 39–40
spiritual motivations, 37–39
talaq, 5
talaq tafweedh, 5
see also civil divorce
religious divorce panels:
expectations from sharia processes, 99–101
gender bias of, 50–51
imam recognition of, 67–68

improvement:
expectations from sharia processes, 99–101
female intake officers, 99–101
inclusion of professionals on panels, 104–5
inclusion of women on panels, 101–4
timelines and delays, 100–1

Sharia Council of Birmingham Central Mosque (UK), 15, 18

tafriq, *see* ***faskh***
talaq, 5, 71–72
Australian National Islamic Council, *29*
Board of Imams Victoria, *26*
consent, 5, 77
costs, 18, 27
Hadith, 154
iddah, 154, 155
juristic opinions, 155
Lebanese Muslim Association, *31*
mahr, 154, 155
mutah, 155
outcomes, 73
Quranic verses, 153–54
revocable v irrevocable, 154
talaq tafweedh **(delegated divorce rights),** 5, 72, 97
consent, 75
Hadith, 159
juristic opinions, 160
marriage contracts, 5, 75–76, 97, 153, 159, 160
outcomes, 75–76
Quranic verses, 159

transparency:
advice, 45–46
available options, 82, 105–6
decision making, 54
financial entitlement, 105–6
sharia policies and processes, 12, 42, 45–46, 106–7, 125
trauma/humiliation, 51–52

United Kingdom:
sharia councils:
formality, 15–16
Islamic Sharia Council, 16–17
Muslim Arbitration Tribunal, 18–19
Muslim Law Sharia Council, 16, 18
Sharia Council of Birmingham Central Mosque, 15, 18
sharia processes, *17*

women's experiences, 42, 53–54, 125–29
acknowledgement of injustice, lack of, 49–50
domestic violence, inadequacy of response, 46–49
faith and religious practice, impact on, 53
forum shopping, 51–53
gender imbalance, 50–51
privacy issues, 51
reconciliation procedures, 42–44
skills/training, lack of, 44–45
transparency, lack of, 45–46
Women's Legal Education and Action Fund (LEAF), 2–3
women's organisations:
importance of, 117–19
see also gender bias of religious divorce panels

www.ingramcontent.com/pod-product-compliance
Ingram Content Group UK Ltd.
Pitfield, Milton Keynes, MK11 3LW, UK
UKHW020819290926
15470UKWH00003B/1243

9 781509 920730